# LITERATURE, ETHICS, AND THE EMOTIONS

Recently there has been a renewed interest in the ethical value of literature. But how exactly does literature contribute to our ethical understanding? In *Literature, Ethics, and the Emotions*, Kenneth Asher argues that literary scholars should locate this question in the long and various history of moral philosophy. On the basis of his own reading of this history, Asher contends for the centrality of emotions in our ethical lives and shows how literature – novels, poetry, and drama – can each contribute to crucial emotional understanding. Individual chapters on T. S. Eliot, D. H. Lawrence, Virginia Woolf, and G. B. Shaw give detailed analyses of how this contribution takes shape even in modernist authors who try to reconfigure the very nature of the self.

Kenneth Asher holds a Ph.D. in Comparative Literature from the University of California, Berkeley. Currently he is Professor of English and Philosophy at the State University of New York, Geneseo, where he serves as Chairman of the Humanities Committee. He has also taught at Stanford University and the Georgia Institute of Technology. He is the author of *T.S. Eliot and Ideology* (Cambridge, 1995; paperback 1997).

# LITERATURE, ETHICS, AND THE EMOTIONS

KENNETH ASHER
*SUNY Geneseo*

# CAMBRIDGE
UNIVERSITY PRESS

University Printing House, Cambridge CB2 8BS, United Kingdom

One Liberty Plaza, 20th Floor, New York, NY 10006, USA

477 Williamstown Road, Port Melbourne, VIC 3207, Australia

4843/24, 2nd Floor, Ansari Road, Daryaganj, Delhi – 110002, India

79 Anson Road, #06–04/06, Singapore 079906

Cambridge University Press is part of the University of Cambridge.

It furthers the University's mission by disseminating knowledge in the pursuit of education, learning, and research at the highest international levels of excellence.

www.cambridge.org
Information on this title: www.cambridge.org/9781107185951
DOI: 10.1017/9781316888643

© Kenneth Asher 2017

This publication is in copyright. Subject to statutory exception and to the provisions of relevant collective licensing agreements, no reproduction of any part may take place without the written permission of Cambridge University Press.

First published 2017

Printed in the United Kingdom by Clays, St Ives plc

*A catalogue record for this publication is available from the British Library.*

ISBN 978-1-107-18595-1 Hardback

Cambridge University Press has no responsibility for the persistence or accuracy of URLs for external or third-party Internet Web sites referred to in this publication and does not guarantee that any content on such Web sites is, or will remain, accurate or appropriate.

*For Colin*

# Contents

| | | |
|---|---|---|
| *Acknowledgments* | | *page* viii |
| | Introduction | 1 |
| 1 | Literature as the Recalibration of Emotions | 14 |
| 2 | T. S. Eliot's Emotive Theory of Poetry | 50 |
| 3 | D. H. Lawrence: Primal Consciousness and the Function of Emotion | 82 |
| 4 | Epistemology and Ethics in Virginia Woolf | 111 |
| 5 | George Bernard Shaw: History as Cosmic Comedy | 144 |
| | Conclusion | 175 |
| *Index* | | 181 |

# Acknowledgments

I am very grateful to Gillian Paku, Eugene Stelzig, Walt Soffer, Carlo Filice, and Melanie Blood for looking over drafts of my manuscript along the way. I have profited, too, from the refreshing and provocative comments of students of my course on Philosophy and Literature who came to the issues with few preconceived notions. I would like to thank both Ray Ryan, my Editor at Cambridge, for his steady support and encouragement, and the two anonymous readers for their extremely thoughtful responses to the manuscript. For their graciousness and constant good advice, I am in debt to Catherine Smith, the Content Manager at Cambridge University Press, and Velmurugan Inbasigamoni, the Project Manager at Integra. Finally, I would like to thank Michele Feeley for her Hogwarts wizardry in helping me assemble things in proper digital format.

Acknowledgement is made to the following for permission to reprint copyrighted material:

Faber & Faber, Ltd. and Houghton Mifflin Harcourt for:
T.S. Eliot, *Selected Essays*
T.S. Eliot, *Complete Poems and Plays 1909–1962*
T.S Eliot, *Selected Prose*

Farrar, Straus and Giroux, LLC for:
T. S. Eliot *Knowledge and Experience in the Philosophy of F.H. Bradley*

Houghton Mifflin Harcourt for:
Virginia Woolf *To the Lighthouse*
*The Diary of Virginia Woolf,* volume II, 1920–1924

The Society of Authors on behalf of the Bernard Shaw Estate for the various works of Bernard Shaw.

An earlier form of chapter 3 appeared in the *Cambridge Quarterly* as "Emotions and the Ethical Life in D.H. Lawrence" (2011, volume 40).

*Introduction*

Over the past twenty-five years there has been a renewed interest in the ethical content of literature. Although the reasons for this change of focus are complex, if one had to identify a single event that marked the turn, a good choice would be the revelation of Paul de Man's wartime journalism and the ensuing, heated debate.[1] Certainly few of de Man's opponents made the irresponsible case that there was a *necessary* connection between his tainted past and his subsequent career as arguably the most prominent deconstructionist in the American academy, but it was not necessary to do so in order to bring about a rethinking of deconstruction. The claim that there was nothing *inconsistent* in his early collaboration and later theorizing proved damaging enough. While defenders sometimes tried to demonstrate that there was an implicit ethics in de Man's theory, this effort proved unconvincing given his explicit disdain for anything that we might normally think of as ethical considerations. In "The Resistance to Theory," he made clear that any contamination of literary studies with either psychology or ethics might lead in a direction vastly inferior to his own method: "The equation of rhetoric with psychology rather than with epistemology opens up dreary prospects of pragmatic banality, all the drearier if compared to the brilliance of the [i.e., my] performative analysis."[2] De Man does recognize that there is something called ethics, but what it amounts to is a recognition of his particular view of epistemology: "In this sense, ethics has nothing to do with the will (thwarted or free) of a subject, nor *a fortiori*, with a relationship between subjects. The ethical category is imperative (i.e., a category rather than a value) to the extent that

---

[1] See Paul de Man, *Wartime Journalism: 1939–1943* (Lincoln: University of Nebraska Press, 1989) and *Responses: On Paul de Man's Wartime Journalism*, ed. by Werner Hamacher, Neil Hertz, and Thomas Keenan (Lincoln: University of Nebraska Press, 1989).
[2] Paul de Man, "The Resistance to Theory," in *The Resistance to Theory* (Minneapolis: University of Minnesota Press, 1986), p. 19.

it is linguistic and not subjective."[3] Morality in its traditional sense, then, is merely a linguistic construct, of necessity tainted by the inadequacy of language to get at truth: "Morality is a version of the same language aporia that gave rise to such concepts as 'man' or 'love' or 'self,' and not the cause or consequence of such concepts."[4] There is nothing in de Man that would suggest any ethical imperative beyond subscribing to the "insight" that we are forever trapped in this linguistic web.

Thus, de Man – and he was hardly alone in this among the deconstructionists – summarily dismissed those who busied themselves with ethical considerations as philosophically naïve. Such concerns were flat-footed, it was intimated, and best left to the sclerotic descendants of Matthew Arnold, unfit for the rigors of continental thought.[5] De Man found support for his position in an early, unpublished essay of Nietzsche's, "Über Wahrheit und Lüge im Außermoralischen Sinn," that "flatly states the necessary subversion of truth by rhetoric as the distinctive feature of all language."[6] This epistemological skepticism quickly leads to an unmasking of morality as "originat[ing] out of lies." While de Man's reading of this youthful essay is legitimate, he took this to be a position that Nietzsche maintained to the end of his life – a far more dubious claim, but one that allowed de Man to enlist the authority of Nietzsche as ratification of his own view.[7] Buoyed by this alliance, de Man felt no need to engage in the rich tradition of moral philosophy, a move that was consistent with deconstruction's overall complaint against Western philosophy as suffering from "logocentrism." The influence of de Man can be seen most clearly in J. Hillis Miller's *The Ethics of Reading* (1987), a book whose limitations are suggested by the very title. Miller's diminished sense of ethical obligation requires nothing more than a willingness to read with the skepticism of a deconstructionist. This alone constitutes "the ethical moment."[8] Schooled in suspicion, the ethical reader would be able to exercise his

---

[3] Paul de Man, *Allegories of Reading* (New Haven: Yale University Press, 1979), p. 206.
[4] Ibid., p. 206.
[5] Alice Jaegar Kaplan recalls how de Man taught his graduate students contempt for such horrors as "New Critical Moral Earnestness." See Alice Jaeger Kaplan, "Paul de Man, *Le Soir*, and the Francophone Collaboration," in *Responses*, p. 278.
[6] De Man, *Allegories of Reading*, p. 110.
[7] De Man claims that Nietzsche's corpus is an "endlessly repeated gesture [in favor of truth as rhetoric]" but for a far more convincing and subtle account of Nietzsche's evolving position on truth see Maudemarie Clark, *Nietzsche on Truth and Philosophy* (Cambridge: Cambridge University Press, 1991). Also helpful is Brian Leiter, "Perspectivism in Nietzsche's *Genealogy of Morals*," in *Nietzsche, Genealogy, Morality*, ed. Richard Schacht (Berkeley: University of California, 1994), pp. 334–57.
[8] J. Hillis Miller, *The Ethics of Reading* (New York: Columbia University Press, 1987), p. 4.

*Introduction* 3

moral intelligence by, for example, enjoying the pages of Kant's *Foundations of the Metaphysics of Morals* as a "comedy."[9] One can see the immediate appeal this might have to faculty and students in literature departments who could now claim a mastery of, and even more intoxicatingly *over*, material they needn't painstakingly work through, yet it had the unfortunate effect of prescinding the study of literature from the long and sophisticated philosophical conversation about ethics.

Thus, when it came time to look for a rejuvenation of ethics, literary scholars turned reflexively to Derrida and Foucault rather than moral philosophy. In a generally even-handed and accurate assessment of the state of ethical criticism near the turn of the century, Lawrence Buell notes: "No major ethical philosopher from Aristotle to Rawls has attracted anywhere near the attention among those currently linking literature and ethics that Derrida and Foucault have attracted (neither of them ethicists in any strict sense)."[10] Buell's estimation of Derrida's relationship to ethical theory is confirmed in Derrida's response to a collection of critical essays devoted to his work:

> What is the ethicity of ethics? The morality of morality? What is responsibility? What is the "What is?" in this case? etc. These questions are always urgent. In a certain way they must remain urgent and unanswered, at any rate without a general and rule-governed response, without a response other than that which is linked specifically each time, to the occurrence of a decision without rules and without will in the course of a new test of the undecidable.[11]

The line of argument is familiar: because we can never know with certainty, insistence on ethical categories and principles can only be an act of *mauvaise foi*. Instead, Derrida finds far more congenial the thinking of the transcendental philosopher Emmanuel Lévinas. Lévinas had studied with both Husserl and Heidegger at Freiburg in the late twenties, and, while deeply influenced by each, began to break away when he came to question the primacy of the Cartesian ego that Husserl took as his starting point. His eventual difference from Heidegger is subtler, but, if I am being fair to both thinkers, appears to consist in a reconfiguration of the relationship between Heidegger's Dasein (being in the world) and Mitsein (being with). For Heidegger Dasein entails Mitsein, but the interpersonal is

---
[9] Ibid., p. 13
[10] Lawrence Buell, "In Pursuit of Ethics," *PMLA*, vol. 114, no. 1 (January 1999), 11.
[11] Jacques Derrida, "Passions: 'An Oblique Offering," in *Derrida: A Critical Reader*, ed. James Wood (Blackwell: Oxford, 1992), pp. 16–17.

subordinate to Dasein's authenticity, its responsibility to itself. Lévinas, in effect, makes Mitsein primordial by positing a "first philosophy" that makes the relationship to Other the ground of being, something prior to the self taken as an intending consciousness in Husserl's sense. This relationship is one of responsiveness and obligation. We might think, then, of Lévinas as providing a transcendental justification for ethics without addressing ethics in any more specific way. One can see the immediate appeal this would have for Derrida since this justification is prior to the cognitive self and the problems of epistemology, but two problems remain with his attraction to Lévinas. The first and most obvious is that it is odd that Derrida, who devoted himself to a critique of any sort of foundational claims – denounced as "the metaphysics of presence" and "logocentrism" – should now embrace a "first philosophy," and one so deeply and clearly influenced by the Biblical tradition of moral responsibility. The second, voiced most pointedly by Edward Said in the early eighties but still worth repeating, is that we look in vain to Derrida for any kind of engagement with ethics on a more mundane level, the pressing world of practical ethics.[12] While Derrida has defenders who detect implied concerns, it is hard not to conclude that there are more direct and fruitful ways to rejuvenate literary studies than by attempting to wring an ethics from deconstruction.[13]

Though not hamstrung by the radical epistemological skepticism of the deconstructionists, Foucault faced difficulties of his own in trying to demonstrate how his work might contribute to a discussion of ethics. For well over a decade Foucault had meticulously evolved a theory of "discourse." Indebted in nearly equal parts to Althusser's elaboration of the

---

[12] See Edward Said, *The World, the Text, and the Critic* (Cambridge, Mass: Harvard University Press, 1983), pp. 178–225. The continued relevance of Said's criticism is underscored when reading Derrida's response to the events of 9/11: "'Something' took place, we have the feeling of not having seen it coming, and certain consequences undeniably follow upon the 'thing.' But this very thing, the place and meaning of this 'event,' remains ineffable, like an intuition without concept, like a unicity with no generality on the horizon or with no horizon at all, out of range for a language that admits its powerlessness and so is reduced to pronouncing mechanically a date, repeating it endlessly, as a kind of ritual incantation, a conjuring poem, a journalistic litany or rhetorical refrain that admits to not knowing what it's talking about. We do not in fact know what we are saying or naming in this way: September 11, le 11 septembre, September 11. The brevity of the appellation (September 11, 9/11) stems not only from an economic or rhetorical necessity. The telegram of this metonymy – a name, a number – points out the unqualifiable by recognizing that we do not recognize or even cognize that we do not yet know how to qualify, that we do not know what we are talking about." Giovanna Borridori, *Philosophy in a Time of Terror: Dialogues with Jürgen Habermas and Jacques Derrida* (Chicago: University of Chicago Press, 2004), pp. 85–86.

[13] For the most sustained defense, see Simon Critchley, *The Ethics of Deconstruction: Derrida and Lévinas* (Oxford: Blackwell, 1992).

Marxian notion of ideology and to Nietzsche's grounding of all activity in the will-to-power, Foucault had posited a web of cultural practices that enmesh all who live within it as it empowers or marginalizes behavior and shapes consciousness accordingly. So helpless is the individual in the toils of discourse that, in *Les Mots et Les Choses* (1966), Foucault announced "the death of man," the end of the illusion of individual autonomy. A few years later, in his much read "What is an Author?" (1969), Foucault drew out one of the implications of his position by arguing that the very idea of an author as creative consciousness was an ideological obfuscation. In reality "the author does not precede the works; he is a certain functional principle."[14] This stark anti-humanism has led Giddens, Lentricchia, and others to note that Foucault has, in effect, elevated Power to a metaphysical principle, with the historical record as its unfolding manifestation. Thus, it comes as a surprise, though a welcome one, to hear Foucault, toward the end of his life, urging that we consider "the axis of ethics" whose pressing question is "How are we constituted as moral subjects of our own actions?"[15] Rightly, but no less surprisingly, he concedes, "Freedom is the ontological condition of ethics. But ethics is the considered form that freedom takes when it is informed by reflection."[16] When questioned about the contradictions between his later and earlier assessments of human agency, Foucault lightheartedly claimed the right to learn and evolve. Yet, apart from the fact that his later position, because of his death, never got elaborated in the same way as the earlier position, there remained the problem that too much academic capital had been invested in the earlier Foucault by his adherents for these late pronouncements to bear much fruit, for they would first have to be acknowledged as a substantial reversal.[17]

So strong had been the influence of Derrida and Foucault that even those politically oriented schools of criticism such as New Historicism and Postcolonialism that located themselves in the vicinity of ethical conversation had to effect unhappy compromises. Stephen Greenblatt, the originator of New Historicism, relied on the historical record to situate and

---

[14] *The Foucault Reader*, ed. Paul Rabinow (New York: Pantheon Books, 1984), pp. 118–19.
[15] Foucault, "What Is Enlightenment," in *The Foucault Reader*, pp. 48–49.
[16] Michel Foucault, "The Ethics of the Concern for Self as a Practice of Freedom," in *Ethics: Subjectivity and Truth*, ed. Paul Rabinow (New York: The New Press), p. 284.
[17] As with Derrida, there were those who claimed that the late writing was not the reversal it seemed. See, for example, Kevin Jon Heller, "Power, Subjectification, and Resistance in Foucault," *SubStance*, vol. 25, no. 1 (1996), 78–110. The case for continuity runs up against not just Foucault's own near admission that he has changed his mind, but also the understanding of his early works by most of those who embraced discourse theory.

clarify literary texts, at times brilliantly, but then wonders whether history is not just one more fiction, a story we tell ourselves, no more valid than a myriad of alternatives.[18] He settles for a subordination of "truth" to power, following Foucault's reading of Nietzsche. Those with power will inevitably arrogate to themselves the right to tell the master narrative. It is in this way that Greenblatt justifies his own power over the texts, both literary and historical, that he interprets. But this theory sits uneasily with the ever-present tone of his readings, one that implicitly but unmistakably asks us to share his indignation at the cruelties occasioned by inequality of power. The ethical norm silently appealed to is belied by a theory according to which the most that can be said against cruelty is simply that Greenblatt doesn't happen to prefer it and has gained enough power to tell the story his way.

Postcolonialism has suffered from a similar contradiction between theory and practice, but one more pronounced since it has tended at times to take on board, along with deconstruction and Foucault, both feminism and Marxism. Gayatri Spivak, who came to prominence as the translator of Derrida's notoriously difficult prose and then emerged as a leading postcolonial critic in her own right, tries to explain, in a passage that defies paraphrase, how all this might be possible:

> Most of the interest in deconstruction has been based upon the fact that at both ends of the deconstructive morphology there is a stalling ...The stalling at the beginning is called *différance* and the stalling at the end is called aporia. This is a focus that one can discuss in terms of the institutional space in which deconstruction has been welcome.
>
> Although I acknowledge the crucial importance of these stallings at beginnings and ends, my interest is much more in the middle, which is where something like a practice emerges by way of a mistake. "Mistake" within quotes because the possibility of this mistake cannot be derived from something that is over against it, "correct." ... Within that space, against what would you declare your own inability since there is no model where anyone is fully able to do anything. That's the declaration of interest as far as I'm concerned, it is in fact a deeply theoretical move, as there is no room there for apologizing for the limits of one's own production.[19]

In the end, like Greenblatt, though he would never be guilty of such prose, she must doubt the factuality of the very events she finds deplorable; under

---

[18] Stephen Greenblatt, *Learning to Curse* (New York: Routledge, 1990), pp. 1–15.
[19] Gayatri Spivak, "The New Historicism: Political Commitment and the Postmodern Critic," in *The Post-Colonial Critic*, ed. Sarah Harasym (New York: Routledge, 1990), pp. 158–59.

the influence of Foucault, she must imprison in brackets the very selves whose chains she would loosen.

Any sorting out of these conceptual muddles has encountered a further hindrance in postcolonial studies, namely the conviction that a normative ethics can only be the product of an Enlightenment ideology that posits the European as universal standard, all others as deviant. On this view, the much-vaunted Enlightenment appeal to reason was invoked merely to justify imperialistic impositions of instrumental reason. This line of thought can be traced back through Horkheimer and Adorno's notorious case in *Dialectic of Enlightenment* that "Enlightenment is totalitarian"; through Heidegger's denunciation of the Cartesian cogito as licensing the technological depredations of the modern world; through Joseph de Maistre's attack on the French Revolution's Rights of Man; and ultimately to Herder's rejection of Reason as an imposition on *Volksgeist*, the unique spirit of an individual people that manifests itself in "prejudice." For most of its history, as even this quick overview makes clear, the case against the Enlightenment was the province of deeply conservative thinkers. It appealed especially to those who would deny any extra-national code of justice, as in the Dreyfus affair when Maurice Barrès insisted that Dreyfus' guilt or innocence must be determined not according to a "Kantian" notion of absolute justice, but according to "French" justice, which had as its sole criterion the welfare of the nation – and arraigned before this tribunal, Dreyfus most certainly must be condemned. (The prestige of the French army was at stake.) The difficulty with the postcolonial adoption of this stance lies not so much in the historical irony that it was typically used by those on the other end of the political spectrum to reject freedom from traditional authority, but that the postcolonial project, if it is to carry any weight, must rely on a universal view of human beings as rational moral agents who can be held to common standards. Without the assumption of an essential element of human nature, cultures would be mutually incomprehensible, a form of multi-culturalism that few would relish; without the possibility of at least some supracultural norms, on what basis condemn colonialism in the first place?

Because of such inconsistencies, a rethinking of these issues eventually emerged in some quarters of postcolonial scholarship. Satya Mohanty, in his lucid and temperate *Literary Theory and the Claims of History*, recognized that "postmodernism does not appear very attractive as a philosophical position or as a political perspective." Persuasively, he urges a "post-positivist realism" that would show "moral universalism and multiculturalism are compatible and indeed complementary ideals."[20] Mohanty's acknowledgment that norms, rather than militating against multiculturalism, are necessary to protect it shows up most fruitfully in a reconfigured "cosmopolitanism." As defended by Anthony Appiah, this new cosmopolitanism would respect both the necessarily "thin" universal moral abstractions and their "thick" elaboration in different cultures.[21] Thus, respect for parents may qualify as a universal good, but find radically different ways of expressing itself, and the same with funeral customs that are meant to honor the departed. Because these practices are enmeshed in a broad set of value-laden assumptions, Appiah regards them as part of an elaborate narrative and considers encounters with such alternate narratives as beneficial in themselves. While he is not specifically concerned with literature per se, the skill in reading another culture's narrative bears obvious affinities to the imaginative expansion of self involved in engaging empathetically with fictional worlds. What, though, are we to do when we find local elaborations to be sharply at odds with the justifying principles – female circumcision as an instance of respect for women, for example – and, more troublesome, discover that these differences are not likely to be solved by reasoned argument? Appiah recognizes this as a real problem. His solution is to extol understanding of the difference as a virtue in itself: "and I stress the role of the imagination here because the encounters, properly conducted, are valuable in themselves."[22] That tends to make the trumping principle of cosmopolitanism the value of tolerantly living together, and, while it is hard not to appreciate the generosity of Appiah's view, more will need to be said about what Nussbaum refers to as "the dark side of the aspiration to community and historical rootedness."

What goes under the general rubric of feminist criticism encompasses such a number of different, and often antagonist, methodologies and theoretical assumptions that it is difficult in short space to speak definitively while still being fair to the variety. At the most basic level, however, what fuels nearly all manifestations of feminist criticism is a justified concern to point out and ultimately correct systematic patterns of unfairness in the treatment of women. In this regard, it is clearly engaged with political and ethical considerations. Sharp splits occur immediately, though, in determining what is entailed by fair treatment. Equity

[20] Satya Mohanty, *Literary Theory and the Claims of History* (Ithaca: Cornell University Press, 1997), p. xii.
[21] Kwame Anthony Appiah, *Cosmopolitanism: Ethics in a World of Strangers* (New York: Norton, 2006).
[22] Ibid., p. 85.

feminists, in the tradition of Wollstonecraft and Mill, do not question liberal, democratic principles, but argue that they have not been evenhandedly applied. Those literary critics sympathetic to this position have sought to highlight this disparity in examining the plight of female characters and the particular burdens of female authors trying to make their voices heard in a male-dominated society. Ranged against this view are those who maintain that women are sufficiently different from men that a much more radical rethinking of social practices and institutions must take place. This group itself quickly divides into those who believe the difference is natural (essentialists) and those who believe it is cultural (constructivists). Among Anglo-American feminists the essentialist position has had markedly less success than it has had on the Continent. There has been a pervasive fear, understandably inspired by the long memory of Victorian gender rigidities, that arguments based on innate differences will once again be taken as warrant for separate and unequal treatment. In addition, there has been a general failure of the essentialists to convincingly demonstrate what precisely the difference is. Attempts to argue the case for a female epistemology, the need for a different language to accommodate it (or even more modestly, the tendency to use the existing language in predictably different ways), have not been persuasive, and this weakness has acted as a further deterrent. Constructivism, then, may be seen as an attempt to argue for female particularism without committing to biological hardwiring.

Constructivism can careen to excesses of its own, certainly, as in the work of Judith Butler, who extravagantly asserts that all gender difference, aside from anatomical details, is culturally produced. The body is reduced to a pure arena of Foucauldian power intersections without prior dispositions or tendencies. Sociology consumes biology. We are left – in some unexplained way – with just enough freedom to parody these arrangements without ever being able to change them.[23] Worthier of more consideration is the constructivist claim that we should make central to morality the virtue of care, a quality deeply important to women in their cultural role as nurturers. Needs would become more important than rights; a flexible, sensitive concern would become more important than duty and its accompanying rules. In the work of both the psychologist Carol Gilligan and the philosopher Nell Noddings this ethic of care is seen as particularly consonant with female experience, maternal solicitude serving as the

---

[23] See Martha Nussbaum "The Professor of Parody," *The New Republic*, November 28, 2000, 37–45, for a sharp criticism of both the content and style of Butler's work.

paradigmatic scenario. Though they acknowledge that men could become full participants, virtually all their examples of care are associated with women. Building on their seminal work, Annette Baier has found mainstream precedent in the sentimental moral theory of Hume, whom she assimilates as the "women's moral theorist."[24] Others, such as Virginia Held and Joan Tronto, worried that the maternal paradigm makes of ethics something too narrowly personal and immediate, have tried to show how the ethics of care might be expanded into the public sphere.[25] Criticisms, as with any theory, have arisen: 1) that the ethics of care is crypto-essentialist; 2) that there is far less new about all this since the talk about care is merely a recasting of the virtue of benevolence; and 3) that insufficient attention has been paid to the indispensable idea of justice, too quickly dismissed as part of the male perspective. Yet, while the ethics of care may not be the radical news some of its proponents take it to be, and while it might profit from greater accommodation with deontology or especially virtue ethics, it does serve a useful function in redirecting attention toward the emotions, of crucial importance in establishing an interrelationship between literature and moral theory.

As Martha Nussbaum has argued – and it seems unfortunate that literary scholars interested in ethics did not enter earlier into conversation with her and other contemporary moral philosophers – a great deal of the ethical import of literature, indeed of the value of literature as a whole, depends on the part played by emotions in our moral lives.[26] Literature clearly does not

---

[24] Annette Baier, "Hume: The Women's Moral Theorist?" in *Women and Moral Theory*, ed. Eva Feder Kittay and Diana Tatowa Meyers (New Jersey: Rowman & Littlefield, 1987), pp. 37–55, at 37.

[25] Virginia Held, *Feminist Morality: Transforming Culture, Society, and Politics* (Chicago: University of Chicago Press, 1993); Virginia Held, "Feminist Moral Inquiry and the Feminist Future," in V. Held (ed.), *Justice and Care* (Boulder: Westview Press, 2006), pp. 153–76; Joan Tronto, *Moral Boundaries: A Political Argument for an Ethic of Care* (New York: Routledge, 1994) and "Women and Caring: What Can Feminists Learn about Morality from Caring?" in *Justice and Care: Essential Readings in Feminist Ethics*, pp. 101–15.

[26] Among Nussbaum's copious writing on the topic, one might single out *Love's Knowledge* (Oxford: Oxford University Press, 1990) and *Upheavals of Thought: The Intelligence of Emotions* (Cambridge: Cambridge University Press, 2001). By her own admission, a strong influence on her interest in this area was Bernard Williams. Of interest in this regard, see his "Morality and the Emotions," in *Problems of the Self* (Cambridge: Cambridge University Press, 1973), pp. 207–29, and *Shame and Necessity* (Berkeley: University of California Press, 1993). A neo-Aristotelian position at significant odds with Nussbaum's might be found in Alasdair MacIntyre's *After Virtue* (Notre Dame: Notre Dame University Press, 1981) and *Whose Justice? Which Rationality?* (Notre Dame: Notre Dame University Press, 1989). Finding the modern liberal state to be a cacophony of unorchestrated self-interest, MacIntyre looks instead to a Thomistic Catholicism that has absorbed Aristotle to provide the necessary grounding authority for virtue. Rejecting the belief in original sin, upon which this view heavily relies, Nussbaum believes that Aristotle can be accommodated to secular modern society. See especially her *Poetic Justice: The Literary Imagination and Public Life* (Boston: Beacon Press, 1995).

attempt to vie with philosophy in the technical analysis of principles, and even if on rare occasion it should approximate such formal abstraction, the estimation of such a passage would more probably hinge on whether or not the pronouncement was consistent with the character who voiced it and the theme of the work than with the flawlessness of the argument. Instead, literature turns much of its attention to recording the emotional density of life, whether it be that of the persona of lyric poetry or that of the characters in drama and fiction. The stuff of literature is not exclusively, but is certainly prominently, a nuanced register of emotional crosscurrents. This is not to claim that literature must rely on irrational insights – though, of course, at times it does. The stronger case for literature's irreplaceable contribution to ethical knowledge rests crucially on the cognitive role of emotions and the necessary implication of appropriate emotional response in actions that would be considered fully moral. Nussbaum follows Aristotle in claiming that emotions may recognize and respond to ethically crucial elements of a situation in a way that can escape detached deliberation. Properly tutored, emotions can have a finely grained perceptiveness "that embody some of our most deeply rooted views of what has importance."[27] Thus, emotions can serve as "judgments of value."[28] Nussbaum finds literature's contribution to be greatest in the genre of the novel by virtue of its dense particularity that most closely resembles the messiness of ordinary experience. Henry James' novels, with their exquisite alertness to the moral implications of quotidian encounters, become for her paradigmatic. In addition to James, Nussbaum has written appreciatively of Proust, Woolf, Emily Brontë, and others.

The case for literature's ethical importance as elaborated by Nussbaum seems to me the most promising starting point. Her view of literary characters as a warehouse of alternative lives that deepen our moral understanding when sympathetically, but not uncritically, regarded strikes me as faithful to the reading experience at its best. Her own interpretations, philosophically informed, yet sensitive to emotional nuance and tone, provide strong examples of what her approach can yield. To cite just one example, her essay "The Window: Knowledge of Other Minds in Virginia Woolf's *To the Lighthouse*" shows how Woolf poses the problem of other minds, something philosophers approach in terms of evidence and certainty, as essentially an ethical problem.[29] The success of entry into the

---

[27] Nussbaum, *Love's Knowledge*, p. 42.
[28] See especially the first chapter of *Upheavals of Thought*.
[29] Martha Nussbaum, "The Window: Knowledge of Other Minds in Virginia Woolf's *To the Lighthouse*," *New Literary History*, 1995 (26), 731–53.

minds of others depends on the desires that motivate us to enter. Knowledge will ultimately rely on the character of the quester, and only those capable of and willing to exercise an emotionally rich attentiveness gain access. Nussbaum, here and in her other literary explications, has limited herself to the novel, but she admits that this in no way implies that her inquiry might not be expanded to other genres. Yet it is clear that if lyric poetry, which typically lacks the dense circumstantiality of the novels that Nussbaum values, is to be included in a neo-Aristotelian justification for literature's contribution to ethical awareness, amendments of some sort will have to be made. But can the lyric's naked emotional intensities be accommodated to her model? Further, there is the problem presented, in its most sophisticated form, by modernist literature's impatience with the traditional conception of character that Aristotle's moral psychology relies upon. Despite the sensitive, nuanced reading of *To The Lighthouse* that Nussbaum provides, is there something about Woolf's conception of the self that she doesn't capture? Looking back from 1924, Woolf famously notes that on or about December of 1910 "human character changed,"[30] and the ironic arbitrariness of the date should not obscure the fact that she staked everything in her fiction on that change. Likewise, D. H. Lawrence, in 1914, explains to his publisher that he "mustn't look in my novel for the old stable ego of character." Between these two statements, T. S. Eliot advances his Impersonal Theory of Poetry that relies on F. H. Bradley's positing of a precognitive relationship to the world. Shaw, even earlier, in the first decade of the new century, detects a transpersonal Life Force that whisperingly seeks to work its purposes through us. All of these, in different ways, present challenges to a view of the properly organized self as a constellation of virtues, conceived of as deeply ingrained dispositions of character, long and carefully cultivated, that allow us to fulfill our human function. In devoting chapters to each of the four, I have endeavored to explore the force of these challenges. The chapters on T. S. Eliot and Shaw serve the additional function of examining whether or not this sort of ethical criticism might be expanded to poetry and drama. Is Nussbaum's view elastic enough to encompass other genres?

To avoid any false expectations, I should mention that, while I hope this study will contribute to an understanding of the ethical value of several modernist writers, I do not intend this book to be primarily an examination of "the ethics of modernism" – a topic that, at the very least, would

---

[30] "Mr. Bennett and Mrs. Brown," in *The Virginia Woolf Reader*, ed. Mitchell A. Leaska (Orlando: Harcourt, Inc., 1984), p. 194.

demand a discussion of Yeats and Joyce, too.[31] I have chosen modernist challenges because their elaborate rethinking of the self and the role of our emotional lives is central to their justly admired literary creations. Any theory of the way literature engages us ethically cannot avoid dealing with the persuasiveness of such examples. And these examples seemed to me to lead most profitably to the boundaries, and at times limits, of what Nussbaum's rich theory could provide. Certainly, it is only fair to add that Nussbaum's Aristotelian assumptions about the role of emotions in our ethical lives have critics, too, among both modern philosophers of emotion and literary theorists, all of whom build on earlier antagonistic views. To speak all too quickly and generally, one could lump the complaints into three large categories:

1) Positions maintaining that emotions are irrational states that tend to cloud the rational assessments necessary for a well-ordered life; hence, rather than valuable components of judgment, they are threats to judgment. They seize us, rather than serve us.
2) Positions that would – like Nussbaum's – grant the emotions powers of appraisal, but insist that the appraisal almost inevitably is a *misappraisal* insofar as, lacking deeper reflection, it leads us to overvalue the transitory and inessential.
3) Positions that untether strong emotion from the constraints of reason, but see this freedom as positive. Emotions are regarded as self-ratifying expansions of the self, at their summit leading to states of rapture or transcendence.

To start with, then, in the next chapter, I will give a more detailed account of the long debate over the role of emotions in our ethical lives and what bearing this has on the role of literature in sustaining such lives.

---

[31] This topic has been treated recently in Lee Oser's *The Ethics of Modernism: Moral Ideas in Yeats, Eliot, Joyce, Woolf, and Beckett* (Cambridge: Cambridge University Press, 2007) and in a global context by Jessica Berman in *Modernist Commitments: Ethics, Politics, and Transnational Modernism* (New York: Columbia University Press, 2012).

CHAPTER I

# *Literature as the Recalibration of Emotions*

Emotions have been notoriously difficult to treat systematically. What precisely is an emotion? Is there a natural class of emotions? Would this grouping differ from something we might categorize as feelings? What is the relationship of emotions to rationality? How responsible are we for the emotions we experience? Most philosophers would agree that emotions have an intentional structure, i.e., that they are directed toward an object, but in what way? Intensely personal but also a source of frequent self-deception, how transparent are emotions to the one who experiences them? And, of most interest to the present study, what role do emotions play in our moral lives? Needless to say, the theorizing on these and related questions has a long and varied history in the philosophical literature, to which one might add the contributions of other fields that reside, though not always with mutual admiration, under the interdisciplinary umbrella of cognitive science, especially psychology, neuroscience, and evolutionary biology. Rather than attempting the virtually impossible task of rehearsing this tradition in a chapter, I have selected several of the most pointed critics and most persuasive defenders of the view that emotions are essential to sound moral judgment. In each instance I will try to draw out the aesthetic implications of the position, especially as it has relevance to the potential ethical value of literature.

Those who regard the emotions as playing a crucial role in moral appraisal are immediately confronted with the daunting opposition of Plato, for whom the emotions represent an essential threat to moral integrity. We might recall that his moral psychology begins with a division of the soul into three parts: the rational, the spirited (*thumos*), and the appetitive.[1] Each of these three parts generates desire, the

---

[1] I will be quoting from the translation of the *Republic* by G. M. A. Grube, revised by C. D. C. Reeve (Cambridge: Hackett Publishing Co., 1992). References to the *Republic* will be given in the text by section number in parentheses.

motivational energy capable of moving us to action. The rational part of the soul desires to know the good, to plan life in accordance with it, and to execute this plan. The spirited part of the soul is that part most closely associated with emotions. Plato at one time or another in the *Republic* sees it as the seat of anger, righteous indignation, and a kind of self-contempt or shame for failure to act nobly. It may also issue forth in admiration of those who do behave nobly. (Such emotions as compassion, nostalgia, grief, and religious awe are not attributed to spirit and are never clearly accounted for by Plato in this model.) Socrates refers to the spirited part of the soul as "victory-loving and honor-loving" (581b), and John Cooper, in his excellent study of ancient moral psychology, is surely right in defining the desire of *thumos* as that for "competitive success and the esteem from others and oneself that comes with it."[2] The appetitive part of the soul, at its most basic, desires the objects that will satisfy such bodily needs as thirst, hunger, and sex. But Plato also includes the oligarch's quest for money among such desires. The whims of the democratic man, a flighty dabbler in music, philosophy, and whatever else is the fad *du jour*, are also lumped with the appetitive urges. Music, philosophy, and exercise can be – indeed, should be – part of the reasonably chosen good life, but the democrat clearly does not choose them for the right reason or pursue them with appropriate persistence. The organizing principle for this broad range of desires is never announced, but perhaps what Plato intends to capture in this grab-bag are unstable desires, desires that attach themselves to the transitory or are themselves transitory. (Both reason that seeks the immutable good and spirit that is concerned with those accomplishments that ensure immortality through reputation would be distinguished from the appetitive desires in this regard.) What is manifestly clear is that the appetitive desires, like the great mass of people who constitute their political analogue, must be excluded from any decision regarding the pursuit of the good. These desires, along with the appetitively driven populace, are performing their function insofar as they allow themselves to be ruled by reason: obedience is their chief virtue.

The role of the spirited part, that part that is most intimately connected with our emotional lives, is more complex. Plato says that in a well-ordered soul the spirited part would be an ally of the rational part (440a–441a). But an ally on what footing? The famous comparison in the *Phaedrus* that likens reason to a charioteer controlling two horses offers the most pointed

---

[2] John M. Cooper, *Reason and Emotion: Essays on Ancient Moral Psychology and Ethical Theory* (Princeton: Princeton University Press, 1999), p. 135.

answer. The good horse, representing the spirited part, is responsive to the direction of reason, while the bad horse, representing the appetitive part, is recalcitrant and must be whipped into obedience. Here there is no hint that the spirited horse is ever to be given its head in guiding the chariot; it is preferred to the wayward horse because it is much more amenable to reason's control and its energy helps keep its partner in line. In the beautifully concise portraits of the eighth book of the *Republic*, Plato sketches what a life dominated by the spirited part of the soul would look like. He refers to this soul as "timocratic," characterized primarily by the love of honor. The timocratic man, who sounds like an abstraction from Odysseus, employs reason in the service of military strategy and various clever manipulations that conduce to reputation-building exploits. Intelligent, but not intellectual, he does not concern himself with the ultimate good. What emerges from Plato's overall position, then, is a view of the self in which the emotions, though corrigible, are never able to detect or respond to what is morally salient in any situation in a way that would enhance the calculations of unaided reason. Even in the well-ordered soul, the emotions are supplementary, never complementary.

The distrust of emotions evident throughout Plato's work feeds into his series of complaints about poetry. In the agonistic manner common to the dialogues, he refers to "an ancient quarrel between [poetry] and philosophy," and it wouldn't be unfair to see what is at stake here as an aggressively conducted curricular debate. We should remember, first of all, though, that Plato conceives ethics in a much broader sense than we do today, where it is typically regarded as a set of obligations that duty demands. Bernard Williams has suggested that we reserve the term "morality" for this narrower modern conception to distinguish it from the more expansive ancient view of ethics as addressing the question "how should one live?"[3] What he has in mind can clearly be seen near the beginning of the *Republic* when Socrates persuades an annoyed Thrasymachus to return to the discussion of justice by reproachfully asking "or do you think it a small matter to determine which whole way of life would make living most worthwhile for each of us?" (343e). Socrates' unwillingness to let Thrasymachus stray from dialectical cross-examination underlines the efforts of both Socrates and Plato to bring this question almost exclusively into the province of philosophy. Prior to this, Greeks had looked for guidance primarily from the tragic stage and the Homeric epics. How and why lives go wrong, and less frequently right, were

---

[3] Bernard Williams, *Ethics and the Limits of Philosophy* (Cambridge, Mass: Harvard University Press, 1985), p. 6.

*Literature as the Recalibration of Emotions* 17

there forcefully and memorably presented. Indeed, it would be hard to overestimate the importance of Homer in this regard. He was the basis of all formal education, with particular attention paid to the ethical implications of his work.[4] In Xenophon's *Symposium*, Nicias' son relates how his father had compelled him to learn by heart all of Homer in his youth and claims that he could still recite both the entire *Iliad* and *Odyssey* from memory.[5] Plato himself, despite his call for massive censorship of Homer, quotes him readily, and apparently from memory, throughout his dialogues to support his points. But at the same time, he is keenly aware that if he is to set ethical knowledge on firmer ground, he must wrest authority away from Homer and his fellow poets.

Plato confesses that he loves Homer, but that the demands of truth require that he reveal him as a seductive danger. Homer cannot always be trusted, either epistemically or ethically. If we required any more evidence of the prestige of Homer, it can be seen in Plato's need to begin his attack with the aesthetically unsophisticated point that Homer was not an expert in the various skills and crafts he chose to portray. (Thucydides, similarly, felt obliged to begin the *Peloponnesian War* by doing a statistical analysis of Homer's armies in order to denigrate him as an accurate military historian of the Trojan War.) More serious charges follow, however: 1) that Homer, along with the tradition of tragic mimesis, solicits identification with characters who are not moral exemplars; and 2) that all art appeals primarily to the emotions and thereby caters to our lesser selves. These two failures have a common set of causes: 1) poets have no special knowledge of the good, so are prone to produce inferior, emotionally driven souls; and 2) audiences demand the titillation of emotional excitation; a philosopher lost in contemplation doesn't make great theater or gripping narrative:

> Clearly, then, an imitative poet isn't by nature related to the part of the soul [the quiet rational faculty] that rules in such a character, and if he's to attain a good reputation with the majority of people, his cleverness isn't directed to pleasing it. Instead, he's related to the excitable and multicolored character, since it is easy to imitate. (605a)

Even the rational, well-ordered soul may lose its bearings when subjected to all this agitation, for the charmed circle of poetry is believed to license

---

[4] H.-I. Marrou, *A History of Education in Antiquity*, trans. George Lamb (London: Sheed and Ward, 1956).
[5] Wilhelm Nestle, "Begründung der Jugendbildung durch die Griechen," in *Erziehung und Bildung in der Heidnischen und Christlichen Antike* (Darmstadt: Wisschenschaftliche Buchgesellschaft, 1976), p. 72.

a Mardi Gras of emotional response that we would be ashamed to indulge in otherwise. The danger, according to Plato, is that we cannot hive off our habitual response to poetry from the everyday motions of the soul (606a–606d). Poetry confirms the weak in their weakness and contaminates the strong. There can be no place for it in the commonwealth.

Kant joins Plato in holding the emotions under steady suspicion of impeding rational judgment, though he conceived of the aim of moral philosophy much more narrowly than Plato. The ancient question "How should one live?" – even if sharpened with the implicit addition "How should one live to achieve true happiness?" – was far too general for Kant. The large promise of Plato's deeply ethicized psychology was that it would lead to happiness, and inevitably so. The right ordering of the soul would make it proof against any external misfortune. No Job-like disasters or unfounded slander could affect the happiness of the noble soul. Plato's extraordinary confidence in the soul's self-sufficiency is dependent on his belief in a rationally ordered universe whose overarching Good it is within the powers of reason to see and incorporate. As Charles Taylor perceptively points out: "The correct vision [in Plato] is criterial. There is no way one could be ruled by reason and be *mistaken* or wrong about the order of reality."[6] Having once seen the Good, one is aware of the relative worth of things and organizes the soul accordingly. Metaphysically ratified in this way, the noble soul is immune to contingency's buffets. Since for Kant all that can be known about the noumenal is that it exists, he cannot link his morality to a hypergood in the manner of Plato. He insists just as strongly as Plato that human beings are distinguished by their rational agency, but he cannot make perception of an ordered universe the test of our rationality. Instead, to fulfill our rational nature and achieve the freedom consonant with our dignity, we – each of us – must discover the universal principle that constitutes the moral law. By acting for the sake of this law, we respect both ourselves and the community of other rational beings who are always to be considered as ends in themselves, not solely as means to our purposes. In this way duty has replaced the quest for the Good and its attendant happiness.

Why moral obligation should be so intimately connected to freedom becomes clearer when we consider the Newtonian background of Kant's philosophy. The phenomenal world, as Newton had demonstrated, is bound by nature's laws. Kant regards these laws as a form of limitation,

---

[6] Charles Taylor, *The Sources of the Self: The Making of Modern Identity* (Cambridge, Mass: Harvard University Press, 1989), pp. 121–22.

and extends the realm of what is determined to the rhythms of animal nature, driven by instincts and desires. Insofar as the human animal acts on these "lower" impulses, it does not transcend the sensible world at whose mercy it must remain. Only through the faculty of reason are we able to conceive of ourselves as belonging to an intelligible realm where we can become our own legislators. Thus, Kant takes it upon himself "to work out for once a pure moral philosophy, completely cleansed of everything that may be only empirical and that belongs to anthropology."[7] To be moral is to avoid the moral contradiction that occurs when the universalization self-destructs. Crucially, Kant divorces the moral worth of an act from the outcome, for the outcome may be influenced by the vagaries of the empirical world. It is the *intention* of the agent that is decisive, and that intention must be to act, not just in conformity with the law, "but for the sake of the law" (*GM* 4.390). In choosing the law for its own sake, we assert the freedom of the rationally autonomous individual.

With unremitting austerity, Kant forbids inclination (*Neigung*) – the motivation inspired by feelings – from playing any part in an act that merits moral approval. Thus, he disqualifies an act of altruism should it be inspired by a pleasurable feeling of benevolence, for "in such a case an action of this kind, however it may conform to duty and however amiable it may be, has nevertheless no true moral worth but is on the same footing with other inclinations"(*GM* 4.398). There is an allusion in this passage to Hutcheson's positing of an innate moral sense that directs us benevolently toward our fellows, an idea echoed in Rousseau's discovery of a deep propensity in the state of nature toward sympathy in the human heart. But Kant rejects sentiment as an adequate guide to morality, for if there are "many souls ... sympathetically attuned," there are some at least who are not. Yet no system of morality can afford to excuse those who have not been naturally blessed with this gift. Moreover, even those who have this propensity may not be disposed to exercise it consistently, either day to day or person to person. Taken together, then, these two shortcomings of moral sentiment will make it an unreliable source of moral behavior, according to Kant. Because it is randomly distributed and volatile, it

---

[7] Immanuel Kant, *Groundwork of the Metaphysics of Morals*, trans. and ed. by Mary Gregor (Cambridge: Cambridge University Press, 1998) (4.389). Citations refer to volume and page number in the standard *Akademie* edition: *Kants Gesammelte Schriften* (Berlin: Königlich Preußische Akademie der Wissenschaft, 1902–). Hereafter, references to *Groundwork* will be cited in the text by *GM* plus volume and page number in parentheses.

cannot guarantee the universalizability and consistency Kant demands of moral principle.

Even those more favorably disposed to emotions might be able to accommodate Kant up to this point in his argument. But in his description of the cold-hearted philanthropist, he pushes his case another step:

> If nature had put little sympathy in the heart of this or that man; if (in other respects an honest man) he is by temperament cold and indifferent to the suffering of others, perhaps because he himself is provided with the special gift of patience and endurance toward his own suffering ... would he still not find within himself a far higher worth than what a good-natured temperament might have? By all means! It is just then that the worth of character comes out, which is moral and incomparably the highest, namely that he is beneficent not from inclination but from duty. (GM 4.398)

The claim that emotional frigidity is consonant with "incomparably the highest" form of morality brings about a radical parting of the ways with – to take the strongest counter-position – Aristotle's moral psychology. In the *Ethics*, which will be discussed in detail shortly, Aristotle distinguishes between the self-controlled person (the possessor of *enkrateia*) and the virtuous (who embodies *aretê*). The former, knowing what the right thing to do is and doing it, will act contrary to his desires; the latter, knowing and *feeling* what the right thing to do is, will do it *while desiring to do it*. It is only the second of these, according to Aristotle, who is fully virtuous.[8]

Central to Kant's admiration for the cold-hearted philanthropist is his mistrust of fellow-feeling in general. Love of others is always subtly, and sometimes not so subtly, implicated in self-love, the pursuit of personal happiness. In Kant, however, happiness never enlarges to the Greek sense of *eudaimonia*; it is always under suspicion as a form of hedonism, since he holds that happiness comes from the gratification of desires, the indulgence in passions. And even in this short-sighted quest for happiness, we must fail, for our notion of what would bring us satisfaction, under constant pressure from uncoordinated desire, is too unstable to allow us to achieve the wished-for results. Worse, because both desires and feelings attach themselves to objects, we are left to the mercy of the empirical world, itself as changing and unreliable as the feelings it inspires (*GM* 4.418). Neither would the problem be solved by positing an unresisting world – the granting of Gyges' ring – "for [human] nature is not so constituted as to

---

[8] Rosalind Hursthouse, in *On Virtue Ethics* (Oxford: Oxford University Press, 1999) notes the distinction between the two types, but believes they are not as far apart as I have suggested here.

rest or be satisfied in any possession or enjoyment whatsoever."[9] In the end, as with Plato, our inclinations can only lead us morally astray.

The picture of moral rectitude that Kant paints is deliberately austere, and, as he seems to realize, in danger of becoming inhumane in its suppression of feeling. Moral activity must be accompanied almost inevitably by varying degrees of psychological pain, depending on the strength of our contrary passions. In fact, as the example of the cold-hearted philanthropist implies, the greater the temptation to act otherwise, the more demonstrably moral the act. The psychological payoff for enduring this pain consists solely in the awareness that we have asserted our rational freedom. Faced with an affectively dead morality, he does, however, manage to smuggle in one of the coolest emotions, self-respect:

> As *submission* to the law, therefore, that is, as a command (announcing constraint for the sensibly affected subject), it [duty] contains in it no pleasure, but on the contrary, so far, pain in the action. On the other hand, however, as this constraint is exercised merely by the legislation of our *own* reason, it also contains something *elevating*, and this subjective effect on feeling, inasmuch as pure practical reason is the sole cause of it, may be called in this respect *self-approbation* ... [T]his feeling obtains a special name, that of respect.[10]

Even here, though, it is important to see that self-respect is not really motivational; it *attends* the will's choosing rightly. Unlike Hume, who held that motivation came through the passions alone, Kant believes that practical reason is itself motivating.[11]

But if morality must preserve its universalizability by excluding emotion, what are we to make of aesthetics? Kant could have answered the question by following his teacher Baumgarten, who believed that rules of beauty could be deduced. To adjudge something beautiful, then, would involve a cognition of properties as beauty-making. Aesthetics would in

---

[9] I have relied heavily in this paragraph on J. B. Schneewind's magisterial study of Kant and his predecessors, *The Invention of Autonomy: A History of Modern Moral Philosophy* (Cambridge: Cambridge University Press, 1998). The quotation from Kant is from *Critique of Judgment* (5.430). Hereafter, references to this work will be taken from *Critique of Judgment*, trans. by Werner S. Pluhar (Indianapolis: Hackett Publishing Company, 1987), and given in the text by *CJ* followed by the *Akademie* volume and page number in parentheses.

[10] Immanuel Kant, *Critique of Practical Reason*, trans. T. K. Abbot (Amherst: Prometheus Books, 1996) (5.80–81).

[11] Here Kant seems to harken back to the classical idea of *boulêses*, purely rational motivation. Schneewind, differing here, believes that Kant is trying to buttress his position by pressing respect into motivational service. See J. B. Schneewind, *The Invention of Autonomy: A History of Modern Moral Philosophy* (Cambridge: Cambridge University Press, 1998), p. 521.

this way approximate the regularity of science.[12] Alternatively, Kant could have dismissed aesthetics as merely subjective talk about the personally agreeable, preferences for which no disputable reasons could be given. If this were so, we could do no better defending an absorption in Dante than an addiction to chocolate ice cream. In the *Critique of Judgment*, Kant, however, rejects both of these possibilities. In answer to Baumgarten, he maintains that aesthetic judgments contribute nothing to the cognition of their objects; they are based on a feeling of pleasure aroused by the objects (*CJ* 5.194). We make no knowledge claims about objects in declaring them beautiful, i.e., we do not assert that the objects possess properties that then can be subsumed under a general principle of beauty. If we could, then we might be persuaded reasonably that an object that we had never experienced must be beautiful in the same way we could be led to hold a firm scientific belief about the atmosphere of Venus (*CJ* 5. 215–16). Kant, at the same time, wishes to avoid a flaccid relativism. The crucial problem of the *Critique* is abstracted by Kant in the famous antinomy of taste:

> 1) Thesis: A judgment of taste is not based on concepts; for otherwise one could dispute about it (decide by means of proof). 2) Antithesis: A judgment of taste is based on concepts; for otherwise, regardless of the variation among [such judgments], one could not even so much as quarrel about them (lay claim to other people's necessary assent to one's judgment). (CJ 5. 338–39)

The focus of Kant's attention here, as always, is objectivity, a concern that links him intimately to most of what has occupied literary theory in recent times.

As it turns out, the solution to this antinomy hinges on the type of pleasurable feeling that determines a judgment of taste. Yet, given Kant's clear mistrust of the capriciousness of feeling, it is not immediately clear what the candidates for such a feeling could be. What sort of feeling could generate a judgment that would make a claim to everyone's assent? To sort out an answer, Kant invokes the notion of "disinterested interest," a concept that had been in circulation in the eighteenth century.[13] While this term does not do all the work that Kant would wish, or as neatly as he would wish, what he intends is clear enough. He hopes to distinguish appetitive pleasures (including an appetite for engaging with putative good involved in didactic appeal) from contemplative pleasure. While a work of art (or natural splendor) may bring about a desirable state of mind, it is not

---

[12] Donald W. Crawford, *Kant's Aesthetic Theory* (Madison: University of Wisconsin Press, 1974), pp. 29–30.
[13] Crawford, *Kant's Aesthetic Theory*, pp. 37–38.

itself an object of desire. To understand the line of Kant's argument in what follows we must recall that his epistemology allows us only a representation of objects. What takes place during the experience of the beautiful is that we organize the representation of the object into a pattern. We do so by means of the interaction of the faculties of imagination and understanding, which together are responsible for giving shape to the manifold of sensory data. Kant refers to the aesthetic organization of an object as "purposiveness without a purpose" (Zweckmässigkeit ohne Zweck), i.e., we understand the structure as if it were caused by a purposeful will, yet this understanding is independent of any such actual will. The disinterestedness and independence of mind involved in aesthetic perception allow a particularly high degree of free-play of our faculties as they order our experience. The pleasure we derive from this contemplation consists of two analytically separable elements: 1) The untrammeled harmonizing of our faculties in an exercise of rational freedom, and 2) The recognition that the world is amenable to the faculties of cognition that we bring to bear on it. Thus, aesthetic pleasure is attributable to both an internal and an external harmony. What allows this aesthetic experience to yield universal judgment – even though it involves no objectively determinate concept – is that it is grounded in the harmony of faculties that enable cognition itself. This interplay of faculties Kant speaks of as a *sensus communis*:

> But this attunement of the cognitive powers varies in its proportion, depending on what difference there is among the objects that are given. And yet there must be one attunement in which this inner relation is most conducive to the (mutual) quickening of the two mental powers with a view to cognition (of given objects) in general; and the only way this attunement can be determined is by feeling (rather than by concepts). Moreover, this attunement itself, and hence also the feeling of it (when a presentation is given), must be universally communicable, while the universal communicability of a feeling presupposes a common sense. (CJ 5. 238–39)

Thus, the precise coordination of understanding and imagination (the two faculties referred to above) in the aesthetic moment gives rise to a feeling that is universally recognizable. Not content to base commonality on a feeling, Kant argues that the feeling itself is generated by a sense common to all and that this sense can be appealed to when trying to justify aesthetic judgments.

While the epistemological assumptions of the *Critique of Judgment* obviously rely on the *Critique of Pure Reason*, what of the moral imperative of the *Critique of Practical Reason*? Does Kant's account of aesthetic pleasure bear any relationship to moral concerns? In terms of the representation of the object, whether it be natural or man-made, the answer is clearly "no." Any response to the moral properties of an object would argue the very interest that localizes rather than universalizes our pleasure. Kant's aesthetics demands that we consider only the *formal* subjective purposiveness of an object. In that regard it bears affinity to the various "art for art's sake" movements of the nineteenth century and, allowing for the more objective formalism of New Criticism, to that critical school in the twentieth century.[14] Indeed, it is precisely Kant's worry that conceptualization in a work of art might play a part in its appeal that leads him in the end to prefer the aesthetic experience of natural scenes. At times Kant suggests that aesthetic sensitivity may be a necessary condition of a morally alert disposition, but at other times seems to know better (*CJ* 5. 298–99). His most sustained argument for a connection between beauty and morality is that beauty is a *symbol* of morality. In the aesthetic experience, we impose an order on the sensible by means of supersensible faculties. In doing so, we regard the natural or artistic objects of our contemplation as amenable to our patternings. In an analogous way, Kant wants to argue, we legislate the moral law, and through practical reason endeavor to impose it on the empirical world. Though consequences are not decisive in judging a will to be good, the choices of the good will are *intended* to have an impact in the realm of phenomena. In this way, beauty and morality resemble one another. Yet it is never made absolutely clear why beauty should be a symbol for morality rather than vice versa.[15] Perhaps what Kant is assuming here is that to be fully moral one must be aware of the purely rational basis for morality, and this is made clearest in the aesthetic reflection on the supersensible freedom of our faculties and their harmonious interaction.

Unlike Plato, Kant establishes a positive connection between art and morality. However, to do so he must first drain a work of its own implied moral positions and sever the observer from any identification with the emotional energies of the work. In this way he avoids the very two complaints that Plato had lodged against art. But what he leaves us with

---

[14] William K. Wimsatt, Jr. and Cleanth Brooks make the connection to the nineteenth-century aesthetic tradition in their *Literary Criticism: A Short History* (New York: Vintage Books, 1957), pp. 490–91. René Wellek, in his *A History of Modern Criticism; 1750–1950*, vol. 6 (New Haven: Yale University Press, 1986), chapters 8 and 9 passim, demonstrates Kant's influence on the New Critics, especially John Crowe Ransom and Allen Tate.

[15] For a discussion of this question, see Ted Cohen, "Why Beauty Is a Symbol of Morality," in *Essays in Kant's Aesthetics*, ed. and introduced by Ted Cohen and Paul Guyer (Chicago: University of Chicago Press, 1982).

is a rarified formal gratification that, at best, fosters the transcendental perspective necessary for the abstraction of the categorical imperative. This is not to say that the formal pleasure in art that Kant stresses is negligible, though it is often clumsily ignored in an age of ideology. Nor is it to deny that art, by engendering a transport beyond the purely sensible, may at some level enhance the similar disposition required of moral consideration. But in salvaging what he has, Kant has had to give up too much. In the end, he himself acknowledges that the foliage on wallpaper would be a purer, because conceptless, example of beauty than – to supply an implied contrast – an idea-laden tragedy of Shakespeare (*CJ* 5. 229).

What underlies both Plato's dismissal of the (positive) ethical import of literature and Kant's attenuation of it is their common refusal to grant emotions a significant role in moral agency. If they are right, then the most literature would have to contribute to our ethical knowledge would be to provide examples of reason-derived rules of behavior, or, only slightly more promisingly, to demonstrate in vivid detail how the morally correct life involves steady suppression of affective interference. We might recall in this regard that even Plato is willing to approve of selected uplifting passages in the much blue-penciled Homer, as in the case of Odysseus' self-exhortations to restrain his rage at the spectacle of the brazen abuse of his household (*Odyssey* 20. 27–28). On this view, literature can at best serve an ancillary role as "Plato for the people," a warehouse of memorable instances of strongly rule-guided behavior derived with technical sophistication elsewhere. Indeed, one too frequently hears varieties of this opinion in philosophy departments today, even from many who would consider themselves sympathetic to literature. For those who think this way, the primary justification for literature's inclusion in cross-disciplinary humanities programs is based almost solely on its aesthetic value and that it has, on account of that value, been traditionally considered a component of "culture." Ethics, properly understood, is to be left to the philosophers. (This is not to claim, by any means, that those in literature are typically more successful at doing justice to philosophy; in fact, the grosser, more partisan errors have tended to come from that direction.)

What seems clear, then, is that if literature is to make a more extensive claim on our ethical attention, a stronger case for the role of emotions will have to be put forward. In particular, emotions will have to be shown to have a cognitive capacity greater than Plato or Kant allow. This capacity must involve both the cognitive corrigibility of emotions and, even more importantly, the ability of properly tutored emotions to shape an ethical response. Such a view would entail Aristotle's recognition that the ethically enriched life requires one to feel the right emotion, on the right occasion, toward the right object, in the right degree. Virtue involves an active emotional response, not suppression or dutiful acquiescence. As an example, we might take the not unusual situation in which one attends by the bedside of a dying parent. The child would pass the Kantian test for moral worth with flying colors if her inclination urged her to be elsewhere more enjoyable, but that nonetheless, she recognized and acted on her obligation to sit with the dying parent. Aristotle's stance – and it certainly seems persuasive – is that a parent who was aware that her child attended her passing *only* out of a sense of duty would be justified in complaining about a lack of humanity in her offspring. Likewise, something would also be missing in the parting if Plato had his way. Because of his complete sequestering of happiness from external misfortune, the nobly equipoised soul would be allowed only a Houynhym-like leave-taking. But Aristotle would rightly remind us that to preclude the ache of grief under such circumstances is to subtract from life, and the life of both parties.

It is important to note that the grief in the preceding example would not be unrestrained or inappropriate, for Aristotle presents a developmental view of moral psychology in which the emotions are highly receptive to modification. There is, first of all, a cognitive element intimately associated with emotion, though this often gets ignored in the facile opposition of the rational (cognition) and the irrational (emotion). To continue with the example, the child who believes in an afterlife and is convinced her parent will cross over to a happier state will very likely feel a grief mitigated by this prospect, a feeling in its particular complexity different from the grief of the non-believer (though, of course, hers may be assuaged by some other consoling belief). An even simpler example would be the situation in which the belief that one had been insulted is accompanied by anger or indignation. If the person so aroused could be convinced that there was no insult intended, the emotion should disappear as this cognitive re-estimation takes place.[16] What follows from these examples is that to talk of emotions as irrational typically means that the belief component is unlikely to be true. The limiting case of this would be the paranoid personality who believes that all conversations involved plots against him and lives in a state of nearly perpetual fear and anxiety as a result.

---

[16] This is most clearly seen in the *Rhetoric* (1378a 8) where Aristotle notes "The emotions are those things through which, by undergoing change, people come to differ in their judgments and which are accompanied by pain and pleasure, for example, anger, pity, fear, and other such things and their opposites."

Because virtually all emotion involves belief about an object, it is important to get these beliefs right as soon as possible. We must be taught what matters and in what degree before we could possibly give a systematic account of why this should be so. With this in mind, Aristotle relies very heavily on childhood habituation in the formation of virtuous character. In a proper upbringing – and it seems almost impossible to compensate later for its lack – children are taught to perform just and noble acts before they fully understand why they are just and noble. Further, because a child's sense of pleasure and pain remain for some the sole source of motivation, feelings of pleasure must be associated with just and noble things, and feelings of distaste for their opposites.[17] Emotions, themselves tutored both in kind and degree, come to attach themselves in the right way in a series of particular situations. From this emotional patterning should emerge sensitivity not reducible to rules or precepts, though it must be assumed that general moral advice will provide guidance.[18] At this point, we are a long way from the almost purely rationalistic position of Plato and Kant. I think this can be seen most clearly in Aristotle's explanation of *akrasia* as a failure to *inhabit* moral knowledge:

> Now it is clear that we must attribute to the morally weak a condition similar to that of men who are asleep, mad, or drunk. That the words they utter spring from knowledge (as to what is good) is no evidence to the contrary. People can repeat geometrical demonstrations and verses of Empedocles even when affected by sleep, madness, and drink; and beginning students can reel off the words they have heard, but they do not yet know the subject. The subject must grow to be part of them, and that takes time. We must, therefore, assume that a man who displays moral weakness repeats the formulae (of moral knowledge) in the same way an actor speaks his lines. (NE 1147a 17–22)

The knowledge necessary for an act to count as virtuous requires a full emotional awareness; the performance of the virtuous act requires an emotional affirmation.

The tight fit between cognition and emotion is evident in his aesthetic theory as well. As is well known, in the *Poetics* Aristotle talks of tragedy as a mimesis that through pity and fear brings about the proper purgation of

---

[17] Aristotle, *Nicomachean Ethics*, trans. Martin Oswald (Indianapolis: Bobbs-Merrill, 1980), 1104b 3–14. References to this work will hereafter be cited in the text by *NE* followed by standard Bekker numbers in parentheses.

[18] For an illuminating discussion of the importance of moral training in Aristotle, see M. F. Burnyeat, "Aristotle on Learning to Be Good," in *Aristotle's Ethics: Critical Essays*, ed. Nancy Sherman (Lanham: Rowman and Littlefield, 1999), pp. 205–30.

the emotions. As Aristotle elaborates this terse description, he arrives at something very close to Eliot's objective correlative, the skillful handling of poetic material in order to elicit a specific emotional response. Of course, exactly to what end these emotions are to be aroused will depend on how one interprets the controversial term *kartharsis*. If it can be shown to include a refinement of the emotions, as I believe, then we will have established an important basis for art's nourishment of our moral lives, relying as they do on affective discrimination.

Despite its prominence in the definition of tragedy, *katharsis* is mentioned only in that definition and no clarification of the term is ever offered elsewhere in the text.[19] What does seem reasonably certain is that Aristotle's use of *katharsis* is intended as a rebuttal to Plato's insistence on the psychological harm produced by tragic poetry.[20] This would mean that the consequences of emotional stimulation brought about by tragedy should, according to Aristotle, enhance the psychological well-being of the onlooker. S. H. Butcher, the nineteenth-century translator and elegant exegete of the *Poetics*, helpfully calls the curative function of tragedy "homeopathic," the treatment of like by like: pity and fear are introduced to restore these emotions to a healthy state.[21] But how radical is this cure to be? There existed a medicinal use of the term *katharsis* to indicate an evacuation of harmful elements from the body; there also existed a religious use of the term to indicate the process of purification necessary for one about to participate in a ritualistic ceremony.[22]

If Aristotle is relying solely on the first of these, then tragedy's goal would be to empty out the emotions of pity and fear. Perhaps the most prominent exponent of this view is Corneille, with Dryden and Johnson subscribing to forms of it. If Aristotle had in mind primarily the second view, we arrive at something closer to a refinement of the emotions (though this may involve a draining off of excess as part of the process). This view is expounded at length by Lessing in the *Hamburg Dramaturgy* and briefly by Milton in the preface to *Samson Agonistes*. As Lessing points out in his criticism of Corneille, those who believe that Aristotle is prescribing an emetic concentrate almost exclusively on fear, which they misleadingly

---

[19] Aristotle does mention *catharsis* briefly in the *Politics* when he ascribes to music educational and cathartic purposes, but unhelpfully refers us back to the *Poetics* for an understanding of the term.
[20] Stephen Halliwell, *Aristotle's Poetics* (Chapel Hill: University of North Carolina Press, 1986), p. 184. My argument on *katharsis* follows Halliwell's closely.
[21] S. H. Butcher, *Aristotle's Theory of Poetry and Fine Art* (London: St. Martin's 1894; rpt. Dover 1951), pp. 247ff. Hereafter references to the *Poetics* will be given in the text by *Poet* followed by standard Bekker numbers in parentheses.
[22] Halliwell, *Aristotle's Poetics*, p. 186.

exaggerate to terror to explain why its elimination is salutary. As corrective, Lessing helpfully directs us to the *Rhetoric*, the work that contains Aristotle's fullest account of the emotions. There Aristotle indicates that both pity and fear are perfectly appropriate responses to certain situations and thus are part of a healthy emotional apparatus even though both involve pain. Either can, like any emotion, become excessive or misdirected, but that certainly need not be the case. If fear needs more justification than pity, Aristotle brilliantly provides it by pointing out that pity would be impossible without fear. We pity where we fear that the same misfortune that befalls the victim might threaten us. As a corollary, Aristotle points out that those deficient in the capacity to fear are incapable of pity. As instances he points out those whose fortunes have fallen so low that they believe they have nothing left to fear and, conversely, those so inflated by happiness that insolent pride (*hybris*) leads them to believe themselves beyond misfortune. In both cases, *not* to fear reduces the range of virtuous response. It is hard to imagine, then, that Aristotle had in mind by *katharsis* the eradication of pity and fear.

The cognitive structure of both emotions, especially pity, is further evidence that Aristotle is addressing more subtle modifications than the radical theory of *katharsis* would allow. In his analysis of the experience of pity, he outlines several necessary preconditions beyond the mere observation of suffering: 1) the evil that befalls the victim must be judged to be undeserved; 2) the evil must be of a kind that could threaten the observer or someone close to him; 3) the victim must be someone considered sufficiently like the onlooker to guarantee sympathetic identification.[23] Far from being an uncontrollable transport that irrationally carries one off, pity entails a great deal of preliminary discrimination. Even fear, more simply, involves at least the belief that one is in immediate danger.

On the basis of similar observations, Lessing sees *katharsis* effecting a subtle adjustment of emotions consonant with the call for a mean advocated in the *Ethics*:

> This purification rests in nothing else than in the transformation of passions into virtuous habits, and since according to our philosopher each virtue has two extremes between which it rests, it follows that if tragedy is to change our pity into virtue it must also be able to purify us from the two extremes of pity, and the same is understood of fear. Tragic pity must not only purify the soul of him who has too much pity, but also of him who has too little; tragic

---

[23] Aristotle, *On Rhetoric*, trans. by George A. Kennedy (Oxford: Oxford University Press, 1991) (1386a 12–15).

fear must not simply purify the soul of him who does not fear any manner of misfortune but also of him who is terrified by every misfortune, even the most distant and improbable.[24]

While it is true that Aristotle never links the aesthetic treatment of art in the *Poetics* directly to ethics as Lessing does here, his theory of *katharsis* would be philosophically trivial if the connection were not implicit. Without it the spectacle of tragic suffering and the strong reaction it arouses would make essentially no difference to us. At most, there would result the relaxation that follows the resolution of temporary agitation. It might, nonetheless, still be argued that aesthetic emotion is of a significantly different kind than non-aesthetic emotion and therefore ethically irrelevant, but in the *Politics* Aristotle expressly denies this.[25] In fact, he concludes the *Politics* with an account of the way various types of music can be influential in cultivating virtue: "But for educational purposes, as we have said, for its purposes we must use tunes and modes too which have *ethical* value" (*Pol* 1342a 28).

This is not by any means to suggest that Aristotle is putting forth a crudely didactic theory of poetry, if by that is meant the inculcation of something amounting to a moral lesson. That sort of abstraction is left to the pedestrian summations of the tragic chorus: "the gods bring things to surprising endings" or "we should judge no life fortunate before it has reached conclusion." Instead, what art and ethical training have in common is the tutelage of emotion, more carefully orchestrated in the stylized presentation of art. Aristotle's demands on plot and character are ground rules for enabling the desired emotive effect. We are led to feel the right emotion for the right reason in just the right intensity. Nor, of course, is Aristotle naïve enough to believe that the emotional experience undergone will inevitably result in nobler behavior. The most he – or any advocate of an essentially emotive connection between art and ethics – can reasonably assert is that the sensitive perceiver will emerge from the artistic encounter with a refreshed, ideally heightened, *disposition* toward virtue.

The similarity between poetry and philosophy is underscored in the *Poetics* in the well-known passage where Aristotle distinguishes poetry from history: "The true difference [between history and poetry] is that one relates what has happened, the other what may happen. Poetry, therefore,

---

[24] G. E. Lessing, *Hamburg Dramaturgy*, trans. by Helen Zimmern (New York: Dover, 1962), sec. 78.
[25] Aristotle, *Politics*, trans. T. A. Sinclair, rev. Trevor J. Saunders (New York: Penguin Books, 1982). (1340a 16–18). Hereafter reference to this work will be cited in the text by *Pol* followed by standard Bekker numbers in parentheses.

is a more philosophical and higher thing than history: for poetry tends to express the universal, history the particular" (*Poet* 1451b 4–8). Here we are immediately aware that this assertion is meant as a rebuttal to Plato's denigration of poetry as an enterprise that never rises above the surface of life, which it vainly imitates, a copy at two removes from the Forms. In a bold stroke, Aristotle declares a truce in "the ancient quarrel between philosophy and poetry" by pronouncing the two antagonists to be allies. Poetry, too, will establish patterns as opposed to immersing us in indiscriminate experience. It will show us what *ought* to follow from an act if we abstract it from the distortions of contingency. Near the end of Jane Austen's *Emma*, Mr. Knightley protests that the caddish Frank Churchill was "too much indebted to the event for his acquittal"[26] – i.e., that the playing out of events spared him from bearing the consequences of his shabby behavior (a complaint that Knightley might have made with equal justness about the meddlesome Emma herself). This is precisely what Aristotle would avoid in the less forgiving genre of tragedy. If the emotions are to be clarified, let it be in response to a pure case, one that follows an internal logic that looks inexorable. The particularism of the everyday will present us with an infinite number of variations from this norm, but the variations can only be evaluated by their deviation from that norm. And, in the end, this is consistent with the balance found in Aristotle's ethical writings where he describes a fixed set of virtues, but counsels a flexible means in their exercise.

There exists, however, a second challenge to this Aristotelian view of poetry as a stage for the cognitive and moral power of emotion, and once again the locus is Plato. In the *Ion*, Plato raises again the question of what kind of knowledge poets possess and ultimately convey in their work. At times Socrates, Ion's interlocutor, will pursue a line of argument familiar from the *Republic*: poets speak of many areas such as warfare, medicine, and navigation; yet surely if one wished to gain knowledge (*technê*) of these crafts, it would be better to consult generals, doctors, and pilots. Once one subtracts all the amateurish claims to domain-specific knowledge, there is little left in poetry to count as wisdom. Yet Plato clearly seems to realize that there is a power to poetry that this unsympathetic analysis does not account for. Ion, the rhapsode, raises the possibility that there may be an independent *technê* that belongs exclusively to poetry – a reasonable enough assumption since all worthwhile crafts are, according to Plato, reliant on such a body of knowledge. According to Ion, the poetic craft

---

[26] Jane Austen, *Emma* (Boston: Riverside Press, 1957), p. 350.

would include the knowledge of "What it is proper for a man to say ... or what for a woman, what for a slave or what for a free man, what for a subject or what for a ruler" (540a–b).[27] This suggestion of Ion would license something like Aristotle's *Poetics*, a parsing of the *technê* of the poet who, among other things, makes his characters say what they ought to say.[28] Yet, Socrates dismisses this almost immediately by choosing to overemphasize the role (e.g., general, pilot) and underestimate the circumstanced individual in that role. Because Socrates will not countenance Ion's suggestion that the poet might master material and convey the product of his mastery, he is left with the option that the poet may be divinely possessed: like a lodestone, the god perforce magnetically attracts the "ring" of the poet, which in turn leads to the compelled concatenation of the "rings" of the rhapsode and finally the audience (*Ion* 533d–536d). This view leaves us with an ecstatic poet conveying a highly emotionally charged language that he cannot fully understand, and in this way echoes Plato's judgment elsewhere that the emotions are irrational. Yet, tantalizingly, Plato leaves open the possibility that they could be irrational *and* of oracular value. Because he never reconciles this view of poetry with his charge about the poet's specious claims to ordinary, practical knowledge, it is hard to know what sort of truth claims can be made for poetry.[29]

This tension in Plato's view needed to be addressed not just by philosophers but also by literary critics and theorists, and here, as in so much else, Plato established a framework for subsequent thought. Perhaps the most insightful response in the classical literary tradition is Longinus' *On the Sublime*. Though there is some debate on who precisely Longinus was and when he lived (sometime from the first to the third century CE), far more relevant is that he was a Greek speaker well acquainted with the Hellenic philosophical and literary tradition. At first glance, the work appears to be yet one more contribution to classical rhetoric, and clearly that is one of its purposes as Longinus, typically with great subtlety, comments on rhetorical devices in poetry and oration. Such commentary

---

[27] I have used W. H. D. Rouse's translation in *Great Dialogues of Plato* (New York: Mentor, 1956). Hereafter references to the *Ion* will be cited in the text by *Ion* followed by the section and line number in parentheses.

[28] For an excellent discussion of the *Ion*, see "To Banish or Not to Banish? Plato's Unanswered Question about Poetry," in Steven Halliwell, *Between Ecstasy and Truth: Interpretations of Greek Poetics from Homer to Longinus* (New York: Oxford University Press, 2011), pp. 155–207.

[29] For a different view, see Suzanne Stern-Gillet, "On (Mis)Interpreting Plato's *Ion*," in *Phronesis*, vol. 49, no. 2 (2004), 169–201. There she argues that the tension is only apparent due to the mistaken Romanticized readings of Shelley and others that make divine inspiration positive, rather than ironically dismissive as Plato intended.

would place Longinus squarely in the tradition of technical discussion found in Aristotle's *Rhetoric*. Yet in the *Rhetoric* Aristotle is content to leave the art of persuasion morally neutral: it can be employed equally by the virtuous speaker enjoining the good or by the depraved advocating the vicious (though he does concede that it is generally easier to convince that the good is good than that the bad is good). Plato, however, is much less willing to divorce the *what* is being said from the *how* it is being said. Rhetoric for him, as the *mere* art of persuasion, is denigrated as sophism. He is fully aware that philosophic dialectic itself tries to seek out the best means to persuade and thus has a rhetorical element, but philosophy tries to convey knowledge, not mere opinion or belief. It is intended primarily to bring all parties closer to the truth, not to achieve personal celebrity or political success. Rhetoric in the service of truth is to be commended; rhetoric in the service of power (Thrasymachus' position) is not. In the latter case, it becomes a sort of beguiling enchantment, and as such Plato will often associate sophistic rhetoric with poetry: neither the sophist nor the poet – witness Homer's ignorance of the various *technai* he sings of – possesses true wisdom, though both are at pains to convince us that they do. How this diminished view of poetry is to be squared with its vatic potential becomes Longinus' starting point.

Longinus begins by pointedly insisting that no level of rhetorical proficiency can ever, by itself, explain true sublimity (*hypsos*) of expression. The sublime moves us in ways different from rhetoric:

> Great writing does not persuade; it takes the reader out of himself. The startling and amazing is more powerful than the charming and persuasive, if it is indeed true that to be convinced is usually within our control whereas amazement is the result of an irresistible force beyond the control of any audience.[30]

This certainly captures Plato's recognition of literature as capable of ecstatic transport. Yet, though Longinus never fully jettisons the idea that the poet may be divinely inspired, he tends to emphasize the qualities of the poet's mind. The two most important sources for sublime creation reside within the poet: "First and most important is vigor of mental conception ... Second is strong and inspired emotion. Both of these are for the most part innate dispositions" (*S* 8.1). This naturalization of sublime creation makes it far more likely that the poet may have cognitive

---

[30] Longinus, *On Great Writing (On the Sublime)*, trans. G. M. A. Grube (Cambridge: Hackett Publishing Co, Inc., 1991), 1.3. Hereafter references to this work will be given in the text as *S* plus chapter and subdivision in parentheses.

control of his ecstatic expression than if he or she were merely a divinely employed conduit. The employment of well-chosen figures of speech (rhetoric) to express these *éclats* furthers the sense of the poet's understanding and control. However, at the same time, in a far more dramatic image than Plato's lodestone with attracted rings, Longinus likens the power of the sublime on the reader to a "thunderbolt." The experience is clearly extra-ordinary, but *how*?

The answer to this question will have serious implications for the cognitive-emotional value of literature that Nussbaum urges. Nor can the issue be sidestepped entirely by noting that Nussbaum confines herself deliberately to the novel. Longinus makes clear that his conception of the sublime transcends genre and can even be found in the great oratory of Demosthenes. (This far-reaching view of the sublime will raise the different problem of whether the emotional effect Nussbaum finds inherent in literature may not also be found in history or biography – but let me table that for later.) If Nussbaum's theory is to survive intact, these passages of intensely elevated emotion must be shown to have a truth content, for Longinus makes clear that it is the occurrence of such passages that distinguishes great literature from the mediocre. The contending position would be that these ecstatic moments constitute rapturous experiences whose value resides in their exercise of a typically untapped potential in us. As such they would serve as an expansion of being, rather than a transmission of knowledge. In this way, they would be purely self-ratifying, needing no further justification. Though he does not cite Longinus as a source, Charles Altieri has essentially staked out this case in his recent rebuttal to Nussbaum and it serves as perhaps the sharpest line of attack.[31]

Let us start with the instance seemingly most difficult to accommodate to Nussbaum's cognitive claims for emotions and literature's representation of those emotions: Longinus' citing of the famous ode by Sappho that we only have because of his citation. Here are the last two stanzas in which the persona is transfixed by the sight of her beloved:

> Yea, my tongue is broken, and through and through me
> 'Neath the flesh, impalpable fire runs tingling;
> Nothing see mine eyes, and a noise of roaring
> Waves in my ears sounds

---

[31] Charles Altieri, *The Particulars of Rapture: An Aesthetic of the Affects* (Ithaca: Cornell University Press, 2003).

*Literature as the Recalibration of Emotions* 35

> Sweat runs down in rivers, a tremor seizes
> All my limbs and paler than grass in autumn,
> Caught by pains of menacing death, I falter,
> Lost in the love trance. (*S* 10.2)

The poem consists solely of the single ecstatic moment of sexual obsession. There is no larger context to help us to a view outside the speaker's. The subtle triangulations of a novel are burned off by the experience. Is the emotional force of this poem in any way cognitive-evaluative, or is its power purely that of amazement (*ekplexis*)? Would the importation of Nussbaum here be a misguided attempt to Apollonize the Dionysian? In his commentary, Longinus praises the concentration of intense details in which the persona's body seems simultaneously alienated and overwhelmingly engaged.[32] Less clear at this point is the value he attaches to this striking example of sublimity. The issue here is the one that Yeats, inheritor of Sappho's eroticism, raises brilliantly in "Leda and the Swan." In the moment when Leda, forced by Zeus in the shape of a swan, intersects with the divine, Yeats wonders what exactly she experienced: "Did she put on his knowledge with his power/ Before the indifferent beak could let her drop?"

Fortunately, Longinus provides other examples of the sublime that, taken together with the Sappho poem, might help us work toward an answer. Two of the most low-key, and thus furthest from Sappho, involve the Homeric representation of Ajax: one from the *Iliad*, the other from the *Odyssey*. In the first of these, Zeus has shrouded the Greeks in a mist, confounding them as the Trojans advance. Unafraid of death, but wishing to engage properly in the one-to-one combat that defines a hero, Ajax pleads:

> Ward off this gloomy darkness, father Zeus,
> Restore the light, grant that our eyes may see,
> And in the light destroy us, if you must. (*S* 9.7)[33]

In the second of these, Odysseus comes across Ajax in the underworld, still bearing his searing grudge against Odysseus, who was granted the honorific armor of Achilles rather than him, a slight that led to Ajax' suicide. In the

---

[32] T. S. Eliot likewise praises the striking corporeal manifestation of emotion in this poem: "You will see that Sappho's great ode ... is a real advance, a development, in human consciousness; it sets down, within its verse, the unity of an experience which had previously only existed unconsciously; in recording the physical concomitants of an emotion it modifies the emotion." "First Clark Lecture" in *The Varieties of Metaphysical Poetry by T. S. Eliot*, ed. and introduced by Ronald Schuchard (New York: Harcourt, Brace and Company, 1993), p. 51.
[33] Quoted from *Iliad*, 17, 645–47.

text of the *Odyssey*, Odysseus beseeches Ajax: "Conquer your indignation and your pride." Yet he is met with stony silence:

> But he gave no reply, and turned away,
> Following other ghosts toward Erebos.
> Who knows if in that darkness he might still
> have spoken, and I answered. (11. 561–66)[34]

Certainly, neither of these two Homeric passages has the feverish tone of Sappho's. But what all three do have in common according to Longinus is that the author has a flawless gift for selecting the significant details of an emotional situation, joining them "harmoniously without inserting between them anything irrelevant, frivolous, or artificial" (*S* 10.5). It is this intense abstraction that lends such passages their timeless appeal: "[c]onsider truly great and beautiful writing to be that which satisfies all men at all times" (*S* 7.4). Too, despite the difference in demonstrativeness of these three passages, all three convey emotion at its highest pitch. In the last passage, for example, one must bear in mind that what Ajax is feeling has led him to kill himself and, even more strikingly, this feeling will remain his most defining inward state *forever* (an anticipation of Dante's Inferno dwellers who will remain for all time the crystallizations of their particular sin). His anguish is boundless. In the second passage in which Ajax implores Zeus for light, he is pleading for nothing less than his chance at immortality, since the Iliadic hero's enduring reputation is based in great measure on his skill and courage on the battlefield. His relative indifference to his own death – "destroy us, if you must" – underscores the much higher stakes for which he is playing. The question remains, however, whether the impact of these three examples is due to the embodiment of deep cognition – the intense emotional states somehow translatable back into an Aristotelian pursuit of "the good life" – or whether their value resides in a self-contained and self-justifying portrayal of the human psyche in extremis.

If we look at the three passages once again, a further, as yet unremarked, similarity emerges that may move this deliberation forward. There are associative links among the three that Longinus does not overtly underscore.[35] All three deal with a state of mind that causes one to court and finally, in Ajax' case, to prefer what Sappho calls "menacing death."

---

[34] Homer, *The Odyssey*, trans. Robert Fitzgerald (New York: Doubleday, 1962). This is the passage Longinus refers to without quoting.
[35] I am indebted for this idea of Longinus moving associatively to Neil Hertz' "A Reading of Longinus," *Critical Inquiry*, vol. 9, no. 3 (March 1983), 580–81.

The imagery of sight/blindness and light/dark is also common to all three: Sappho's persona sees the beloved, but then is blinded by this very vision; Ajax on the battlefield is shrouded in darkness, but prays for light so that he might see his opponents; in the underworld, the mute Ajax disappears into the darkness, never to see or be seen by Odysseus again. Let me import one more example cited by Longinus in this associative thread, this time atypically from the Bible. Attributing the writing of Genesis to Moses, he praises him for the *fiat lux* passage: "And God said 'What? Let there be light,' and there was light; 'Let there be land,' and there was land." Hertz sees the connection between the words of God and Iliadic warriors to be that "heroes may mimic the speech of the gods, but at their peril," something that sounds close to a warning against hubris.[36] But much more likely is that Longinus wants to elevate humans as they themselves become vitally concerned players in creation and destruction, illumination and darkness. There are certain things – a consuming eroticism, the immortality of a brilliant reputation – that we will undo our own creation for.

If this reading is correct, what Longinus has done is to change the Platonic emphasis on divine inspiration to that of divine aspiration. This is further evident in the oratory of Demosthenes, who spurs the Athenians to risk their lives for liberty in emulation of "those who faced death at Marathon ... who fought from the ships at Salamis" (*S* 16.4). Longinus comments:

> He seemingly deifies their ancestors by suggesting that one may invoke those who died such a death as if they were gods ... he turns what is essentially an argument into a supremely great and passionate passage by the appeal of this strange and extraordinary oath; he impresses it like some paean or charm upon the minds of his hearers ... grips his audience and carries it along with him. (*S* 16.2)

What Longinus wants to highlight in this excerpt is not the persuasion but the transport, for as he had said earlier, "[g]reat writing does not persuade; it takes the reader out of himself" (*S* 1.3). It is precisely this claim that makes quick agreement with Nussbaum's cognitive-emotional view impossible. But quick agreement with Altieri's position that "the arts inspire accounts that make affective experience not just something we understand, but something we pursue as a fundamental value"[37] is undercut by Longinus'

---

[36] Ibid., p. 581.   [37] Altieri, *Rapture*, p. 4.

crucial passage on the importance of reflection on passages of sublimity and what is yielded by that reflection:

> nature judged man to be no lowly or ignoble creature when she brought us into this life and into the whole universe as into a great celebration, to be spectators of her whole performance and most ambitious actors. She implanted into our souls an invincible love for all that is great and more divine than ourselves. That is why the whole universe gives insufficient scope to man's power of contemplation and reflection, but his thoughts often pass beyond the boundaries of the surrounding world. Anyone who looks at life in all its aspects will see how far the remarkable, the great, and the beautiful predominate in all things, and he will soon understand to what end we have been born. (*S* 35.2)

The value of the sublime, then, consists of two moments: 1) the ecstatic transport, and 2) reflection on that transport.

In the English tradition, it is Wordsworth's articulation of "spots of time" that best exemplifies what Longinus identified.[38] In the most famous of these, from early in *The Prelude*, the young Wordsworth, rowing across a lake in a stolen boat, has a terrifying vision of a menacing mountain striding toward him. The young boy retains the striking vision, but it is left to the adult poet, reflecting on the scene, to see in this episode evidence of the transformative power of the human mind. The boy has intuited the divine energy in nature and responded to it with his own creative energy, but would certainly not be able to abstract this synergy from the experience. Even for the mature Wordsworth there remains a gap between the riveting vision and the meditation that lends it meaning. In the concluding book, as Wordsworth climbs Mt. Snowden, he ascends suddenly from the mist that had enshrouded him at the lower levels into the full illumination of the moon:

> For instantly a light upon the turf
> Fell like a flash, and lo! as I looked up
> The Moon hung naked in the firmament
> Of azure without cloud, and at my feet
> Rested a silent sea of hoary mist.
> A hundred hills their dusky backs upheaved
> All over this still ocean; and beyond,
> Far, far beyond, the solid vapours stretched,

---

[38] It is not clear whether Wordsworth actually read Longinus or was relying on Kant and Burke's revival of interest in his ideas. Certainly, though, there is no question that Longinus had re-entered discussion of poetic theory and practice during the eighteenth century. For the fullest account, see Thomas Weiskel, *The Romantic Sublime: Studies in the Structure and Psychology of Transcendence* (Baltimore: Johns Hopkins University Press, 1976).

> In headlands, tongues, and promontory shapes,
> Into the main Atlantic, that appeared
> To dwindle, and give up his majesty,
> Usurped upon far as the sight could reach. (XIV. 39–49)

This is almost a textbook example of the Longinian "thunderbolt" of amazement and shares the darkness/light imagery that typifies a number of his citations. But it requires something more to lend it full worth, as Longinus knew and Wordsworth here goes on to confirm. The billowing mist envelops both the Atlantic itself and the audible "roar of waters, torrents, streams/Innumerable," yet subsumes them as it appears to the poet's imagination to be an "ocean," all of which gives rise to the following meditation:

> When into air had partially dissolved
> That vision ... in calm thought
> Reflected, it appeared to me the type
> Of a majestic intellect ...
> There I beheld the emblem of a mind
> That feeds upon infinity ...
> The power, which all
> Acknowledge when thus moved, which Nature thus
> To bodily sense exhibits, is the express
> Resemblance of that glorious faculty [imagination]
> That higher minds bear with them as their own. (XIV. 63–90)

Without the meditation the vision is merely startling without being significant. The only aspect that separates this episode from the passages in Longinus is that the poet here supplies the reflection along with the experience, but that does not preclude the further reflections of the reader. The sublime need not be purely "egotistical," to borrow Keats' designation of the Wordsworthian variety.

The Longinian–Wordsworthian sublime is an exercise in meta-cognition: the ecstatic moment, upon reflection, makes us aware of a capacity of mind/soul/imagination that transcends our ordinary entanglements in the world. We realize, in Longinus' words, that "the whole universe gives insufficient scope to man's power of contemplation and reflection, but his thoughts often pass beyond the boundaries of the surrounding world." Such a realization brings us close to the Kantian aesthetic, an experience that reveals to us the faculties of the mind itself. In this way, there would certainly be a truth-content involved in moments of ecstatic transport, though it would be a long way from the practical wisdom that Nussbaum finds in the delicate calibrations of Henry James.

Perhaps it would be fairer to say that reflection on the sublime provides a background for *phronesis*. While Nussbaum may not have sufficiently considered these moments of transport individually, their occurrence does not seem to jar violently against her overall position. One could account for the downplaying of such moments in Nussbaum since she, following Aristotle, concentrates on the *unity* of a work rather than its sublime *disruptions*.[39] In all fairness, too, it is worth mentioning that Nussbaum is aware of the problems philosophers have had in accommodating anything like the erotic love of a Sappho into normative ethical systems. The obsession with the beloved all too often occludes the rest of humanity, toward whom we ought to have commitments.[40] Even the less feverish forms of love are not something particularly amenable to being investigated by analytic philosophical prose, as she wryly notes. Yet, despite these difficulties she does pay attention to the "upheavals of thought" that attend intense passion and writes with sympathy of the tempestuous relationship of Cathy and Heathcliff in *Wuthering Heights* as possessing a value missing in the Nellies, Lockwoods, and even the more admirable Catherines and Haretons of the world.

What, then, is missing according to Altieri? Most centrally, his complaint is that Nussbaum is never willing to bracket evaluation and simply *experience* the portrayal of emotion. He wishes to let the intense representations of emotion play out unmediated in the theater of the mind – to at least start from a purely phenomenological perspective. The subtle transformation of the reader's consciousness in the instant of perception is for Altieri constitutive of much of the value of these passages of sublimity. Thus, he stresses the adverbial quality of such moments: the *how* we experience them. In doing so, Altieri seems to be following the current interest of philosophy of mind in *qualia*, though he never makes that connection explicit. The range of experiences that might be profitably thought of in terms of *qualia* extends from experiencing something redly, to the taste of a wine, to the pain of a toothache, all the way to feelings and moods. In all of these there is a subjective *texture* that might be said to transform consciousness.[41] (Realizing this instinctively,

---

[39] Northrop Frye, *Anatomy of Criticism* (1957; rpt. New York: Atheneum, 1968), p. 326.

[40] Martha Nussbaum. *Upheavals of Thought: The Intelligence of Emotions* (Cambridge: Cambridge University Press, 2001), p. 472.

[41] The best of the most recent discussions of this quality of perception is Ned Block's "Attention and Mental Paint," in *Philosophy Issues, 20, Philosophy of Mind*, 2010, 23–63. "Mental paint" is his metaphor for these non-intentional, intrinsic properties. Also helpful is S. Shoemaker "A Case for Qualia" in *Contemporary Debates in Philosophy of Mind*, ed. Brian McLaughlin and Jonathan Cohen (Oxford: Blackwell, 2007).

## Literature as the Recalibration of Emotions 41

Dostoevsky's Underground Man revels in the pain of his toothache because it ratifies his own subjectivity; no one else will experience the agony in precisely the way he does). These finely grained experiences elude propositional summations, and according to some proponents, are essentially ineffable. Because Nussbaum, in Altieri's opinion, tries to compel these delicate states to do ethical service, he accuses her of participating in "the benign imperialism of philosophy's reaching out to the arts only so long as the arts turn out to sustain the hegemony of its modes of reflection."[42]

Yet, if Altieri is displeased with what he takes to be Nussbaum's instrumentalism, he knows at the same time that he must provide some sort of alternative purpose for these inward states or risk having his aesthetics turn into a Pater-like aestheticism in which being in such states is telos enough. At times he veers close to Pater: "There is a strong temptation to reduce our concerns about the affects to concerns about identifying them, rather than enjoying them or extending them into related possibilities for intensity", and again, "there are many self-dramatizing possibilities within affective life that tend to establish their own rewards."[43] In the end, however, he opts for authenticity. Affective states, especially those that are intense, reveal to us dimensions of ourselves, capacities that might otherwise lie dormant and unremarked. The arts help us realize who we are. Altieri is too well versed in intellectual history not to immediately see that this presents him with another problem. Suppose one's authentic self is deeply flawed, even vicious? The discovery of intense possibilities in such a case is hardly cause for celebration. With a self-probing honesty that typifies all his writing, Altieri acknowledges an impasse here:

"Works of art help us test the boundaries of such states: At what point does pursuing ends in themselves transform us into heroes? At what point into monsters? And how do we tell the difference between those alternatives? I have no answers to such questions."[44]

This unresolved tension in Altieri's position is nowhere more in evidence than in his initial example of what he has in mind: an examination of Othello's extreme jealousy. Rather than hurrying to place Othello's emotional excess in a moral framework, Altieri asks us to consider instead "[w]hat modes of intensity and what kinds of involvement with others become possible because he yields to his own inordinate demands?"[45] But in Altieri's efforts to keep Nussbaum's ethical evaluations at arm's length, he resorts to the following disturbing reflection: "Othello does not simply

---

[42] Altieri, *Rapture*, p. 5.   [43] Ibid., pp. 16–17.   [44] Ibid., p. 20.   [45] Ibid., p. 21.

murder Desdemona; he sacrifices her. And in that process he manages to develop an identity based on an amazingly intense awareness of what must be put at risk if one is to stay true to one's deepest sense of human possibility."[46] And perhaps even more dubiously, and worth quoting at length:

> For one can argue that we have to be very careful in making negative judgments about Othello. It is possible that if one could actually participate in Othello's way of experiencing both love and justice, one just might choose these values as worth living for and dying for. It is difficult to imagine any more complete measure of love than one in which an agent both sacrifices the other and destroys himself in its name ... Some ways of experiencing the world just might be worth dying for.[47]

The most charitable observation one can make here is that Altieri may be trying to enlist Othello as a Kierkegaardian Knight of Faith: an Abraham who, true to his intensely held commitments, is to be admired for his willingness to sacrifice Isaac. Clearly, both Altieri and Kierkegaard share a common Romantic inheritance of passionate subjectivity as the final court of appeal. Yet even if the Kierkegaardian teleological suspension of the ethical were informing Altieri's position, the connection would serve rather to show its potential dangers rather than licensing his example. Are we really expected to believe that murdering one's wife in a frenzy of jealousy and then committing suicide is evidence of the most complete love of which we are capable? Things only get worse when Altieri grumpily suggests that we would be convinced of this were it not for the fact that we inhabit an "intellectual culture."[48] Presumably this is a world where something like Nussbaum's moral distinctions hold sway.

In the end, one is certainly sympathetic to Altieri's attempts to reassert the aesthetic against those who flatten subtleties as they scurry to enlist or condemn works in the name of "sociopolitical historicism."[49] One hears throughout his pages a salutary reminder of Cleanth Brooks' warning not to lapse into the heresy of paraphrase. But even the New Critics had to engage in *some* sort of analysis that was less than a pure replication of the

---

[46] Ibid., p. 21.   [47] Ibid., p. 22.
[48] That Altieri believes grand passions contain intrinsic value is confirmed in a later chapter when he treats the hypothetical case of the man who wastes his family's fortune to become an opera singer in the hope that this will sufficiently impress a woman he desires to return his love. Approvingly, Altieri notes: "This is clearly imprudent, but the imprudence is part of the conditions that make me feel satisfied by my passion: the passion must have some nobility if I am willing to take such risks" (ibid., p. 158).
[49] Ibid., p. 2.

text or Altieri's interior staging of our affective responses to it. Literary theory must of necessity be a distinction among shorthands. In his desire to defend the aesthetic, Altieri too quickly lumps Nussbaum in with the historical-sociological abstracters, what Bloom sarcastically refers to as "the School of Resentment."[50] Admittedly, philosophers are trained to detect nuances of argument, literary scholars delicacies of tone and connotation, with the result that each, on occasion, will overlook something apparent to the other. But Nussbaum as a philosopher with a strong interest in literature and Altieri as a literary scholar with a strong interest in philosophy occupy much ground in common. Let us listen to them both on Proust, an author for whom they share admiration. First Altieri, here on Swann's jealousy of Odette:

> Were jealousy more subject to rationality, it would not be so able to intensify eros. Without jealousy's modes of producing salience, many of the details of their lives would remain inert, victims of rationality's high standards for significance. Conversely, caring for that very significance makes him continually aware of what one can gain when love provides release from habits of calculation fundamental for rational practical action. And his jealousy creates a theater for Odette because she can then perform delays and signs of affection to others that afford the two of them a highly detailed lover's world securing their intimacy. Jealous passion here does not overcome reason; it finesses reason so as to win for itself a more capacious immediacy.[51]

Nussbaum quotes as epigraph to *Upheavals of Thought* the following passage from Proust that lends her book its title:

> It is almost impossible to understand the extent to which this upheaval agitated, and by that very fact had temporarily enriched, the mind of M. de Charlus… In [his] mind, which only several days before resembled a plane so flat that even from a good vantage point one could not have discerned an idea sticking up above the ground, a mountain range had abruptly thrust itself into view, hard as rock – but mountains sculpted as if an artist, instead of taking the marble away, had worked it on the spot, and where there twisted about one another, in giant and swollen groupings, Rage, Jealousy, Curiosity, Envy, Hate, Suffering, Pride, Astonishment, and Love.

She then comments on this eruptive geology of emotion:

> If emotions involve judgments about the salience for our well-being of uncontrolled external objects, judgments in which the mind of the judge is projected unstably outward into a world of objects, we will need to be able

---

[50] Harold Bloom, *The Western Canon* (New York: Riverhead Books, 1995), p. 4.   [51] Ibid., p. 23.

to imagine those attachments, their delight and their terror, their intense and even obsessive focusing on their object, if we are ever to talk well about love, or fear, or anger.[52]

Altieri and Nussbaum see almost exactly the same thing: that erotic energy often fuels our attachments and perceptions. The difference is that Altieri wants to stress the way it bends us, Nussbaum how we can bend it. To borrow the title of her earlier book, she focuses on the *therapy* of desire.

At times, it must be conceded, one senses a surplus of somatic urgency that Nussbaum's cognitive-evaluative model of the emotions doesn't quite capture, and Altieri is aware of the gap. Her humane neo-Aristotelianism may not always take full account of these darkest corners, the mind-flooding obsession of a Sappho that dwarfs therapy. Perhaps in these instances literary criticism should just remain silent; no context will help. But such moments are rarer than Altieri would have us believe. With the exception of Sappho's poem, not even the other Longinian sublimities would qualify. To take once more the case of Othello, our reaction to his enormous jealously is, *even as we experience it,* colored by our awareness of Desdemona's innocence, our apprehension for her, as well as our sharp dismay that Iago has seduced him into such a state. It is this network of feelings that temper a full-fledged absorption in Othello's passion. We are awe-struck, but not uncritical, not outside *our*selves. Further, if it is inevitable that we must translate Altieri's moments of rapture back into patterns of responsibility and obligation, we will need more help than he provides in sorting out the monsters from the heroes. In the end, then, I think it is most useful to see his criticism as staking out the limits of the large territory Nussbaum does cover rather than seeing her occupation of that territory as an act of philosophical imperialism.

If we trace Altieri's view back to the eighteenth-century sentimental tradition that undergirds the Romantic valorization of grand passions, the fundamental distinctions between his view and Nussbaum's can be made even clearer. Hume, like Aristotle, ties his moral theory tightly to the role of emotions and aesthetics. Since I have highlighted the importance of emotions for Aristotle, one should not forget that it is reason that identifies what a properly led life should look like. While emotional affirmation is necessary to lead such a life, and while the emotions, like bright students, can at times see what the teacher misses, nonetheless it is reason that provides both the guidance and motivation to seek the good

---

[52] Nussbaum. *Upheavals of Thought*, p. 2.

life in the first place. Strikingly, Hume demurs: "Reason is, and ought only to be the slave of the passions, and can never pretend to any other office than to serve and obey them."[53] Reason, in Hume's view, is reduced to ascertaining facts, determining the relationship between ideas as in mathematics or analytic truths, and providing the most probable means of fulfilling our desires. *It is not motivational in itself.* If we were to contemplate the sheer facts of a murder, for example, we could not derive a sense of vice that would move us either to condemn such an action or avoid it ourselves. Thus, reason does not direct the passions by shaping them to serve a vision of the good life. Altieri's complaint against Nussbaum's Aristotelian view of the interplay between reason and emotions is squarely in this tradition.

Yet, by definition, morality is motivational; it inspires us to choose one course of action over another. Hume concludes, then, that one can never find the source of moral response "till you turn your reflection into your own breast and find a sentiment of disapprobation which arises in you towards this action. It is a matter of fact; but it is the object of feeling, not of reason. It lies in yourself, not in the object."[54] It is the nature of our desires that move us in attraction or repulsion from the object, and this impetus is first experienced as pleasure or pain: "An action, or sentiment, or character is virtuous or vicious; why? because its view causes a pleasure or uneasiness of a particular kind."[55] Our desires, the source of moral motivation, are inspired by hedonic energy. These desires, or passions, or what we today would more commonly refer to as emotions, take the particular shape they do – pity, anger, hatred, benevolence – depending on their phenomenological content, and once again, the connection to Altieri should be apparent. Yet Hume will work hard and largely successfully to sort out his position from psychological hedonism and psychological egoism through the positing of a natural capacity for sympathy. Because of this capacity we have a natural tendency to vibrate to the emotional states of others. As Mark Collier succinctly observes in this regard, "We care about their welfare, in other words, because we vicariously feel their pain."[56] Here there is no corresponding move in Altieri, and it is this lack that permits the occasional lapse into a disturbingly deflationary view of obligation to others.

---

[53] David Hume, *A Treatise of Human Nature* (Oxford: Clarendon Press, 1967), p. 415.
[54] Ibid., p. 469.   [55] Ibid., p. 471.
[56] Mark Collier, "Hume's Theory of Moral Imagination," *History of Philosophy Quarterly*, vol. 27, no. 3 (July 2010), 255.

There remains only to consider whether Hume's moral conativism, as it links to his aesthetics, might present itself as a more persuasive account of the way emotions figure in the ethical value of literature than Nussbaum's.[57] Certainly appealing in his moral theory is its allowance for expansion of concern beyond the narrow circle of our acquaintances whose emotional states we mirror. While the mirroring of emotional states requires that we actually observe the other, Hume argues that our sympathies need not remain constrained by time or space. Through the moral imagination we can project ourselves back in history or abroad contemporaneously to share what must have been the reaction of those in proximity to the moral agent in question.[58] In effect, we see through the eyes of those directly affected. Hume does concede that this metaphoric looking will not partake of the same intensity as an unmediated vision, yet it is sufficient to pass moral judgment.[59] Perhaps we should categorize this sort of relationship as empathy rather than sympathy to register the distinction.

Hume's positing of an active moral imagination brings him into the company of a range of scholars who concern themselves with the intersection of ethics and aesthetics – Curry, Carroll, Railton, Levinson, Zunshine, and, of course, Nussbaum herself, to name just a few. Common to all is the belief that the ability and willingness to participate in the fictional representation of lives allows us to refine our own emotional-evaluative sensibility. Literature presents us with a warehouse of alternative lives. While the depth of our engagement may not replicate the real-life analogue, the difference is one of degree, not of kind. Moreover, the very fact that the experience is a simulation makes possible a greater imaginative venturesomeness.[60] The environment is risk-free. We bear no consequences for temporarily misguided investments; nor do we have to sit up all night commiserating with a distraught Pip on the loss of Estella. Too, the moral salience of richly complex situations that the best authors create for us is not something we can typically reproduce for ourselves. Nor, though strangely it is not often remarked upon, do we *ever* have infallible knowledge of the workings of other minds as we get in indirect discourse or Shakespearean asides. But none of this should in any way be mistaken for didacticism, for our imaginative participation is solicited to fill in the "gap" in moral sense-making, as Wolfgang Iser put

---

[57] See John Bricke, *Mind and Morality: An Examination of Hume's Moral Psychology* (Oxford: Clarendon Press, 1996) for the most spirited defense of Hume's conativism.
[58] Hume, *A Treatise of Human Nature*, pp. 602–3.   [59] Ibid., p. 603.
[60] Gregory Currie, "Realism of Character and the Value of Fiction," in *Aesthetics and Ethics*, ed. Jerrold Levinson (Cambridge: Cambridge University Press, 1998), p. 164.

*Literature as the Recalibration of Emotions* 47

it some years ago.[61] Iser's particular brand of reader response is faithful to the Humean model of a subjectivity that avoids the pitfalls of relativism. There is both a "world-to-mind" and "mind-to-world" fit.

In light of all this, why has Hume not proven more fruitful in the theory and practice of literary criticism that concerns itself with ethical understanding? I think there are two reasons, the second more crucial than the first. The first reason is that Hume's most extended treatment of aesthetics, "On Taste," does not directly address ethical issues. It tries to sort out whether or not there is any objective standard for preferring one work to another. His conclusion that the test of time and the opinion of experts provide such a standard can too easily appear – however unfairly – as merely an antiquated and untimely justification for "the canon." While Dabney Townsend has produced a detailed and sophisticated explanation of the ways that Hume's aesthetics and his moral theory are interrelated, literary scholars have not been much inspired to pursue this avenue.[62] The second and more deep-seated obstacle to Hume's adoption has to do with his metaphysics of the self. Pointedly, Hume rejects the idea of personal identity as anything more than a collection of perceptions:

"The mind is a kind of theater, where several perceptions successively make their appearance; pass, glide away, and mingle in an infinite variety of postures and situations. There is properly no *simplicity* in it at one time, nor *identity* in different; whatever natural propension we may have to imagine that simplicity and identity."[63]

Yet when Hume turns to moral psychology, he is perfectly willing to grant that our moral judgments arise when we ascribe motivation to the actions of others, and, when these motivations make patterns, to talk of character, virtuous or otherwise. Reconciling the metaphysical rejection of self with the positing of character has engaged philosophers, predictably with quite different explanations.[64] While this often dense and

---

[61] Wolfgang Iser, *The Act of Reading: A Theory of Aesthetic Response* (Baltimore: Johns Hopkins University Press, 1978).
[62] Dabney Townsend, *Hume's Aesthetic Theory: Sentiment and Taste in the History of Aesthetics* (London: Routledge, 2001). E. M. Dadlez' recent study *Mirrors to One Another: Emotion and Value in Jane Austen and David Hume* (Chichester: Wiley-Blackwell, 2009) is the work of a philosopher reaching from Hume toward Austen, rather than a literary scholar moving in the other direction.
[63] Hume, *A Treatise of Human Nature*, p. 253.
[64] Among the many contributions one might single out Jane L. McIntyre, "Character: A Humean Account," *History of Philosophy Quarterly*, vol. 7, no. 2 (April 1990), 193–206, and Timothy M. Costelloe's response "Beauty, Morals, and Hume's Conception of Character," *History of Philosophy Quarterly*, vol. 21, no. 4 (October 2004), 397–413. Of earlier interest is David Fate Norton, *David Hume: Common Sense Moralist, Sceptical Metaphysician* (Princeton: Princeton University Press, 1982).

technical discussion is not likely to have been followed with rapt attention by literary scholars, the metaphysical shadow cast over character has prevented it from assuming the robust centrality it has, for example, in Aristotle where the metaphysics (we are by nature creatures who seek eudaimonia) and the moral psychology (the possession and exercise of virtues are the means to this telos) fit seamlessly together. The deep commitment to the importance and exploration of character that typifies literature is ratified by Aristotle in a way that it is not by Hume.[65] In fact, though it is clear that behavior is corrigible according to Hume, it is dubious whether character is. Reason can aid us in strategizing better, but it does not seem to have much ability to reorganize our emotional dispositions.[66] Though postmodern interest in decentered and destabilized selves might have taken advantage of the metaphysical skepticism in Hume, sexier continental sources have proved more appealing, perhaps because, captured in the "Enlightenment Project" dragnet, he cannot avoid being under ideological suspicion. Thus, neither the more moderate nor the more radical theorists have been able to turn Hume to account.

In the last twenty years, there has been a revival of interest in Aristotelian virtue ethics that has run parallel to the turn toward ethics in literature. Nussbaum remains the most sophisticated and vigorous proponent of cross-fertilization, basing her case on the claim that emotions are deeply constitutive of the virtues that cohere and persist as character. Because literature is uniquely suited to capturing the nuances of emotional response, the fictional mimesis of "character" can potentially enhance the development of the reader's own character. But, as I am sure she would be the first to admit, the validity of employing a largely Aristotelian view of the self to the study of literature depends both on the philosophical strength of the position as well as its appropriateness to fictional texts. In other words, her approach to literature does not just serve a heuristic function in the manner, say, of the Lacanian influence that survives apart from serious problems in foundational assertions in the field

---

[65] For the most fair-minded and well-informed survey of this problem, see Kristján Kristjánsson, *The Self and Its Emotions* (Cambridge: Cambridge University Press, 2010). Kristjánsson defends what he calls the "soft realism" of Hume's position: the objective reality of an emotionally based moral self despite the lack of metaphysical justification. The problem shows up *tonally* as well, something noted in Hume's contemporary Hutcheson's complaint that the *Treatise* "lacked a certain warmth in the cause of virtue."

[66] Schneewind, *The Invention of Autonomy*, p. 360. Hume himself writes: "it being almost impossible for the mind to change its character in any considerable article, or cure itself of a passionate or splenetic temper, when they are natural to it." Hume, *A Treatise of Human Nature*, p. 608.

of psychiatry.[67] Altieri, whatever the strength of his counterarguments, recognized this insofar as he attacks both her cognitive-evaluative view of the emotions and the way in which what he regards as a skewed view distorts the reading of literary texts. In the chapters that follow, I examine four authors – T. S. Eliot, D. H. Lawrence, Woolf, and Shaw – who, in various, and often related ways, challenge the view of the self, the role of emotions, and the possibility for individual agency on which the Aristotelian view relies. They do so in a flotilla of essays, prefaces, letters, and even, in the case of Eliot, a dissertation. Of course, more importantly, they do so in the fictional incorporations of these views. My purpose will be to determine to what extent an emotionally dependent, virtue-based view of character can meet this challenge.

---

[67] The Lacanian term "the imaginary" is still routinely used in literary studies even though the "mirror stage" on which it relies, if it is to make any sense at all, has no clinical support. See Raymond Tallis, *Not Saussure: A Critique of Post-Saussusrean Literary Theory* (New York: St. Martin's Press, 1995), pp. 131–63.

CHAPTER 2

# T. S. Eliot's Emotive Theory of Poetry

On first reflection, it would be hard to call to mind any significant modernist author less likely than Eliot to locate the emotions near the center of our moral life. One thinks immediately of his Impersonal Theory of Poetry, which strictly quarantines the passional self from the creative mind: "the more perfect the artist, the more completely separate in him will be the man who suffers and the mind which creates."[1] Indeed, it is the desire of the poet to be rid of this very aspect of the self that provides the initial creative energy: "Poetry is not a turning loose of emotion but an escape from emotion."[2] Such passages, and one could easily multiply them, are clearly intended as a pointed rebuttal to Wordsworth's famous claim that all good poetry originates in "the spontaneous overflow of powerful feelings." The quarrel with Wordsworth is itself, however, merely part of a much larger animus against an emotionally soaked Romanticism that allegedly jumps quickly and illegitimately from personal affects to large-scale truths. Keats may insist that philosophical axioms must await the ratification of "our pulses," but Eliot, much like the surly philosopher revealing Lamia as a fraud, dispels such illusion with an unyielding stare: "the only cure for Romanticism is to analyze it."[3]

The ostensible case for Eliot's thoroughgoing distrust of emotion gains even more weight when his anti-Romanticism is placed in its original intellectual framework. As I have tried to demonstrate at length elsewhere, Eliot's anti-romanticism, with its attendant praise of classicism, is taken over nearly wholesale from the French reactionary response to the Revolution of 1789, extending from Joseph de Maistre up through Charles Maurras.[4] What

---

[1] T. S. Eliot, "Tradition and the Individual Talent," in *Selected Essays* (New York: Harcourt, Brace, 1932), pp. 7–8.
[2] Ibid., p. 10.
[3] T. S. Eliot, "Imperfect Critics," in *The Sacred Wood* (London: Methuen, 1920; rpt. New York: Barnes & Noble, 1960), p. 31.
[4] See Kenneth Asher, *T. S. Eliot and Ideology* (New York: Cambridge University Press, 1995).

this tradition taught was that the French Revolution was the source of nearly all the modern ills of the country and that the father of these horrors was Rousseau. By the time this tradition reached Eliot, the charge against Rousseau – originally that he was the quintessential man of the Enlightenment, erecting false ideals in the name of reason – had given way to the opposite indictment: Rousseau heeded only the peculiar rhythm of his own untutored sensibility and was therefore the proto-Romantic. While from an English point of view this may have seemed a strangely literary complaint to lodge against the alleged transformer of a society, it did not seem so in France, where classicism was typically regarded as part of an authoritarian tradition that included Catholicism, royalism, and a rigidly hierarchical social organization culminating in hereditary aristocracy. The Romantic attack on classical decorum was thus understood to imply rebellion in much wider spheres. And it was certainly in this way that Eliot understood it. The self-indulgent emotiveness that Eliot detects in Romanticism, then, does not just spoil sonnets, but our political and religious lives as well. When Eliot announces himself in 1928 as "classicist in literature, royalist in politics, and anglo-catholic in religion,"[5] (a verbatim echo, if we substitute anglo-catholic for Catholic, of the *Nouvelle Revue Francaise's* 1913 description of Maurras' beliefs), this is an intimately related constellation of positions.

While ethics is not specifically mentioned in Eliot's triumvirate of commitments, he makes clear elsewhere that no viable ethical system can do without religious underpinnings. In two essays written shortly after his conversion, Eliot respectfully takes his former teacher Irving Babbitt to task for imagining that a non-religious humanism can organize our moral lives. Babbitt, in an effort to fuse the internal equilibrium of Aristotle's virtuous man with American individualism, had held out hopes that a self-imposed "inner check" would be sufficient to curb excessive emotions and wayward desires without the imposition of any institutional authority. This "inner check," Babbitt was forced to concede – though he didn't consider this a drawback – would only appeal to a small elite who, thoroughly grounded in the ancients, would willingly elect the discipline necessary for the Aristotelian model. Apart from the fact that this would reduce ethical behavior to little more than a cult practice, Eliot denies that Babbitt's secular "inner check" could ever justify itself:

---

[5] T. S. Eliot, "Preface," in *For Lancelot Andrewes* (Garden City: Doubleday, Doran, 1929), p. vii.

> Where do all these morals come from? One advantage of an orthodox religion, to my mind, is that it puts morals in their proper place ... I can understand, though I do not approve, the naturalistic systems of morals founded upon biology and analytic psychology (what is valid in these consists in things that were always known); but I cannot understand a system of morals which seems to be founded on nothing but itself – which exists, I suspect, only by illicit relations with either psychology or religion or both, according to the bias of mind of the individual humanist.[6]

While Eliot is in complete agreement with Babbitt that America suffers from lack of restraint, as evidenced in the sloppy emotionalism of much of its letters and the rampant greed of post-Civil War industrial capitalism, and he would probably freely concede that Babbitt's purely ethical solution may be the most intelligent one on offer by an American, it is the ultimate indefensibility of such a solution that causes Eliot to prefer Maurras' alternative and England as a country more congenial to its propagation.

Assembled in this way, the evidence would seem to give the impression that Eliot had built a career essentially on the suppression of emotion, a perception that could only be enhanced when one considers his own studied formality of manner. While this, naturally enough, has inspired some Freudian excavation, both of the man and of his art, there has been very little recognition of how deeply committed Eliot was to a view of a common culture as the objectification of feelings, the organization (not repression) of emotions.[7] Contributing to critics' general failure to recognize the importance of the emotions for Eliot is undoubtedly the fact that the foundations of his view are set forth in the relatively obscure and often technically daunting pages of his doctoral dissertation on F. H. Bradley. This work of 1916 was only published in 1964, a few months before Eliot's death, at the urging of his wife, who thought she detected a stylistic similarity between Bradley's work and her husband's. Whatever scant incentive this might have provided to plow through a graduate exercise was even further diminished when, in the brief introduction, and with very little evidence of false modesty, Eliot claimed that he could no longer understand his own terminology.

When Bradley has been taken into account in Eliot studies it generally, and understandably, has been to show how the particular mixture of skepticism and belief in his philosophy has resonance for Eliot's own

---

[6] Eliot, "Second Thoughts about Humanism," in *Selected Essays*, p. 432.
[7] A noteworthy exception is Raymond William's chapter on Eliot in *Culture & Society: 1780–1950* (New York: Columbia University Press, 1983), pp. 227–43.

intellectual and spiritual development.[8] Although Bradley might not have approved of the categorization, his metaphysics seems to conform to the Biblical pattern – common to so much nineteenth-century thought, as M. H. Abrams has exhaustively shown – of an original prereflective wholeness, succeeded by a fall into fragmentation and alienation, followed by the promise of assumption into an absolute reality.[9] The first of these stages Bradley refers to as "immediate experience," a state in which "no division can be found between an awareness and that of which it is aware."[10] Consciousness is fully absorbed in the intending of its objects. There is a felt totality. It is only subsequently that we fall into false dichotomies by sorting out subjective from objective. Virtually the whole realm of human discourse is a trafficking in the corollary distinctions we create as we negotiate our way through what, ontologically considered, is merely Appearance. But Bradley posits the existence of an Absolute that is consistent, harmonious, and all-inclusive. Because it is all-inclusive it must contain the totality of individual errors and evils; because it is harmonious and consistent these must somehow be resolved. (And here, again, is the echo of another line of theological thought, one that claims all evil is merely so when viewed with local, partial vision, ignorant of God's larger

---

[8] J. Hillis Miller in *Poets of Reality* (Cambridge, Mass: Belknap Press of Harvard University, 1965, pp. 131–99) regards the poetry immediately following the dissertation as populated with characters groping for an Absolute they cannot achieve. Walter Benn Michael ("Philosophy in Kinkanja: Eliot's Pragmatism," *Glyph* 8 [1981], pp. 170–202) likewise stresses the skeptical Eliot, but eager to assimilate him to deconstruction, makes him, on the basis of his distrust of Presence, an honorary "grammatologist" *avant la lettre*. Lyndall Gordon, in *Eliot's Early Years* (Oxford: Oxford University Press, 1977, p. 53), posits a young Eliot "torn between the truth of his visions and his rational distrust of them," the latter finally giving way in the process of conversion. Michael Levinson in *A Genealogy of Modernism: A Study of English Literary Doctrine 1908–1922* (Cambridge: Cambridge University Press, 1984, pp. 176–86) charts Eliot's growing dissatisfaction with Bradley's version of an Absolute that "towered majestically" over empirical individualism. The most philosophically rigorous of these comparisons is that of Richard Wollheim in *On Art and Mind* (London: Allan Lane, 1973, pp. 220–49), who cautions against connecting the philosophy to the literary criticism in any but the most general way, an opinion seconded by Louis Menand in *Discovering Modernism: T. S. Eliot and His Context* (Oxford: Oxford University Press, 1987), p. 43. Two more recent and welcome exceptions that acknowledge the link that I will attempt to elaborate between Bradley's "immediate experience" and Eliot's thinking about emotion are: 1) Charles Altieri, "Theorizing Emotions in Eliot's Poetry and Poetics," a chapter in Cassandra Laity (ed.), *Gender, Desire, and Sexuality in T. S. Eliot* (Cambridge: Cambridge University Press, 2004). Altieri has excellent observations to make on the newness of Eliot's lyric voice. His concentration is almost exclusively on the poetry, however, since he claims that "Eliot never sets himself explicitly to developing a theoretical account of the affects." His point is true, but I have tried to piece together such an account from the critical writings; 2) see also Lewis Freed "T. S. Eliot's Impersonal Theory of Poetry and the Doctrine of Feeling and Emotion as Objects," *Yeats/Eliot Review*, 17 (Winter 2001), 2–18.

[9] M. H. Abrams, *Natural Supernaturalism* (New York: Norton and Company, 1971), esp. chapters 3–5.

[10] T. S. Eliot, *Knowledge and Experience in the Philosophy of F. H. Bradley* (1914; rpt., New York: Columbia University Press, 1989), p. 29.

Good.) Yet Bradley does not demonstrate how we might work dialectically through the morass of relational contradictions to arrive at the Absolute. He can offer little more than the assurance that because his system needs the Absolute to exist in this way and that it is not manifestly impossible that it does, we may assume its reality: "For what is *possible* and what a general principle compels us to say *must be*, that certainly *is*."[11]

In the dissertation, Eliot only occasionally points out places of tension in Bradley's work, for, as is typical of this type of scholarship, most of the effort is devoted to an explication of difficult material, less to evaluation from outside the philosophy. Yet within a year of the completion of the thesis, Eliot has gained the distance and confidence to speak more critically. In an essay published in *The Monist* (October 1916) on Leibniz and Bradley, Eliot shows his dissatisfaction with Bradley's blank notion of the Absolute (Bradley: "The Absolute is not personal, nor is it moral, nor is it beautiful or true")[12] and its hasty, unexplained absorption of the individual instances of experience known as "finite centres":

> [S]o Bradley's universe, actual only in finite centres, is only by an act of faith unified. Upon inspection, it falls away into the isolated finite experiences out of which it is put together. Like monads they aim at being one; each expanded to completion, to the full reality latent within it, would be identical with the whole universe. But in doing so it would lose the actuality, the here and now, which is essential to the small reality which it actually achieves. The Absolute responds only to an imaginary demand of thought, and satisfies only an imaginary demand of feeling. Pretending to be something which makes finite centres cohere, it turns out to be merely the assertion that they do. And this assertion is true so far as we here and now find it to be so.[13]

This essay, coupled with the dissertation, has inspired most of those critics who find the Bradleyan connection formative to read Eliot's subsequent conversion as the attempt to find a better explanation of how the Absolute collects its manifestations. Alert to the theological skeleton of Bradley's metaphysics, they see Eliot's turn to Christianity as finally making explicit what had been implicit in the philosophy. At that level of generality, the case seems unimpeachable and loosely helpful. But I would like to direct attention to what I consider a far more fruitful line of inquiry, the status of feeling and emotions in Bradley's work, for this aspect, never rejected, has both a more specific and a more foundational influence on Eliot.

---

[11] F. H. Bradley, *Appearance and Reality* (1893, rpt. Oxford: Clarendon Press, 1930), p. 173.
[12] Ibid., p. 472.
[13] T. S. Eliot, "Leibniz's Monads and Bradley's Finite Centers," *Monist* 26 (October 1916), 570.

Indeed, what is perhaps most striking about Bradley's account of reality and our knowledge of it is the primordial role played by feeling. The state of immediate experience that constitutes naïve sentience Bradley refers to as one of feeling. It exists prior to all cognition:

> In the beginning there is nothing beyond what is presented, what is and is felt, or rather is felt simply. There is no imagination or hope or fear or thought or will, and no perception of difference or likeness. There are in short, no relations and no feelings, only feeling.[14]

The distinction between feeling and feelings is intended to sort out an all-enveloping reaction to the sensation of wholeness from smaller, more finely directed feelings that can only arise after the process of discrimination has begun. Seen in this way, this state bears resemblance to Freud's "oceanic feeling," the absorption of the external world into the infantile ego. But whereas for Freud this stage is chronologically prior to the shrunken ego of the adult (though vestiges, unfortunately, may persist), for Bradley the stage is only, moment to moment, epistemically prior to the subsequent distinction of self and world. As Eliot quite correctly notes, "it is not ... more pure in the animal or the infant mind than in the mind of the mathematician engaged upon a problem."[15] In fact, Bradley wants to insist that all articulation of thought and specificity of feeling is derivative of this original state. What is experienced in primordial feeling is the non-relational nature of reality that when fractured, and thus distorted, supplies the stuff of our cognitive and affective lives.

This claim is certainly large enough, but Bradley wants to go further. Since the state of primitive feeling allows us to experience a non-relational reality, it provides a foretaste, or, more properly speaking, serves as an analogue to the Absolute itself. The Absolute is a recapitulation, at much greater level of complexity, of immediate experience. Our immediate experience lies below thought; the Absolute, gathering up and transcending thought, lies beyond it:

> And feeling and will must also be transmuted in this whole, into which thought has entered. Such a whole state would possess in a superior form that immediacy which we find (more or less) in feeling; and in this whole all divisions would be healed up. It would be experience entire, containing all elements in harmony. Thought would be present as a higher intuition ... But if truth and fact are to be one, then in some such way thought must

---

[14] F. H. Bradley, *Collected Essays* (Oxford: Clarendon Press, 1935) 1: p. 216
[15] Eliot, *Knowledge and Experience*, p. 16.

reach its consummation. But in that consummation thought has certainly been so transformed, that to go on calling it thought seems indefensible.[16]

Now, Bradley admits he cannot say in any detail how all this might look, but since metaphysics itself is, of necessity, part of the fallen world of Appearance, a gesture in the right direction rather than a blueprint might be the more modest and consistent position. For the purposes of the present study, however, it is more important to see what Eliot might have gleaned from this connection between immediate experience and the Absolute. And in this regard, when one draws out the theological implications of the Absolute, a move consistent with Eliot's own inclinations, it would not be unfair to conclude that it is only in primitive feeling that we are able, however distantly and dimly, to experience the divine.

About the nature of primitive feeling it is difficult to say much more "for it cannot without transformation be translated into thought."[17] At this point there might be a temptation to identify it as the self, the matrix from which individual personality must evolve. This, however, would be a mistake since the very notion of self is an abstraction from the undifferentiated unity of experience. To think in terms of a discrete self is already to inhabit the world of appearance.

If Bradley were to dismiss all judgments of appearance as equally flawed, there would be little more to be said about the self or any other coinage of human thought. But he rejects this radical position, instead maintaining that, while absolute clarity about the nature of reality must forever elude us, there are degrees of truth possible. Individual estimations of things will contain more or less of the plenitude of reality. Because, then, despite its metaphysical status, the notion of a self does press on us with the force of something close to psychological necessity, we are not being frivolous in trying to offer a richer rather than a more impoverished account of this insistent perception.

Proceeding with this relatively modest aspiration, Bradley puts aside views of the self that would identify it with body, memory, continuity of consciousness, and so on as he struggles to arrive at the least flawed account possible. When he achieves this point, he announces it without the tentativeness we might have expected:

> Let us take ... then a man's mind and inspect its furniture and contents. We must try to find that part of them in which the self really consists, and which makes it one and not another. And here, so far as I am aware, we can

---

[16] Bradley, *Appearance and Reality*, p. 152.  [17] Ibid., p. 462.

get no assistance from popular ideas. There seems, however, no doubt that the inner core of feeling, resting mainly on what is called coenesthesia, is the foundation of the self.[18]

Here we are left to wonder if the striking centrality of "the inner core of feeling" owes its prominence in personal identity in any way to primitive feeling. What connection, if any, obtains between the former that we know as little more than speculative necessity and the latter that relies on a more ordinary use of feeling as something akin to disposition? We are helped to an answer in Eliot's analysis as he tries to sort out what Bradley intended:

> In describing immediate experience we must use terms which offer a surreptitious suggestion of subject or object. If we say presentation, we think of a subject to which the presentation is present as an object. And if we say feeling, we think of it as the feeling of a subject about an object. And this is to make of feeling another kind of object . . . Nevertheless we can arrive at this metaphysical use of the term feeling in its psychological and current use, and show that "feelings," which are real objects in a world of objects, are different from other objects, are feelings, because of their participation in the nature of feeling in the other sense. The feeling which is an object is feeling shrunk and impoverished, though in a sense expanded and developed as well: shrunk because it is now the object of consciousness, narrower instead of wider than consciousness; expanded because in becoming an object it has developed relations which lead it beyond itself.[19]

Understood in this way (and once again, it is Eliot's understanding that is of paramount importance), our feelings would seem to be more faithful guides to the truth than cognition since they retain a continuity with the intimation of Being available only in primitive feeling.

To place this much importance on feelings to guide us through a world of appearance creates great difficulties, however, for intersubjectivity.[20] As is the case with any object in Bradley's metaphysics, we can only assume the existence of discrete others in the first place at the price of falsification. How can feelings that, in their more extended, ordinary sense at least, we think of as relatively subjective give us any access to the minds of these shadowy others? How can we possibly intend a common world? The weight of these questions can be gauged by the separate chapters both Bradley and Eliot must devote to defending Bradley's idealistic schema

---

[18] Ibid., p. 68.   [19] Eliot, *Knowledge and Experience*, pp. 22–23.
[20] For an excellent recent attempt to sort out the role of emotions in intersubjective understanding, see Peter Goldie *The Emotions* (Oxford: Oxford University Press, 2000), especially the chapter "How We Think of Others' Emotions." Goldie helpfully distinguishes among sympathy, empathy, and what he calls "in-his-shoes imagining."

from the charge of solipsism. Here, though neither Bradley nor Eliot do so, it might be helpful to sort out metaphysical solipsism from epistemological solipsism. The former maintains that only the self is real; the latter that private experience is the only source of knowledge. Now the first of these Bradley can dismiss summarily by reminding us that in immediate experience there is no distinguishable self at all, and even later when self is sorted out, it could only be from a non-self that must exist over and against it. All this is convincing enough. It is the second, epistemological solipsism that proves more troublesome to put aside.

It is, of course, open to Bradley in order to demonstrate the existence of a plurality of perspectives merely to point to the myriad finite centres each with a limited angle that his metaphysics posits. This sort of move resolves the epistemological question by metaphysical assertion and Bradley does begin his discussion by reminding us that he could foreclose the whole issue in this way from the outset. Nonetheless, he is willing, albeit grudgingly, to examine the origin of our *belief* in other selves and justify it within the realm of appearance. Here he takes over, without much enthusiasm, what looks to be essentially J. S. Mill's argument: 1) I am aware of my own body and find it intimately connected with pleasure and pain; 2) I am aware of other bodies but find that they don't correspond with my feelings; 3) Therefore a foreign body must have, by inference, a foreign self of its own. Bradley is well aware that this inferential argument is not a watertight proof, but it is, he maintains, the best we can do and we must be content with that.

Eliot, though, seems less than content as he struggles, in the most original part of his dissertation, to supplement Bradley. Whereas Bradley classifies other minds as objects, atypical only in being known indirectly, Eliot focuses on the uniqueness of objects that can intend us even as we intend them. The difference in Eliot's view is radical enough that he coins the term "half-object" to capture the special status of other minds. In what sounds very much like an anticipation of Sartre's endless merry-go-round of mutually determining consciousnesses, each exposed mercilessly to the gaze of the Other, Eliot records the fragile, unstable nature of selves as simultaneously subject and object:

> The self we find seems to depend upon a world which in turn depends upon it; and nowhere, I repeat, can we find anything original or ultimate. And the self depends as well upon other selves; it is not given as a direct experience, but is an interpretation of experience by interaction with other selves ... The self is a construction.[21]

[21] Eliot, *Knowledge and Experience*, p. 146.

A striking corollary of this situation – one that leads dramatically away from solipsism – is that even feelings, generally thought to be the most personal and idiosyncratic of mental states, may be better known by another than by the possessor.[22] Eliot states it baldly in the essay on Leibniz: "My emotions may be better understood by others than by myself; as my occultist knows my eyes."[23]

How, then, we might ask, does a common world take shape? Very gingerly, Eliot offers what he calls a "provisional account":

> The first objects, we may say, with which we come into contact are half-objects, they are other finite centres, not attended to directly as objects, but are interpretations of recognized resistances and felt divergences. We come to interpret our own experience as the attention to a world of objects, as we feel obscurely an identity between the experiences of other centres and our own. And it is this identity which gradually shapes itself into the external world. There are two (or more) worlds each continuous with a self, and yet running in the other direction – *somehow* – into an identity. Thus in adjusting our behavior to that of others and in cooperating with them we come to intend an identical world.[24]

What we must do here, apparently, is to contrast the intentions of finite centres by inference from their bodies; regard the similarities as the common world; register the differences as evidence of other minds. Gradually the network of assumptions grows; the communal world becomes more populous.

Even at the advanced stage, though, there is a ghostly quality in all this as selves that "somehow" cohere come to deduce the existence of a world by abstraction from the behavior of other intentional centres.[25] (The endlessly circling hollow men of Eliot's verse of the twenties are the poetic heirs to this view, despite an increasingly religious coloration that tends to smudge the lineage.) What lends this vision vitality, or at least the hope of vitality, is the current of feeling that emanates from these monads. Because our feelings are the direct descendants, however attenuated, of primitive feeling, they seem for Eliot to retain something of the impersonality of immediate experience. To stress this, Eliot tends to portray our feelings as intimately connected with the objects that inspire them; at times, indeed, he speaks as if the self had been evacuated, having deposited its feelings in the objects of its attention. This emptying out lends one's

---

[22] Ibid., p. 24.  [23] Eliot, "Leibnitz's Monads and Bradley's Finite Centres," 572.
[24] Eliot, *Knowledge and Experience*, pp. 142–43.
[25] See Wohlheim's *On Art and Mind*, pp. 233 ff., for a very useful analysis of the implications of this blank view. I am indebted to his discussion in this and the next paragraph.

feelings the public quality noted previously: "so far as feelings are objects at all, they exist on the same footing as other objects: they are equally public, they are equally independent of consciousness."[26] As these projected feelings accumulate around objects, a common world of emotional intention presumably takes shape.

René Wellek, in his magisterial study of modern criticism, judges this particular assertion of Eliot's to be "incomprehensible," and at first glance it is hard not to share his bewilderment.[27] The radical estrangement of feeling that Eliot's position would require is sharply at odds with what we normally take to be ordinary experience. But we can perhaps make some advance toward intelligibility by filling in part of the argument that is never made explicit. Although there is, according to Eliot, no world of fixed objects that serve as common reference points, he does maintain "that we are able to intend one world because our points of view are essentially akin."[28] The only way this would be possible is if there exists *some* similarity on the subject side of intention, and the only real candidate would be the residue of primitive feeling, which is our one universal experience. That which binds us, then, are those feelings that most resemble primitive feeling in being most impersonal. Such feelings would be those that seem to be inevitable responses to objects (in part massaged into shape by these very feelings). These felt objects are the building blocks of our common world as we trace the tendrils of feeling back to their intending centres.

At this point an obvious connection can be made to one of the most well known of Eliot's concepts of literary criticism, the "objective correlative," originally described in the essay on *Hamlet* (1919):

> The only way of expressing emotion in the form of art is by finding an "objective correlative"; in other words, a set of objects, a situation, a chain of events which shall be the formula of that *particular* emotion; such that when the external facts, which must terminate in sensory experience, are given, the emotion is immediately evoked.[29]

With the dissertation as background, we can see that what is at stake in this pronouncement is a great deal more than just an aesthetic preference; in creating an objective correlative, the artist heightens our communal life by establishing a *consensus* at the most foundational level. Now, it may appear

---

[26] Eliot, *Knowledge and Experience*, p. 24.
[27] René Wellek, *A History of Modern Criticism 1750–1950* (New Haven: Yale University Press, 1986), 5: p. 186.
[28] Eliot, *Knowledge and Experience*, p. 144.
[29] Eliot, "Hamlet and His Problems," in *Selected Essays*, pp. 124–25.

at this point that Eliot has illegitimately extended the realm of objects to include their verbal signifiers, but he has tried to account for this equivalence as well in the dissertation. There he asserts

> the object which we denote ... is the object *qua* object, and not the bundle of experiences which the object means. The object *qua* object would not exist without this bundle of experiences, but the bundle would not be a bundle unless it were held together by the moment of objectivity which is realized in the name.[30]

In a roundabout way Eliot has arrived here at something very like the Romantic theory of poetry as a secondary creation in imitation of God's, for the poet can manipulate words to lay bare a reconfigured reality that calls forth an emotional response beyond that elicited by things themselves – and metaphysically he is entitled to. St. Augustine may have castigated himself for responding too effusively to the plight of Dido, as does Hamlet for wasting tears on Hecuba, but they could have both spared themselves the self-reproach. The emotional response to a well-crafted work of art *should* be a heightened analogue to that evoked by the corresponding set of non-fictive circumstances.

At this point, one may wonder how the prominence given to the emotional quality of art can possibly be made to square with the disdainful anti-Romanticism noted earlier. The problem becomes even more acute when we find scattered throughout Eliot's criticism a string of observations about the gestation of poetry that seemingly jar with the impersonal theory of a poem's creation: "He [the poet] is oppressed by a burden which he must bring to birth in order to obtain relief. Or, to change the figure of speech, he is haunted by a demon,"[31] later identified as "his unknown, dark, *psychic material* – we might say, the octopus or angel with which the poet struggles."[32] These subterranean pressures cause the poet to "choose whatever subject matter allows [him or her] the most powerful and secret release."[33] Which is it to be? Is the poet the self-estranged manipulator of evocative images or merely the harried amanuensis of his own desire?

To make sense of these two apparently contradictory sets of claims will get us to the core of Eliot's poetic theory. Now, of course, one solution would be to despair of any reconciliation and simply pronounce Eliot's

---

[30] Eliot, *Knowledge and Experience*, p. 133.
[31] T. S. Eliot, "The Three Voices of Poetry," in *On Poetry and Poets* (London: Faber and Faber, 1957), p. 98.
[32] Ibid., p. 100.
[33] T. S. Eliot, "Introduction," in *Selected Poems by Marianne Moore* (London: Faber and Faber, 1935), p. xi.

thinking to be hopelessly muddled on these issues. And, in all fairness to this conclusion, that would be the inevitable outcome if we took these bald statements as purely self-sufficient distillations of Eliot's thought. But if we take the trouble to revert to the dissertation one more time for help, we can, perhaps, find some coherence in what Eliot intends. In particular, what is crucial is that he considers our emotions themselves to be objects. Originally, of course, these emotions have attached themselves to something external that had called them up in the first place. But because it is possible for the emotions themselves, qua objects, to arouse further emotions, we can be led further and further from the original external stimulus. The subjective element, if you like, tends to detach from its objective stimulus and become the occasion for an affective chain that becomes more and more personal and idiosyncratic, having lost its moorings. When emotions feed off themselves in this way we have the self-indulgence typical of, though not confined to, Romanticism. The most grandiose practitioner of this inward referentiality is Hegel: "Finally Hegel arrived, and if not perhaps the first, he was certainly the most prodigious exponent of emotional systematization, dealing with his emotions as if they were definite objects which had aroused these emotions."[34] The preferred point of contrast comes from the classical procedure of Aristotle: "in whatever sphere of interest, he looked solely and steadfastly at the object."[35]

This sorting out of inward- from outward-turning emotions, while it distinguishes Eliot's preference from that of Romanticism (as he conceives it), still doesn't help much in determining whether poetic creation should be cathartic or merely an exercise where "emotions which he [the poet] has never experienced will serve his turn as well as those familiar to him."[36] It might be tempting to assume that the lack of ventilation in an inwardly associative emotional life would be more likely to amass the pressure that would require catharsis, but nowhere does Eliot indicate he believes this. It would also mean that his occasional admissions of the need for catharsis would place him in the abhorred category of Romantic excess, clearly something he spent a lifetime denying. Instead, then, of fruitlessly trying to reconcile the two sorts of claims – how, after all, can one purge oneself of feelings one never experienced – it seems more instructive to try to get at what Eliot intends on this issue when he is being less quotable, but more

---

[34] T. S. Eliot, "The Perfect Critic," in *The Sacred Wood* (London: Methuen, 1920), p. 9. I am much indebted to the excellent article of Sanford Schwartz, "Beyond the Objective Correlative: Eliot and the Objectification of Emotion" in Laura Cowan (ed.) *T. S. Eliot: Man and Poet*, vol. 1 (Orono: National Poetry Foundation University of Maine, 1990), pp. 321–41.
[35] Eliot, "The Perfect Critic," p. 11.   [36] Eliot, "Tradition and the Individual Talent," p. 58.

consistent. A good place to begin in this regard is the simple assertion: "What every good poet starts from is his own emotion."[37] From there, Eliot, as we piece him together, wants to sort out emotion from feelings. When he makes this distinction, emotion gets demoted to the inwardly turning, associative affects, while feelings, undoubtedly in recognition of the residue of primitive feeling that endures, refer to the outwardly directed, more impersonal set of responses. The task of the poet – under whatever degree of internal pressure – is to transmute emotion into feelings.[38] The personal must be universalized, made impersonal in that sense.

The clearest example of what Eliot has in mind by this distinction occurs in the *Divine Comedy*. Brilliantly, Dante has transmuted his love for the earthly Beatrice, replete with personal associations, into the adoration of her divine manifestation, a figure that should similarly compel his readers in a way the earthly Beatrice need not have. But Eliot would insist that the literary image of the divine Beatrice does not cancel out or replace the earthly one; it subsumes her. Maurras, his mentor in this as in so much else, makes the point elegantly:

> Mais premièrement le poète [Dante] commença par l'aimer, par la perdre, et par la pleurer. Heureux et bienheureux le lecteur, le critique d'assez jugement pour avoir compris que voilà bien la chair et le sang du poème, sa matière et sa vie ardente, ce qui vibre de fort et de chaleureux dans sa voix.[39]

This ability of Dante to push personal affections and animosities toward typologies, a skill perfectly suited to his task of creating an anatomy of the afterlife, earns Eliot's unreserved praise. This is not to say that Eliot never shows signs of vacillation on the issue of whether or not poetic creation must originate in personal experience. Even with Dante he can be seduced into a rare, blinkered reading because of this confusion, as when he wrongly imagines that the Ulysses episode engages emotions which have nothing personal in them. (Dante the pilgrim, it might be recalled, pleads as nowhere else in the *Inferno* to be allowed to hear Ulysses. Having nearly tumbled in amongst the sinners in his original eagerness, he draws the reader's attention to the analogy between Ulysses' unrestrained quest for knowledge and his own temptation to be led astray by his vast learning.

---

[37] Eliot, "Shakespeare," in *Selected Essays*, p. 117.
[38] Wellek briefly but very clearly and accurately tries to chart Eliot's use of these two terms. See *A History of Modern Criticism*, vol. 5: pp. 184–85.
[39] Charles Maurras, *Le Conseil de Dante* (Paris: Nouvelle librairie nationale, 1913; rpt. 1920), p. 28 ["First the poet [Dante] began by loving her, losing her, and mourning her. Happy and more than happy the reader, the critic of enough judgment to have understood that here is the flesh and blood of the poem, its matter and ardent life, that which vibrates so strong and passionately in its voice."].

To my mind, this is one of the most highly personal cantos in the *Inferno*.) But if one is willing to prune these occasional aberrations, a considered, coherent body of theory can be found.

What we are left with, then, is a theory that is almost exclusively emotional, both in terms of the poem's origin and its effect on the reader. Good poetry is born in the heat of emotional intensity but must articulate itself coolly, impersonally, and precisely in order to properly arouse a corresponding intensity. Once this basic position is recognized, the unity in Eliot's criticism becomes strikingly apparent. Poets are praised or blamed, compared and ranked, according to the depth and range of emotion for which they can construct an appropriate equation. Consistent with this theory, greatness depends, first of all, on an individual poet's capacity for emotional experience. Thus, even apart from considerations of artistic execution, Eliot judges Shakespeare superior to Jonson because he felt more, and more finely:

"This will mean, not that Shakespeare's [characters] spring from the feelings or imagination and Jonson's from the intellect or invention; they have equally an emotional source; but that Shakespeare's represent a more complex tissue of feelings and desires, as well as a more supple, a more susceptible temperament."[40]

Shortly thereafter, Eliot describes the emotions to which Shakespeare is susceptible as being not only more various than Jonson's, but also "deeper and more obscure." Whether one posits the origin of these obscure emotions in something like the Freudian unconscious or, more faithful to Eliot's own explanation, in the Bradleyan notion of primitive feeling, there is the suggestion that they may very well remain opaque to the artist even as he is inspired by them. Indeed, it is Shakespeare's inability to understand fully the emotions he invests in Hamlet that leads to the mutual confusion of character and author: "the supposed identity of Hamlet with his author is genuine to this point: that Hamlet's bafflement at the absence of objective equivalent to his feelings is a prolongation of the bafflement of his creator in the face of his artistic problem."[41]

Eliot's belief that even the strongest of poets may not be completely in control of his materials shows up most significantly in his steady denial that an author is the privileged interpreter of his own work. Because "the meaning of a poem may be something larger than its author's conscious purpose," it naturally follows that "a poem may appear to mean very different things to different readers, and all of these meanings may be

---

[40] Eliot, "Ben Jonson," in *Selected Essays*, p. 137.  [41] Eliot, "Hamlet," in *Selected Essays*, p. 125.

different from what the author thought he meant."[42] With a fair-minded consistency that he generously applied to interpretations of his own works, he concludes that a reading different from the author's own "[may] be equally valid – it may even be better."[43] That Eliot is willing to talk in terms of better and worse distinguishes his position from the relativism associated with most postmodern theory. Unless there were a high degree of similarity of response, the whole concept of an objective correlative would make little sense. Clearly aware of this himself, Eliot works to place constraints on what may count as valid interpretation: "To understand a poem comes to the same thing as to enjoy it for the right reasons . . . to enjoy a poem under a misunderstanding as to what it is, is to enjoy what is merely a projection of our own mind."[44] Specifically, what right understanding entails, beyond linguistic competence, is to appreciate how a poem fits into the larger tradition of literature, both so that one can perceive what a poet was trying to do and also how well he did it compared to others who attempted similar works. Taken together these two elements make possible a cultivated "taste." And it is only at that point that Eliot will trust the nuances of an individual's emotional reaction. The subsequent theory this most resembles is Wolfgang Iser's carefully controlled version of reader response.

Essentially, what is left for the reader of taste to do as critic is to ascertain precisely the effectiveness of a work's use of the objective correlative. And in essay after essay this becomes the touchstone for Eliot's own judgments. The norm is found in Dante, whose achievement is to have rendered in the *Divine Comedy* "a complete scale of the *depths* and *heights* of human emotion."[45] The theology, though not dispensable, serves mainly as scaffolding for the creation of this architectonic of feeling: "the insistence throughout is upon states of feeling; the reasoning takes only its proper place as a means of reaching these states."[46] Dante's particular strength lies in his nearly uncanny ability to find concrete visual correlatives for states "so remote from ordinary experience" that they approach mysticism.[47] In the end, it is not the doctrine but "the logic of sensibility" that holds this magnificent structure together.[48]

With an almost Dantean predilection for ranking by deviation, Eliot proceeds to judge poets against this benchmark.[49] Tennyson fails, and

---

[42] Eliot, "The Music of Poetry," in *On Poetry and Poets*, p. 90.  [43] Ibid., p. 31.
[44] Eliot, "The Frontiers of Criticism," in *On Poetry and Poets*, p. 115.
[45] Eliot, "Dante," in *Selected Essays*, p. 229.  [46] Ibid., p. 226.  [47] Ibid., p. 227.
[48] Ibid., p. 229.
[49] As early as the Clark Lectures at Cambridge in 1926, Eliot takes Dante, enabled by the thirteen century's superlative fusion of thought and feeling, to be the pinnacle of artistic creation: "I have tried to show . . . that in the poetry of the thirteenth century the human spirit reached a greater sum of *range, intensity* and *completeness* of emotion than it has ever attained before or since"; T. S. Eliot,

generally pretty badly, because he represses the intense emotions of which Eliot believes him capable:

> here is plenty of evidence of emotional intensity and violence – but of emotion so deeply suppressed, even from himself, as to tend rather towards the blackest melancholia than towards dramatic action. And it is emotion which, so far as my reading of the poems can discover, attained no ultimate clear purgation. I should rather reproach Tennyson not for mildness, or tepidity, but rather for lack of serenity.[50]

At his best, Tennyson is a highly skilled elegist of his own frustration, but rarely more. As a result of the congestion of his poetic gifts, Eliot finds him "less capable of expressing complicated, subtle, and surprising emotions" than at least half a dozen of Shakespeare's contemporaries.[51] Tourneur, possibly one of these unnamed six, nevertheless suffers from the opposite vice: an excess of emotion going far beyond even that which Eliot thought he detected in *Hamlet*. Unable to control his own loathing of humanity, Tourneur tries to account for it, in *The Revenger's Tragedy*, by the creation of a gallery of grotesques. This is an "immature" attempt at objective equivalence that has the unintended result of drawing attention away from the creation to the mind that creates. Instead of inspiring a Swiftian loathing of mankind, Tourneur only succeeds in causing the audience to recoil from him, with the reflection "how terrible to loathe human beings as much as that."[52]

But there is an admirable kind of precision in Tourneur, according to Eliot. If he has had to warp reality to fit his vision, at least he has taken the trouble to warp it uniformly; his caricatures "are all distorted to scale." More importantly, he has looked at his own personages steadily and described them with a vivid economy even as the verse moves at a pell-mell pace consonant with their unsatiated desires. It is this care that earns him Eliot's final approbation: "What gives Tourneur his place is this one play [*The Revenger's Tragedy*], in which a horror of life, singular in his own or any age, finds exactly the right words and the right rhythms."[53] Conversely, the failure to match words and things in this way is what damns the amorphous poetry of Swinburne and Morris. Objects are always indistinct

---

*The Varieties of Metaphysical Poetry*, edited Ronald Schuchard (New York: Harcourt Brace & Company, 1993), p. 222.
[50] Eliot, "In Memoriam," in *Selected Essays*, p. 171.
[51] Eliot, "Marlowe," in *Selected Essays*, pp. 100–1.
[52] Eliot, "Cyril Tourneur, in *Selected Essays*, p. 167. This play is now more commonly attributed to Middleton, though that should not substantially affect Eliot's comments on the play itself.
[53] Ibid., p. 169.

in the ground fog of their verbiage: "he [Swinburne] uses the most general word, because his emotion is never particular, never in direct line of vision, never focused; it is emotion reinforced, not by intensification, but by expansion."[54] Did anyone, Eliot implicitly asks, ever visualize "Snowdrops that plead for pardon/ And pine for fright"? William Morris, with a similar penchant for vagueness, would pass it off as an indication of the spirituality of the emotion, but Eliot exposes such verse for what it is by juxtaposing it with the hard edges of Marvell.[55] The concentrated images of "To His Coy Mistress" marshaled in syllogistic form make Morris' softer focus in "The Nymph's Song to Hylas" on a related theme seem not elevated, but flaccid. Morris' "tottering" persona on the brink of death yearns

> To seek the unforgotten face
> Once seen, once kissed, once reft from me
> Anigh the murmuring of the sea

These lines – who could disagree? – do not jolt the reader in the same way as Marvell's conclusion:

> Let us roll all our strength and all
> Our sweetness up into one ball,
> And tear our pleasures with rough strife
> Through the iron gates of life.

Thus, Eliot places Marvell squarely in the tradition of Dante; Morris represents the final enervation of Romanticism.

At this point one may well feel that, despite the justness of much of what he says, Eliot is too much under the influence of Pound as he winnows poetry for emotional ideograms. Precision is in danger of shading into aesthetic preciousness. It is but a short step – one that, to his credit, Eliot never took – from here to the New Critical elevation of the poem itself to an emotionally laden icon. (With the sole exception of Dante's poetry, Eliot's critical intelligence remained far too skeptical and comparative for him ever to display such veneration). But what saves Eliot from the force of such a charge is that, at the deepest level, he essentially sought the union of affective centres across alien space. In this regard, he looked to the compelling coherence of an author's emotional vision as a guarantor of fidelity. This was a litmus test that, though harder to demonstrate than the objective correlative, was at least as important. It is because of his superiority in this regard that Middleton is to be preferred to Ford:

---

[54] Eliot, "Swinburne as Poet," in *Selected Essays*, p. 283.
[55] Eliot, "Andrew Marvell," in *Selected Essays*, pp. 257–59.

> Even without an *oeuvre*, some dramatists can effect a satisfying unity and significance of pattern in single plays, a unity springing from the depth and coherence of emotions and feelings, and not only from dramatic and poetic skill. *The Maid's Tragedy*, or *A King and No King*, is better constructed, and has as many poetic lines, as *The Changeling*, but is inferior in the degree of inner necessity in the feeling: something more profound and more complex than what is ordinarily called "sincerity."[56]

The primacy of emotion for Eliot makes consistency and depth of "feeling tone" more crucially binding than the structure of plot. In the best poetic drama there will be a dominant tone, "and if this be strong enough, the most heterogeneous emotions may be made to reinforce it."[57] Understood aright, poetic drama is a more multifarious lyric. For this reason, if we attend carefully enough, we can find Shakespeare behind his characters.[58]

This takes us very close to the harmony of the Aristotelian soul strongly marked by its emotional intelligence. It is the job of the poet to record the movements of this kind of intelligence with the same rigor that the philosopher uses in sorting out abstract thought. When a poet indulges in systematic thinking in this latter sense it ought to be only as a vehicle for transmitting the attendant emotions. As long as the thought is not distractingly immature (as Eliot considered Shelley's) it seemed to Eliot, at his critical best, not to make a great deal of difference. In fact, he goes so far as to claim that had Shakespeare been a better philosopher he would have been a worse poet.[59] The clearest expression of Eliot's position is set forth in "Shakespeare and the Stoicism of Seneca" (1927):

> We say in a vague way, that Shakespeare, or Dante, or Lucretius, is a poet who thinks, and that Swinburne is a poet who does not think, even that Tennyson is a poet who does not think. But what we really mean is not a difference in quality of thought, but a difference in quality of emotion. The poet who "thinks" is merely the poet who can express the emotional equivalent of thought. But he is not necessarily interested in the thought itself. We talk as if thought was precise and emotion was vague. In reality there is precise emotion and there is vague emotion. To express precise emotion requires as great intellectual power as to express precise thought.[60]

In the end, Eliot's ideal poet is the one who is able to tap into a reservoir of feeling so deep that it seems to lie beneath the vagaries of selfhood, follow its articulation through a range of personal emotions, and, in artistic

---

[56] Eliot, "John Ford," in *Selected Essays*, p. 171.
[57] Eliot, "Philip Massinger," in *Selected Essays*, p. 190.
[58] Eliot, "The Three Voices of Poetry," in *On Poetry and Poets*, p. 102.
[59] Eliot, "Shakespeare and the Stoicism of Seneca," in *Selected Essays*, p. 117.　[60] Ibid., p. 115.

creation, deposit these emotions in objective correlatives with a precision and consistency that makes them seem impersonal.

This process, in turn, presupposes a thick culture, itself in part the product of earlier poetry. Only within this context can a poet find the public vocabulary, the network of common reference, that allows an objective correlative to be understood. Clearly, Eliot's theory requires that values be held in common, and even more importantly, be *felt* in common. When there is a severing of belief and feeling in a society it shows up most prominently in artistic failure. Relying on this indexing of art to a society's moral health, Eliot gets at the essence of what goes wrong in Massinger's drama:

> As soon as the emotions disappear the morality which ordered it [sic] becomes hideous. Puritanism itself became repulsive only when it appeared as the survival of a restraint after the feelings which it restrained had gone. When Massinger's ladies resist temptation they do not appear to undergo any important emotion; they merely know what is expected of them; they manifest themselves to us as lubricious prudes.[61]

The opposite – a clinging to the emotions when the concomitant beliefs have been discarded – is also possible and nearly as bad, as Eliot indicates in his sarcastic dismissal of Arnold's desire to "affirm that the emotions of Christianity can and must be preserved without the belief" as nothing more than a cost-free stimulant:

> "The power of Christianity has been in the immense emotion which it has excited," he says; not realizing at all that this is a counsel to get all the emotional kick out of Christianity one can, without the bother of believing in it; without reading the future to foresee *Marius the Epicurean*, and finally *De Profundis*.[62]

Within a generation, in Pater and Wilde, Arnold's misguided advice corrupts literature.

Eliot's own early, pre-Bradleyan poetry may be seen as a struggle against this dissociation, or perhaps, more pessimistically, as a record of our helplessness in the face of it. In poem after poem what we find are emotionally charged images that fail to forge a communal world. Typically the persona will have an intermittent connection with these affective nodal points, but be incapable of drawing anyone else into the circuitry. "Preludes," for example, is essentially a series of such dampered images with no narrative

---

[61] Eliot, " Philip Massinger," in *Selected Essays*, p. 190.
[62] Eliot, "Arnold and Pater," in *Selected Essays*, p. 385.

thread. These themselves are a mere sample of "The thousand sordid images/Of which your soul was constituted." Properly speaking, these are images of sordidness, not sordid images, insofar as they provide the only oasis of hope in this world. The second prelude shows the potential for empathy in its otherwise bleak last image:

> The morning comes to consciousness
> Of faint stale smells of beers
> From the sawdust-trampled street
> With all its muddy feet that press
> To early coffee-stands.
> With the other masquerades
> That time resumes,
> One thinks of all the hands
> That are raising dingy shades
> In a thousand furnished rooms.

But the experience remains private, with no affective resonance for anyone else, as the succeeding prelude makes clear: "You had a vision of the street/As the street hardly understands." This leads in turn to a cynical rejection of the vision in the last prelude:

> His soul stretched tight across the skies
> That fade behind a city block,
> Or trampled by insistent feet
> At four and five and six o'clock;
> And short square fingers stuffing pipes,
> . . .
> I am moved by fancies that are curled
> Around these images, and cling:
> The notion of some infinitely gentle
> Infinitely suffering thing
>
> Wipe your hand across your mouth, and laugh;
> The worlds revolve like ancient women
> Gathering fuel in vacant lots.

Poignant sentiment is dismissed as sentimentality.

A similar inability to trust the image enough to make it the basis for emotional regeneration plagues Prufrock in his more widely known poem. While we may never be absolutely sure if the "you" addressed is internal or external, and the precise nature of Prufrock's infinitely deferred question is not made clear, Eliot does give us something definitive: the image that generates the question. In the poem's most optimistic moment, Prufrock tries to frame a beginning that recalls the abandoned images of "Preludes":

> Shall I say, I have gone at dusk through narrow streets
> And watched the smoke that rises from the pipes
> Of lonely men in shirt-sleeves, leaning out of windows?

This is immediately abandoned, however, jostled aside without comment by the fractured, private image: "I should have been a pair of ragged claws/Scuttling across the floors of silent seas," a degeneration of touch that runs through much of the early verse. We see it in the "hand of the child, automatic" ("Rhapsody"), "the murderous paws" of Rachel Rabinovitch ("Sweeney Among the Nightingales"), the "meagre, blue-nailed phthisic hand" of Princess Volupine ("Burbank"), and the typist's "automatic hand" that mechanically smoothes her hair and plays the gramophone after enduring the greedily grasping hands of the clerk (*The Waste Land*). In one sense, though, Prufrock does represent an advance on the persona of "Preludes" insofar as he does not doubt the value of his image of the lonely men; he doubts instead its ability to engage the drawing room *Kulturträger*. While we suspect his fear of ridicule is hyperbolic, we do not mistrust his judgment that any appeal to the image will be largely misunderstood. In a society devoid of powerful, endemic belief, the emotional harkening to an objective correlative is impossible.

Because these images cannot be fitted into any coherent pattern in Eliot's early poetry, he tends to bead them along a time line. In "Preludes" we follow random impressions from evening to morning to awakening to evening. Only a tonal consistency enables us to assume a single consciousness. In "Rhapsody" the time is marked at street lamps from midnight to 4 A.M. This chronological progression holds together the wandering, nameless consciousness that otherwise only exists weakly in the associative links among abruptly appearing external images and those dredged from memory. The stunted emotional life of an anonymous young man in "Portrait of a Lady" moves seasonally in the poem's three parts from winter to spring to autumn departure; it is this progressless progression through time that links the otherwise disparate vignettes of his cowardice. Prufrock is granted a name, or at least a last name, but even here it is the temporal flow from "there will be time" to "and would it have been worth it after all" that lends the poem what little narrative structure it has.

By 1920 Eliot abandons even this skeletal chronology, for though it allowed him to play off ironically the passage of time against the paralysis of the emotional life, perhaps it seemed to hold out the false hope that something *might* have developed. In "Gerontion" he creates a persona that is nothing more than hypostatized consciousness, a warehouse of wildly achronological images. By the time of *The Waste Land* (1922) this contrived container is also dispensed with, leaving us at last with nothing but the images themselves. (Although confidently, Eliot tells us in the notes that Tiresias is the spectator who views "the substance of the poem" thereby "uniting all the rest," this is an artificial assertion of cohesion rather than a demonstration, the same sort of thing Eliot had rightly complained about in Bradley's unity by fiat.) The source that generally has been appealed to by those who would defend the radical disjunctions of the poem is Eliot's praise of Joyce's mythic method in *Ulysses*:

"In using the myth, in manipulating a continuous parallel between contemporaneity and antiquity, Mr. Joyce is pursuing a method which others must pursue after him ... It is simply a way of controlling, of ordering, of giving a shape and a significance to the immense panorama of futility and anarchy which is contemporary history."[63]

And immediately such defenders put into play the panoply of footnotes, most especially the reference to Jessie Weston's *From Ritual to Romance*. But the clue to whatever unity the poem does contain is more accurately found in Eliot's less familiar introduction to St. John Perse's *Anabase*:

> any obscurity of the poem, on first readings, is due to the suppression of "links in the chain," of explanatory and connecting matter, and not to incoherence, or to the love of cryptogram. The justification of such abbreviation of method is that the sequence of images coincides and concentrates into one intense impression of barbaric civilization. The reader has to allow the images to fall into his memory successively without questioning the reasonableness of each at the moment; so that, at the end, a total effect is produced.[64]

In other words, this is a poem – like *The Waste Land* – that must rely *solely* on what Eliot referred to as "feeling tone," the emotive unity of the author's sensibility. Eliot, in his poem, has all but given up on objective correlatives, a deficiency that the supplied footnotes presumably tried, unsuccessfully, to remedy. Nothing in the content of the poem could possibly redeem the form if a shared emotional life is Eliot's goal. What we end up with is a reversion to something like the imagism of Pound, a poetry that relies on the strikingly precise use of imagery, but, devoid of context, is affectively thin.

---

[63] T. S. Eliot, "Ulysses, Order, and Myth," *Dial* 75 (November 1923), 483.
[64] T. S. Eliot, Preface to *Anabasis* (London: Faber & Faber, 1930; rpt. *Selected Prose of T. S. Eliot*, ed. Frank Kermode (New York: Harvest, 1975), p. 77.

Certainly aware of this himself, Eliot attempts to re-establish context by asserting a faith-based common culture in the poetry that he writes immediately after his conversion. This intent can be seen most clearly in a shift of emphasis away from the spiritually perplexed consciousness to a religious reality that awaits those of better understanding. In "Journey of the Magi," the Magi themselves do not comprehend the Christian imagery marking a landscape that they register merely as barren geography. Even when they witness the nativity, confused, they ask "were we led all that way for/Birth or Death?" In the early work, whether, for example, Prufrock can get an answer to (or even ask) his "overwhelming question" looms up with paramount importance. In "Magi," by contrast, the religious event dwarfs the question. The ironic failure of the half-comprehending Magi need not absorb us. The Christian narrative merely needs a better audience, and Eliot hoped to produce it. To this end, the very diction of the *Ariel Poems* tries to convert consciousness into liturgical rhythms:

> Before the time of cords and scourges and lamentation
> Grant us thy peace.
> Before the stations of the mountains of desolation,
> Before the certain hour of maternal sorrow,
> Now at this birth season of decease,
> Let the Infant, the still unspeaking and unspoken Word,
> Grant Israel's consolation
> To one who has eighty years and no tomorrow.
>         ("A Song for Simeon")

It is perhaps not altogether unfair to see what Ronald Bush perceptively notes as the willed aspect of Eliot's efforts to write in this condensed religious mode – nowhere more evident than in the ponderously assembled "Now at the birth season of decease" – as emblematic of the enormous pressure he had to exert to contrive a viable community.[65]

Eager to absorb others into his vision, Eliot's poetic interest during the thirties began to turn from the lyric to the more broadly engaging drama. Having built his own reputation on a poetry the complex allusiveness of which deterred all but a highly educated elite, he knew full well that even his starker, more accessible religious verse was not likely to have widespread appeal. The drama, however, born in religious ritual and cutting across class lines, might still enjoy popular favor without sacrificing artistic seriousness. Indeed, it seemed to Eliot at this point that along with the

---

[65] Ronald Bush, *T. S. Eliot* (Oxford: Oxford University Press, 1983), pp. 108–9.

celebration of the Mass, drama could provide a way of re-establishing a meaningful sense of community otherwise absent in the liberal state:

"The most useful poetry, socially, would be one which could cut across all the present stratifications of public taste – stratifications which are perhaps a sign of social disintegration. The ideal medium for poetry, to my mind, and the most direct means of social "usefulness" for poetry, is the theatre."[66]

A promising possibility presented itself when the Bishop of Chichester commissioned a play from Eliot on the martyrdom of St. Thomas. The fact that the production was to be mounted within fifty yards of Becket's actual assassination undoubtedly underscored for Eliot an important connection to Greek tragedy, that traced its origin, thematically and geographically, to the festival commemorating the slain Dionysus. Here, then, was a unique chance to reawaken spiritual community in the most deeply traditional way imaginable. In keeping with this tradition, Eliot chose to employ a chorus, a device doubly appealing to him at this point in his career because of its abstraction of the purely personal. A great deal is at stake for Eliot in the chorus, for if he can show that Thomas' struggle bears on the spiritual well-being of the uneducated women of Canterbury in the same way that the Greek hero's moral disposition affects the polis, then he will have gone a long way toward establishing communal sensibility. But it is precisely this that Eliot cannot do. Unlike the situation in Greek tragedy in which the chorus often comments perceptively on the career of the protagonist and is thereby intimately involved in his or her fate, Eliot's chorus is denied all understanding of Thomas' agon with the tempters. Comprehension of orthodoxy, according to Eliot, is available only to the very few; the many, dimly patient, receive the trickle-down:

"These things had to come to you and you to accept them./This is your share of the eternal burden,/The perpetual glory."[67] The problem is that Eliot has no real sympathy with "the scrubbers and sweepers of Canterbury" and even less belief that the remote and rarified Thomas could learn anything from them. Conversely, his effect on them is attraction at a distance, the magnetism of his martyrdom aligning the lives of these women like iron filings. What we are left with then is a tenuous and unconvincing relationship between the self-sufficient orthodoxy of the spiritual elite and the mores of the great mass of believers. The levels of

---

[66] T. S Eliot, *The Use of Poetry and the Use of Criticism* (London: Faber & Faber, 1933; rpt. 1980), pp. 152–53.
[67] T. S. Eliot, *The Complete Poems and Plays 1909–1950* (New York: Harcourt, Brace & World, 1962), p. 208.

awareness are so radically different that one can hardly imagine what a shared emotional life would look like.

During the late thirties and early forties, in *The Idea of a Christian Society and Notes Towards the Definition of Culture*, Eliot worked systematically on this very problem. Despite his occasionally crabbed, inquisitorial winnowing of authors for orthodoxy in the decade following his conversion, Eliot had known as early as his Harvard years that what it meant to be part of a culture was not primarily the acceptance of a set of beliefs, but a felt understanding of the deeply embodied life particularized by those beliefs. After having dutifully attempted to comprehend Buddhism by learning Sanskrit and immersing himself in the sacred writings and philosophy, he concluded that, as an outsider – however well intentioned and eager – he could not become a Buddhist because he would never feel in his bones as a Buddhist would. A variety of the problem that we see in this respectful cross-cultural diffidence can also become a difficulty *within* a culture when thought and feeling begin to disentangle. This, of course, is the very malaise Eliot famously laments in his notion of England's "dissociation of sensibility," a process set in motion at or around the time of the Civil War.

By the time of his major critical writings, though, Eliot had thoroughly abandoned the early hope that an individual poet, however deeply versed in the past, could save him- or herself by immersion in the great tradition. Ultimately, he concedes: "At the moment when one writes, one is what one is, and the damage of a lifetime, and of having been born into an unsettled society, cannot be repaired at the moment of composition."[68] With this in mind, Eliot obliquely criticizes his own past attempt at the private remedy of unifying thought and feeling through the mastery of disparate vocations: "For a poet to be also a philosopher he would have to be virtually two men: I cannot think of any example of this thorough schizophrenia, nor can I see anything to be gained by it: the work is better performed inside two skulls than one."[69] Eliot now acknowledges that even the most exquisitely cosmopolitan and learned poet is imbedded in his own contemporary culture; indeed, the more perceptive, the more imbedded, for the more in tune with its essential rhythms. Though a poet can and should learn from the poetry of other languages, and may himself come to have an international appeal, he belongs first and foremost to his own linguistic community:

[68] T. S. Eliot, *After Strange Gods: A Primer of Modern Heresy* (London: Faber & Faber, 1934), p. 26.
[69] T. S. Eliot, *The Use of Poetry and the Use of Criticism* (London: Faber & Faber, 1933; rpt. 1980), p. 99.

in a homogeneous people the feelings of the most refined and complex have something in common with the most crude and simple, which they have not in common with those of people of their own level speaking another language. And, when a civilization is healthy, the great poet will have something to say to his fellow countrymen at every level of education.[70]

The social function of poetry requires a people who feel in the same *kind* of ways.

But Eliot will demand more than just shared linguistic competence to guarantee a common emotional lexicon. In the above passage he calls for a "homogeneous" population, just as he had a decade earlier in his 1933 Page-Barbour lecture that was published as *After Strange Gods*. There, notoriously, he had labeled the presence of "free-thinking Jews" undesirable; no myth-questioning gadflies need apply. The rationale for this intolerance comes in *Notes Towards the Definition of Culture*, where Eliot posits a definition of culture that is practically coterminous with religion, the two being distinguishable only for the sake of analysis, much like form and content: "We may go further and ask whether what we call the culture, and what we call the religion, of a people are not different aspects of the same thing: the culture being, essentially, the incarnation (so to speak) of the religion of a people."[71] Not surprisingly, given this definition, in *The Idea of a Christian Society*, Eliot unabashedly advocates a theocracy: "I conceive then of the Christian State as of the Christian Society under the aspect of legislation, public administration, legal tradition and form."[72] The managers of this state would consist of an intellectual and spiritual elite that he designates the "Community of Christians." The ordinary mass of believers would make up the "Christian Community" (the inversion of terms betrays the great distance between similars that marks all of Eliot's social thinking). For this lower order Christianity will be largely unconscious, consisting of habitual observance. The care and maintenance of orthodoxy will be left to the sophisticated elite. Despite the difference, a thoroughly Christian culture will result, embracing the following disparate list:

"It includes all the characteristic activities and interests of a people: Derby Day, Henley Regatta, Cowes, the twelfth of August, a cup final, the dog races, the pin table, the dart board, Wensleydale cheese, boiled cabbage

---

[70] T. S. Eliot, "The Social Function of Poetry," in *On Poetry and Poets* (London: Faber & Faber, 1957), p. 20.
[71] T. S. Eliot, "Notes Towards the Definition of Culture," in *Christianity and Culture: The Idea of a Christian Society and Notes Towards the Definition of Culture* (New York: Harcourt Brace Jovanovich, 1968), p. 101.
[72] Eliot, "The Idea of a Christian Society," p. 21.

cut into slices, beetroot in vinegar, nineteenth-century Gothic churches and the music of Elgar."[73]

Once again, though, Eliot's attempt to posit a common culture looks forced. One can readily see how the spirit of Christianity manifests itself in a Gothic church or the music of Elgar, but remain utterly clueless how it might show up in a piece of cheese or boiled cabbage.

Much like Aristotle, Eliot is keenly aware of the importance of habit for an ethical life. But as he made clear in his criticism of the neo-Aristotelianism of Irving Babbitt, his Harvard mentor, the return to classical humanism is an impossibility. At this point in the development of Western sensibility a virtuous life must, of necessity, be avowedly Christian, or parasitic on Christianity. Any call for a purely humanistic self-restraint is at root motivated by Christian sentiment that goes unacknowledged. This being the case, moral/spiritual renewal depends upon a large-scale societal revivification of Christianity. Leaving aside the validity of this profoundly anti-Nietzschean assessment, we must question whether Eliot could ever be the architect of this renewal. At a minimum we might expect that this Christian utopia would require an embrace of the humble, not a mere toleration. And it seems that this is precisely what Eliot cannot provide. He is willing to endure cabbage-eating Sweeneys, but no more. The habits of ritual are intended to *regulate* them rather than fully include them. Too, because their habits can never generate reflection, they could not, on any Aristotelian account, be numbered among the virtuous, and Eliot marks this kind of distinction in his sorting out of the Community of Christians from the Christian Community.

One can see the same problem in more purely literary terms in Eliot's struggle to accommodate his emotive theory of poetry to his increasing insistence on the importance of Christian belief. In his 1927 essay "Shakespeare and the Stoicism of Seneca," he still insists on what sounds like a purely emotive theory. In comparing a line of Dante "la sua volundade e notra pace" and Shakespeare's "As flies to wanton boys, are we to the gods;/They kill us for their sport," Eliot claims that, although the philosophy behind Dante is superior, Shakespeare's poetry is equally great:

"But the essential is, that each expresses in perfect language, some permanent human impulse. Emotionally, the latter is just as strong, just as true, and just as informative – just as useful and beneficial in the sense in which poetry is useful and beneficial, as the former."[74]

---

[73] Eliot, *Notes*, p. 104.
[74] Eliot, "Shakespeare and the Stoicism of Seneca," in *Selected Essays*, p. 116.

But by 1929, he is no longer so sure that the quality of belief is artistically irrelevant. As his belief in the truth of Dante has increased, so has his poetic appreciation:

> And that statement of Dante seems to me *literally true*. And I confess that it has more beauty for me now, when my own experience has deepened its meaning, than it did when I first read it. So I can only conclude that I cannot, in practice, wholly separate my poetic appreciation from my personal beliefs . . . Actually, one probably has more pleasure in the poetry when one shares the beliefs of the poet.[75]

A year later he tries to balance the emotive and doctrinal evaluations of poetry:

> Yet we can hardly doubt that the "truest" philosophy is the best material for the greatest poet; so that the poet must be rated in the end both by the philosophy he realizes in poetry and by the fulness and adequacy of the realization. For poetry . . . is not the assertion that something is true, but the making that truth more fully real to us; it is the creation of sensuous embodiment. It is the making the Word Flesh, if for poetry we remember that there are various qualities of Word and various qualities of Flesh.[76]

The specific role of poetry would be to enable us to experience the truth of Christianity in its emotional density; poetry allows us to *feel* what it means to *believe*. The capacity for appropriate feeling presupposes the prior belief, however. Just as Eliot had endorsed St. Thomas' assertion *credo ut intelligam*, so he would add *credo ut sentiam*. This claim allows Eliot to move beyond what he considered the bankrupt Arnoldian position of embracing Christian sentiment without allegiance to the beliefs, as one wanders "between two worlds, one dead/The other powerless to be born."

Rightly, Eliot saw that belief was an essential component of emotions and wanted to align our beliefs so that he might bring us together feelingly.[77] Where I think he erred was in assuming that Belief was necessary to guarantee regularity in more limited beliefs. This assumption was based on his own insistence that religion, politics, and literature formed a trinity, analytically separable, but essentially one. His own mature poetic practice is consistent with this position. In the late poetry

---

[75] Eliot, "Dante," in *Selected Essays*, p. 231.
[76] T. S. Eliot, "Poetry and Propaganda," *Bookman*, vol. 70 no. 6 (1930), 601.
[77] Sue Campbell in *Interpreting the Personal* (Ithaca: Cornell University Press, 1997) emphasizes the role of interpretive communities as influence on one's own emotional repertoire. She refers to her position as "externalist," to be distinguished from social constructivism that she rightly takes to task for rigidly insisting that publicly shared meaning must be publicly generated according to social convention.

of *Four Quartets* he gives us what amounts to an imaginative extrapolation of liturgy: an extended meditation on the soul's cyclical journey back to its otherworldly origins and its need to unburden itself of mundane cares in preparation. Moreover, it might be argued reasonably that the narrowing of focus demands an urgency and intensity of execution consistent with creation under high pressure that Eliot had always championed. And certainly the justly admired George Herbert worked successfully in a similar limited range. The problem is not, then, that there is not a place for such poetry, and a respected place, but in the social theorizing that Eliot uses to license it. An emotively charged poetry does not require the religiously homogeneous society that Eliot insists upon. In the end we can see the tension that plagued Eliot during his post-conversion career: that between the expansive nature of the religion he adopted and his own exclusionary temperament. His ecumenical theory of poetry sits awkwardly with the narrowness of his vision for a renewed society. And, even within this society of the like-minded, his arm's-length relationship to the mass of believers – at best, clumsy-footed peasants circling a fire ritualistically – detracts from the putative reach of the poetry. But this failure should not cause us to overlook what is valuable. Eliot worked throughout his creative and critical career to craft and justify a poetry that would solder community through a shared emotional intelligence. Steadily he sought the precise image around which feeling might coalesce, drawing us together in the assurance of a common world. The objective correlative, understood in all its complexity, was an idea of deeply humanizing import. Like the dinner party in Woolf's *To The Lighthouse*, it provided an oasis of solidarity against the surrounding darkness, the indifferent flux of time.

In this regard, it is good to remember that there are moments when Eliot's poetry shows a forgiveness and tenderness markedly absent from the prose. Let me return briefly to *Four Quartets*. The temptation is to read these poems solely against the background of Eliot's often narrow construal of a Christian commonwealth and to find them an eloquent case of special pleading.[78] And certainly there are parts, even many parts, of these poems that can be read that way. But there is at least one striking moment when Eliot shows us – makes us experience – the kind of deeply felt transcendence of contrarieties that he had been struggling to achieve ever since the chaotic assemblages of the earliest verse. I am referring to the rose-garden scene in *Burnt Norton*. The poem itself starts with the heavy shuffling

---

[78] In *T. S. Eliot and Ideology*, I believe I succumbed to this temptation myself, failing to properly acknowledge passages where the poetry transcended the contemporary prose.

of abstractions that calls to mind the ponderousness of some of the early religious verse already noted. This quickly leads to a deflationary conclusion all too familiar from the earliest poetry in which one is borne along by life, inanimate, volitionless, through the mausoleum of missed opportunity:

> What might have been and what has been
> Point to one end, which is always present.
> Footfalls echo in the memory
> Down the passage we did not take
> Towards the door we never opened
> Into the rose-garden.

But unexpectedly – and we should not underestimate the advance, the newness here – Eliot allows us access to the rose-garden. We are summoned there by the song of a thrush:

> And the bird called, in response to
> The unheard music hidden in the shrubbery,
> And the unseen eyebeam crossed, for the roses
> Had the look of flowers that are looked at.

The obvious allusions to Keats and Donne in neighboring lines, poets not positively paired in the old classic/romantic dichotomy, serve to usher in a new ecumenical grace in Eliot. This grace manifests itself in the vision we are suddenly granted of the interwoven pattern of all the lives that were within us, the éclat lending the experience much of its intensity:

> Dry the pool, dry concrete, brown edged,
> And the pool was filled with water out of sunlight,
> And the lotos rose, quietly, quietly,
> The surface glittered out of the heart of light,
> And they were behind us, reflected in the pool.

Eliot grants us access to the rose-garden, not as a purgatorial reminder, but as an influx of plenitude. In substituting the Buddhist lotos for the Christian rose, Eliot embraces universality, yet a universality of vision that yields a dense particularity, for the web of alternative lives that reveals itself is uniquely one's own.[79] Here he achieves the coalescence of what he had distinguished in the *Dante* essay as feeling (the universal affective response) and emotion (the personal skein of emotive associations).

---

[79] I am indebted here and throughout this discussion of the rose-garden to the insightful essay by Alan Williamson, "Simultaneity in *The Waste Land* and *Burnt Norton*," in *T. S. Eliot: The Modernist in History*, ed. Ronald Bush (Cambridge: Cambridge University Press, 1991), pp. 153–66.

Insofar as the reader is being allowed, encouraged, to bring in more of him- or herself, Eliot here acknowledges that the personal, of which he had ever been highly suspicious, is a necessary component of an integrated life. Consensus requires not just a marshaling from without, as he typically insists in the prose, but a gathering up and preservation of the idiosyncratic. The objective correlative is granted a subjective side. We gather to us, yet each one of us separately, the lost siblings of our unlived lives. A deeply felt inner life is evoked, but not detailed. The explicit particularity, the "messiness" that Nussbaum valued in the novel here remains implicit, but no less central to our comprehension of a *vita integra*.

CHAPTER 3

# D. H. Lawrence: Primal Consciousness and the Function of Emotion

If initially it seemed counterintuitive to claim Eliot for an emotive theory of poetry, conversely it may seem almost too easy to enlist D. H. Lawrence on the importance of the affective life in fiction and hardly be worth a chapter's attention. Strident spokesman for the passionately engaged self in both his essays and in the didactic passages that mark virtually all his major novels, Lawrence is our most thoroughgoing advocate of emotional intelligence. Little effort is required to find him in the following vein:

> My field is to know the feeling inside a man, and to make new feelings conscious. What really torments civilised people is that they are full of feelings they know nothing about; they can't realise them, they can't fulfill them, they can't *live* them. And so they are tortured. It is like having energy you can't use – it destroys you. And feelings are a form of vital energy.[1]

But like a number of the great modernists, determined to distinguish themselves from impressionistic fin-de-siècle aesthetics, Lawrence wants to ground inwardness in the impersonal. Just as Eliot builds on Bradley's monad-like finite centres, Lawrence, too, posits a crucial substratum beneath what we ordinarily take to be our emotional and cognitive life. Let us look at the famous letter to Edward Garnett in which Lawrence tries to distance himself from the derivative treatment of character that has occupied earlier authors:

> that which is physic – non-human, in humanity, is more interesting to me than the old-fashioned human element – which causes one to conceive a character in a certain moral scheme and make him consistent. The certain moral scheme is what I object to. In Turgenev, and in Tolstoi, and in Dostoievsky, the moral scheme into which all the characters fit – and it is nearly the same scheme – is, whatever the extraordinariness of the characters themselves, dull, old, dead ... You musn't look in my novel for the old

[1] D. H. Lawrence, "The State of Funk," in *Assorted Articles* (New York: Alfred A. Knopf, 1930), pp. 113–14.

## D. H. Lawrence: Primal Consciousness and Emotion

stable ego of the character. There is another ego, according to whose action the character is unrecognisable, and passes through, as it were, allotropic states which it needs a deeper sense than any we've been used to exercise, to discover are states of the same single radically-unchanged element. (Like as diamond and coal are the same pure single element of carbon. The ordinary novel would trace the history of the diamond – but I say, "diamond, what! This is carbon." And my diamond might be coal or soot, and my theme is carbon.)[2]

This interest in a carbon-based self would certainly seem to place Lawrence much closer, for example, to the deterministic world of Zola's *Thérèse Raquin* – innately various nervous systems reacting inevitably in a given environment – than to the moral psychology of Aristotle. The problem Lawrence presents, then, in terms of literature's connection with ethics, is whether in delving beneath "character" he doesn't threaten to reduce human agency to a set of physiological responses. Is his view of the self so profoundly irrational that all talk of ethics is ultimately trivial?

Because, understandably, most critical discussion from the very beginning has been absorbed with Lawrence's sexual politics, too little sustained attention has been paid to the radical implications of his rejection of traditional character.[3] To be fair, his most detailed attempts to clarify what he meant occur in *Psychoanalysis and the Unconscious* and *Fantasia of the Unconscious*, both mixtures of insight and silliness in almost equal measure. (The related, slightly earlier "Education of the People" should have served as warning.) Lawrence's champions, with the notable exception of Leavis, have seemed generally embarrassed by these two volumes; his detractors believe themselves to have found better ammunition in more accessible places. And certainly, if these works merely lay inertly beside the literary output, there would be good reason also to pass by in silence. But Lawrence himself is clearly committed to the fundamental insight he struggles to describe in these two works and relied on it heavily, especially in his greatest novel, *Women in Love*, written just prior.[4] (He reveals in the

---

[2] *The Letters of D. H. Lawrence*, ed. A. Huxley (New York: Viking, 1932), pp. 78–79.
[3] The most valuable of the few extended treatments of this issue are Calvin Bedient's excellent study, *Architects of the Self* (Berkeley: University of California Press, 1972). See esp. chapter 5 "The Vital Self" for a chapter that approaches this problem with a seriousness it deserves; and also, Michael Bell's *D. H. Lawrence: Language and Being* (Cambridge: Cambridge University Press, 1992), which sees Lawrence as an ontologist of the self with affinities to the Germanic philosophic tradition of Kant, Schopenhauer, Nietzsche, Heidegger, and Cassirer.
[4] A recent sympathetic treatment of these texts and their importance is offered by Jennifer Spitzer "On Not Reading Freud: Amateurism, Expertise, and the 'Pristine Unconscious' in D. H. Lawrence," in *Modernism/modernity*, vol. 21, no. 1 ((January 2014), 89–105, in which she argues "that the value of these texts lies precisely in their eccentricity, for they reveal the philosophical underpinnings of

forward to *Fantasia* that the theoretical works are abstractions from novels and poems, not the reverse.) In that novel, Birkin's wooing of Ursula is largely consumed by an ongoing struggle to convince her of the reality of "the impersonal plane" where he hopes to rendezvous once she has let go of her insistent ego. Throughout most of the novel, Ursula, joined in my experience by the majority of student readers, listens with bewilderment, suspicion, and outright anger to Birkin's lectures. When Birkin finally acquiesces and mumbles a conventional "I love you" just before they become sexual partners, readers again join Ursula in letting out a long-deferred sigh of relief. But it is clear that neither Lawrence nor Birkin joins this chorus, and, for the moment, neither should we if we hope to get at Lawrence's essential view of the self.

Written in the aftermath of World War I, the works in which Lawrence sets forth his views of the self – "Education of the People" (late 1918), *Psychoanalysis and the Unconscious* (1919), and *Fantasia of the Unconscious* (1921) – are deeply colored by a sense of Armageddon survived. In a letter of 1916 he wrote of the nearly completed *Women in Love*: "The book frightens me: it is so end-of-the-world."[5] And more famously in the postwar *Kangaroo* (1923), Lawrence has his protagonist Sommers reflect "it was in 1915 the old world ended."[6] Of course, Lawrence is far from alone in such opinions. Spengler's monumental *Decline of the West* (1918) had a host of assenters on both sides of the war. But Lawrence sounds much more like Freud than Spengler in insisting that history is a function of psychology, not an inexorable force that bears us along: "What is wrong, then? The system. But when you've said that you've said nothing. The system, after all is only the outcome of the human psyche, human desires ... The system is *in us*, it is not something external to us."[7] This view places Lawrence squarely in an English tradition of seeing societal problems as failures of character, evident prominently in such writers as Austen, Dickens, and George Eliot. Where he differs though – and this is what will make him so problematic – is in his radical assertion of an individual disposition that is inexplicable and perhaps incorrigible.

Of profoundly religious sensibility, Lawrence responded with febrile fertility to an apocalyptic age that demanded all-encompassing visions. Just as Yeats shortly thereafter in *A Vision*, Lawrence did not hesitate to justify

---

Lawrence's body of work and inform the kind of formal and stylistic choices that Lawrence makes elsewhere."

[5] Lawrence, *Letters*, p. 380.    [6] D. H. Lawrence, *Kangaroo* (New York: Viking Press, 1973), p. 220.

[7] D. H. Lawrence, "Education of the People," in *Phoenix: The Posthumous Papers of D. H. Lawrence* (New York: Viking Press, 1974), p. 590.

his view of the self by cosmological speculation. Much to the disapproval of the orthodox Eliot in both cases, each cobbled together a mythology meant to replace – indeed, in many ways, invert – the outmoded Judeo-Christian one. Here is Lawrence on the origin of the universe:

"In the beginning was a living creature, its plasm quivering and its lifepulse throbbing. This little creature died, as little creatures always do. But not before it had had young ones. When the daddy creature died, it fell to pieces. And that was the beginning of the cosmos."[8]

This fanciful *creatio ex individuo* is a preamble to Lawrence's more seriously intended reinvestiture of authority. The cloak of divine mystery is transferred from God to the individual consciousness: "[i]n every individual organism an individual nature, an individual consciousness, is spontaneously created at the moment of conception. We say *created*. And by created we mean spontaneously appearing in the universe out of nothing."[9] Self-generating, such consciousness owes no biological debt: "We deny that the nature of any new creature derives from the nature of its parents ... There is in the nature of the infants something entirely causeless. And this something is the unanalysable, indefinable reality of individuality" (*PU* 14). Individuality, as thus described, seems little different from the Christian concept of the soul, but Lawrence, ever wary of associating man's essential nature with the spiritual, prefers to identify individuality with the unconscious, or primal consciousness as he alternatively calls it, and thereby identify it with the instinctual body – hardly a traditional Christian position. Like both Nietzsche and Freud, Lawrence is distinctly post-Darwinian: man can only be understood along a continuum that links us to the animals. To attempt to argue a priori special status is an act of utter hypocrisy. Thus, not surprisingly, all three are psychobiologists who see the human being essentially as a dynamic bundle of drives, the mind or ego serving as negotiator of somatic energies.

Lawrence's objection to the inherited body of ideas regarding man's nature is twofold. First of all he rebels against the very notion of a norm of self-realization applicable to every individual. Like Nietzsche and Kierkegaard before him, and the existentialists later, Lawrence protests

---

[8] D. H. Lawrence, *Fantasia of the Unconscious* in *Psychoanalysis and the Unconscious and Fantasia of the Unconscious* (New York: Viking Press, 1960), p. 63. Hereafter cited in the text as *F* plus page number.

[9] D. H. Lawrence, *Psychoanalysis and the Unconscious* in *Psychoanalysis and the Unconscious and Fantasia of the Unconscious* (New York: Viking Press, 1960), p. 14. Hereafter cited in the text as *PU* plus page number.

the promiscuity of such a view: "This is all the trouble: that the invented *ideal* world of man is superimposed upon living men and women, and men and women are thus turned into abstracted, functioning, mechanical units."[10] The call here is for recognition of a relativism deeper than that of epistemology. Lawrence is arguing that human beings are ontologically incommensurable. Each of us possesses a unique mode-of-being, if for the moment we can employ an opaque term. The second line of attack against received opinion, predictable from the first, is directed toward the rationalist view of man. This view errs seriously, according to Lawrence, in its overestimation of the importance of mind. Because, he believes, we have failed to realize that most of consciousness is not cerebral, we have mistaken man's nature and aims: "And the goal of life is not the idea, the mental consciousness is not the sum and essence of a human being. Human consciousness is not only ideal; cognition, or knowing, is not only a mental act. Acts of emotion and volition are acts of primary cognition and may be almost entirely non-mental."[11] Fond of electrical metaphor to describe psychological processes, Lawrence likens the mind's perception of the activity of primal consciousness to that of a radio station which of all the "infinite currents and meaningful vibrations in the world's atmosphere" registers only those of a certain wave length "like some strange code."[12] The mind then attempts to decode the message as faithfully as possible (i.e., without any ideal of what the message *should be*), "to act as medium, as interpreter, as agent between the individual and his object" (*F* 165). And even at that the transmission is fitful.

> For, let us realize once and for all that the whole mental consciousness and the whole sum of the mental content of mankind is never, and can never be more than a mere tithe of all the vast surging primal consciousness, the affective consciousness of mankind.[13]

Individuality thus can remain safely unfathomable while still functioning as the source of our drives.

Lawrence's unconscious, though, because of this inaccessibility, threatens to become a kind of Kantian thing-in-itself: an entity whose existence we posit and yet have no direct experience of. Apparently aware of the difficulties involved in such a position, Lawrence takes care not to sever (as did Kant) the causal link between unknown and phenomena. Although

---

[10] Lawrence, "Democracy," in *Phoenix*, p. 704–5.
[11] Lawrence, "Education of the People," p. 618.   [12] Ibid., p. 628.   [13] Ibid., p. 629.

the unconscious as creative mystery lies beyond all cause and effect in its totality, "yet in its process of self-realization it follows the laws of cause and effect" (*PU* 16). Indeed, because Lawrence derives everything from the unconscious, the very laws of cause and effect are merely the abstraction of habitual psychic workings reapplied to their original source. Again, the unconscious seems to have assumed the traditional status of God, inscrutable as creator yet deducible from the orderly functioning of His creation. In his investigations, Lawrence hopes to develop a "science of the creative unconscious," not in order impose a new ideal on the unconscious, but to free it from the encumbrance of past ideals. What, though, does Lawrence understand by primal consciousness or the unconscious? How is it related to its derivative, character? These questions lead directly to the core of his psychology.

In *Psychoanalysis and the Unconscious* and *Fantasia of the Unconscious*, Lawrence tries to explain his beliefs by distinguishing them from the Freudian. What Lawrence dislikes in Freud, or at least Freud as he reads him, is the characterization of the unconscious as an unwholesome cave of repressed desires containing "nothing but a huge slimy serpent of sex, and heaps of excrement, and a myriad repulsive little horrors spawned between sex and excrement" (*PU* 5). Now, though this is a parody of the early Freud, it is not an unrecognizable one, and does get at an essential difference between the two. In opposition to Freud's unconscious that puppeteers us largely in detrimental ways, Lawrence wants to posit an innocent unconscious, one that can motivate us in healthy directions. His use of the term "primal consciousness" captures more clearly what he intends: a somatic awareness that is as close to the integrity of pure being as we are ever likely to get: "the spontaneous origin from which it behooves us to live" (*PU* 13). And in all fairness to Lawrence, when Freud moves away from the conscious-unconscious model to the tripartite superego–ego–id view of the psyche after 1923, his amoral id is a move in the direction of Lawrence. A distinction still remains, however: Lawrence's unconscious, to identify it in Freud's idiom, would be one that is made up purely of eros, with no innate death instinct twisting itself into external aggression. Yet there is a further striking difference between the two men, and one that never moves closer to resolution. Though both Lawrence and Freud have a common source in Nietzsche, Freud retains a faith in the powers of reason to plumb the darkness and subject it to therapy that is remote from the irrationalism of Lawrence and Nietzsche. Despite the fact that Freud, looking back at Nietzsche, claimed that no man who ever lived had a deeper insight into himself than did Nietzsche, Nietzsche himself believed that the Socratic exhortation "know thyself" was largely an impossibility:[14]

> My idea is, as you see, that consciousness does not really belong to man's individual existence, but rather to his social or herd nature; that, as followed from this, it has developed subtlety only insofar as this is required by social or herd utility. Consequently, given the best will in the world to understand ourselves as individually as possible, "to know ourselves," each of us will always succeed in becoming conscious only of what is not individual but "average." Our thoughts themselves are continually governed by the character of consciousness – by the "genius of the species" that commands it – and translated back into the perspective of the herd. Fundamentally, all our actions are altogether incomparably personal, unique, and infinitely individual; there is no doubt of that. But as soon as we translate them into consciousness *they no longer seem to be* ... whatever becomes conscious *becomes* by the same token shallow, low, thin, relatively stupid, general, sign, herd signal.[15]

Again and again, we find Lawrence reminding us of the same thing: "The goal [of education] is *not* ideal. The aim is *not* mental consciousness. We want *effectual* human beings, not conscious ones. The final aim is not *to know* but *to be*. There never was a more risky motto than that: *Know thyself*" (*F* 105). We may come to know just enough of ourselves to realize that it is counterproductive to try to know further.

In light of this sort of diffidence, it might seem contradictory that Lawrence is boldly willing to unfold his "science of the unconscious," but as it turns out this "science" investigates a secondary process – the evolution of primal consciousness – and not its original impenetrable nature. Primal consciousness may be as mysterious as life itself, but it does seem to operate in patterns of rhythmic attraction to and withdrawal from other beings. It is this dynamic that Lawrence attempts to trace in the two volumes compounded of Yoga, Plato, Frazer, St. John, Heraclitus, Freud, and Frobenius. Lawrence freely acknowledges in his forward to *Fantasia* what in any case it wouldn't have taken the reader long to realize: that this is not science in any modern sense, but mythic vision cast in scientific metaphor. He admits that we are "free to dismiss the whole wordy mass of revolting nonsense, without a qualm" (*F* 54). But the tone

---

[14] According to Ernest Jones in his biography of Freud, more than once Freud is reported as saying that Nietzsche "had a more penetrating knowledge of himself than any other man who lived or was ever likely to live." See *The Life and Works of Sigmund Freud*, Vol. II (New York: Basic Books, 1955), p. 344.

[15] Friedrich Nietzsche, *The Gay Science*, trans. Walter Kaufmann (New York: Vintage, 1974), sec. 354.

of the forward suggests that we would do so to the detriment of our well-being.

Committed to the notion of a somatically based consciousness, Lawrence begins by dividing the body in half: the lower half he identifies as the subjective, sensual plane; the upper half as the objective, cognitive plane. But apparently realizing that this centaur-like self is not going to allow much subtlety, he subdivides the two planes vertically. In the front of the body is located the love impulse that strives for absorption, identification; in the back is located the will, which causes us to seek separation, independence.

The first mode of consciousness to develop is that located in the solar plexus (lower, frontal quadrant). From this center the infant is drawn toward the mother in an effort to "re-establish the old oneness." The impulse to seek out the mother's breasts Lawrence refers to as "an anterior knowledge almost like magnetic propulsion" (*PU* 21). At this stage of development the wisdom of the infant consists of the knowledge "I am I, the vital center of all things" (*F* 75). Thus, Lawrence would hold that for Descartes to have to prove his existence to himself by means of self-reflection is misguided, superfluous. We have such knowledge before mental consciousness ever develops:

> Primarily we know, each man, each living creature knows, profoundly and satisfactorily and without question, that *I am I*. This root of all knowledge and being is established in the solar plexus; it is dynamic, pre-mental knowledge, such as cannot be transferred into thought ... The knowledge that *I am I* can never be thought: only known. (*F* 74)

Next to develop is the first volitional center, which Lawrence locates in the lumbar ganglion (lower back). The impulse that emanates from here pulls in a direction opposite to the merging instincts of the solar plexus; the infant recoils in independence, sundering union with the mother. In a fit of temper, it asserts its will as it becomes aware of its separate identity. Flashing into consciousness (still pre-mental) is the knowledge "that I am I in distinction from a whole universe which is not as I am" (*F* 75). Lawrence thinks of the two centers as "poles" which establish the body's first internal "circuitry." Such poles we all have in common, but their relative strength and the resulting circuitry is traceable only to the mystery of individuality:

> The first relationship is neither personal nor biological – a fact which psychoanalysis has not succeeded in grasping.

> For example. A child screams with terror at the touch of fur; another child loves the touch of fur and purrs with pleasure. How now? Is it a complex? Did the father have a beard?
>
> It is possible. But all-too-human. The physical result of rubbing fur is to set up a certain amount of frictional electricity ... one of the sundering forces. It corresponds to the voluntary forces exerted at the lower spinal, the forces of anger and retraction into independence and power. An oversympathetic child will scream with fear at the touch of fur; a refractory child will purr with pleasure. It is a reaction which involves even deeper things than sex – the primal constitution of the elementary psyche. (*PU* 30)

Lawrence does hold, however, that the circuitry can be obstructed by the interference of mental consciousness which develops later, but the individual must pay in neuroses for the blockage.

Following the development of the psyche further, we find that the beginnings of discriminatory knowledge at the first volitional center have prepared the way for the upper, objective plane. On this plane the infant begins to experience objects in their otherness, although the knowledge is still pre-mental. Corresponding to the lower sympathetic pole of the solar plexus is the cardiac plexus (upper front). From this pole emanates devotional love, a "love which gives its all to the beloved," emptying out all sense of self leaving it "as nothing" (*F* 78). Were there no negative pole to counterbalance this outpouring of energy "the self would utterly depart from its own integrity." Fortunately, just such a negative pole exists in the thoracic ganglion (upper back). This center, like the lumbar ganglion of the lower plane, propels us away from the object of desire into singleness. Now, for the first time we come to a "recognition of abysmal *otherness*," the sense that the beloved is separated from us by "an irreparable, or unsurpassable, gulf."

This, then, is Lawrence's basic schema of the primal consciousness. But lest it seem too schematic, too much like a mere obfuscation of an older faculty psychology, he emphasizes that the system is essentially a dynamic one with energy flowing continually from pole to pole.[16] And because all the energy directs us either toward or away from some other, the nature of this particular other's flow must also be considered. Thus, the energy flows along a circuit with eight total points, and from this complexity the psyche takes its shape: "It is the circuit of vital flux between itself and another being or beings which brings about the development and evolution of every individual psyche" (*PU* 46). For the child, this other is the

---

[16] Mary Freeman, *D. H. Lawrence: A Basic Study of His Ideas* (New York: Grosset and Dunlap, 1955), p. 135.

mother (the father is conspicuously absent in Lawrence's account of early development, a faithful reproduction of the psychic fidelities of his own childhood), but as the child matures into adolescence, the love object, of course, changes. But to follow this evolution further we must first make clear how mental consciousness affects primal consciousness.

For Lawrence, mental consciousness is a secondary kind of knowing "in order that [man] may effect quick changes, quick readjustments, preserving himself alive and integral through a myriad environments."[17] To effect these quick changes, the mind is presented with a "shadow" from the primal consciousness, indicating the organism's desires. Similarly, knowledge of the external world is of a rough and ready sort. Vision, which Lawrence identifies as the sense most closely associated with mental consciousness (hence his horror at making love with the lights on) gives us a far more superficial knowledge than primal consciousness:

> When a boy of eight sees a horse, he doesn't see the correct biological object we intend him to see. He sees a big living presence of no particular shape with hair dangling from its neck and four legs. If he puts two eyes in the profile, he is quite right. Because he does *not* see with optical, photographic vision. The image on his retina is *not* the image of his consciousness. The image on his retina just does not go into him. His unconsciousness is filled with a strong, dark, vague prescience of a powerful presence, a two-eyed, four-legged, long-maned presence looming imminent.
>
> And to *force* the boy to see a correct one-eyed horse-profile is just like pasting a placard in front of his vision. It simply kills his inward seeing. We don't *want* him to see a proper horse. The child is *not* a little camera. He is a small vital organism which has direct dynamic *rapport* with the objects of the outer universe. (*F* 125–26)

This recalls Dickens' nearly identical complaint in *Hard Times* where Gradgrind, calling for the definition of a horse, scoffs at the speechless Sissy Jupe who knows horses with a Lawrentian intimacy and praises instead the soulless Bitzer as he proudly recalls that it is a gramnivorous quadruped. Without much difficulty, we can detect the influence on both authors of the visionary children of Wordsworth, no friends of dreary classrooms.

Clearly, then, for Lawrence the stimuli the mind perceives, both from within and without, and the mental image subsequently formed and stored should be seen as limited. Yet it is on the basis of these images that the mind constructs ideals and seeks to impose them on primal consciousness. This

---

[17] Lawrence, "Education of the People," pp. 614–15.

ascendancy of mind is a perversion, and for Lawrence the anti-rationalist, it lies at the root of all our unhappiness. Whereas Socrates had claimed that the intellect determines the good and no sane person could know the good and not choose it, Lawrence is squarely in the opposing voluntarist tradition that grants primacy to the will. For Lawrence it is the healthy will that unerringly chooses the good. As the faculty that maintains the instinctive homeostasis of primal consciousness, it possesses a subtlety unavailable to consciousness:

> Originally it is a purely spontaneous control-factor of the living unconscious. It seems as if, primarily, the will and the conscience were identical, in the premental state. It seems as if the will were given as a great balancing faculty, the faculty whereby automatization is *prevented* in the evolving psyche. The *spontaneous* will reacts at once against the exaggeration of any one particular circuit of polarity … And against … degradation from the spontaneous-vital reality into the mechanic-material reality, the human soul must always struggle. And the will is the power which the unique self possesses to right itself from automatism. (*PU* 47–48)

The will, when performing its function, keeps our impulses in a state of finely tuned balance, which mental consciousness could never achieve with its ideals. And this leads crucially to Lawrence's most pointed assertion about ethics: "Pure morality is only an instinctive adjustment which the soul makes in every circumstance, adjusting one thing to another livingly, delicately, sensitively" (*F* 116). This statement brings him very close to the Rousseauistic belief in the innate morality of human beings, who are only subsequently seduced from their true nature. But he must also take on the burden of Rousseau's argument: if we are innately good, how did we ourselves bring about the social conditions that end up corrupting us? Rousseau suggests that it is the enclosure of private property, followed by unequal social relations, and the envy that inevitably follows, that bring about our malaise. But whence the impulse to stake out the property in the first place? Must we not at least have had the potential desire for such ill-considered acquisition? In Lawrentian terms, how does the pure will allow itself to be corrupted by mental consciousness which is part of our natural development?

Lawrence, I believe, offers two answers to this question, one considerably more promising than the other. Both figure in his fiction and will take us directly to the core of his engagement with ethics. The first and less satisfactory answer if he wants to maintain a kind of primordial innocence is that the beautifully calibrated will is disrupted by establishing circuitry with an unbalanced other. For Lawrence, understandably, this is most typically the result of a mother who comes too close to a child and thereby overstimulates the sympathetic pole of the upper plane, that which impels us to devotional love. This is especially disastrous for the male, whose volitional centers should be the positive, stronger poles allowing him to venture forth in "creative or constructive activity." In addition, the impoverishment of the lower or sensual sympathetic center leaves men sexually inhibited. Why should mothers be so pernicious? Lawrence describes a vicious circle in which debilitated men cannot command their wives' respect, causing the wives, in frustration, to turn to their sons for (spiritual) lovers, which, of course, results in another generation of weak husbands. It is just such a circle that Paul Morel endeavors to break at the end of *Sons and Lovers*. Now this is certainly a recognizable, if unfortunate, syndrome, and we can see it in Charles Bovary and other fictional characters who predate both Lawrence and Freud's isolation of the problem. The difficulty, then, is not that Lawrence's analysis is implausible, but that it is impossible to square with his insistence on the innately pure self. How did the first mother lose her psychic equilibrium in order for the whole process to get underway? Lawrence merely defers the question endlessly without bothering to answer.

If Lawrence's first answer is Rousseauistic, his second is far more Nietzschean. On this view, while it is true that everyone's will is keenly attuned to the prospering of his or her particular individuality, not every self is equally fortunately endowed. In Nietzschean language, there are innately various levels of will-to-power. This secularized Calvinism leads to a division in Nietzsche between the minority of spiritual aristocrats and the herd of weak-willed. As in Calvin, the reason why some are saved, others damned is locked in mystery. We can probe no further. This is a view to which Lawrence is strongly drawn. It allows him to save his notion of the will as a pure expression of the primal self. He does, however, have to give up the ideal that we are all by nature equally healthy in our primitive state, something he was unwilling to do in his Rousseausitic answer. Although Lawrence is more strongly drawn to the Nietzschean answer, especially as he gets older and more disillusioned, he never completely abandons the Rousseauistic answer, and this duality of solution lends his work its deepest tension.

This tension can be seen most clearly in the best of Lawrence's novels: *Women in Love*. There, a good bit of the mounting frustration of Birkin, Lawrence's alter ego in the novel, comes from his inability to sort out the two views even as he tries to convince – at times, bully – others to embrace his philosophy. In an early conversation with Hermione, Birkin offers the clearest expression of the Rousseauistic belief in pure and incommensurate selfhood as he outlines his thoughts on "disquality":

> We are all different and unequal in spirit – it is only the *social* differences that are based on accidental material conditions. We are all abstractly or mathematically equal, if you like. Every man has hunger and thirst, two eyes, one nose and two legs. We're all the same in point of number. But spiritually there is pure difference and neither equality nor inequality counts ... In the spirit, I am as separate as one star is from another, as different in quality and quantity. Establish a state on *that*. One man isn't any better than another, not because they are equal, but because they are intrinsically *other*, that there is no term of comparison.[18]

But scattered throughout the novel are contrasting Nietzschean reminders that there is such a thing as a spiritual aristocracy: we are not just different, but distinctly unequal. In explaining to Gerald why his sister Winnie ought not to be sent to boarding school, Birkin argues for her innate superiority:

> "Well," said Birkin, "I begin to think that you can't live unless you keep entirely out of the line. It's no good trying to toe the line, when your one impulse is to smash up the line. Winnie is a special nature, and for special natures you must give a special world."
> "Yes, but where's your special world?" said Gerald
> "Make it. Instead of chopping yourself down to fit the world, chop the world down to fit yourself. As a matter of fact, two exceptional people make another world." (*WL* 197)

Of Mrs. Brangwen we learn that there is a natural "rightness" about her "such an aristocrat she was by instinct" (*WL* 148), a quality she shares with the elderly Mrs. Crich who "had an amazing instinctive critical faculty, and was a pure anarchist, a pure aristocrat at once" (*WL* 212). Clearly, too, Birkin considers himself and Ursula to belong to this elite that, much like the perpetual émigré Lawrence, must ferret out the world's "chinks," devoid of the unfavored many. In regard to these others, as Birkin says confidingly to Mrs. Crich early in the novel: "Not many people are anything at all ... They jingle and giggle. It would be much better if they were just wiped out. Essentially they don't exist, they aren't there" (*WL* 19).

What the Rousseauistic and Nietzschean views do have in common is that both maintain that false social ideals have twisted better natures out of shape. For Rousseau this was due to the artificial distinctions of vain social hierarchy; for Nietzsche the paralyzing effect of a resentment-driven sense

---

[18] D. H. Lawrence, *Women in Love* (New York: Penguin, 1983), p. 96. Hereafter all citations will appear in the text as *WL* plus page number.

of guilt. And Lawrence, too, laments unrelievedly the oppressive nature of what he would call the imposition of mental consciousness on primal consciousness. But soon Lawrence is forced uncomfortably into deciding who exactly is being substantially hurt by this – all of us, as Rousseau would have it, or the few with their innately superior will-to-power, as Nietzsche would have it? (For Nietzsche it is the weakly endowed many who have concocted, self-protectively, the Judeo-Christian morality in the first place.) To his credit, here as so often, Lawrence has those closest to Birkin pose these hard questions. In this instance it is Gerald, dismayed at his sister's unconventional behavior at her wedding and Birkin's approval of it, who initiates the following exchange:

> "You don't believe in having any standard of behaviour at all, do you?" he challenged Birkin censoriously.
> "Standard – no. I hate standards. But they're necessary for the common ruck.
> Anybody who is anything can just be himself and do as he likes."
> "But what do you mean by being himself?" said Gerald. "Is that an aphorism or a cliché?"
> ... "It's the hardest thing in the world to act spontaneously on one's impulses – and it's the only really gentlemanly thing to do – provided you're fit to do it."
> "You don't expect me to take you seriously, do you?" asked Gerald.
> "Yes, Gerald, you're one of the very few people I do expect that of."
> "Then I'm afraid I can't come up to your expectations here, at any rate. You think people should just do as they like."
> "I think they always do. But I should like them to like the purely individual thing in themselves, which makes them act in singleness. And they only like to do the collective thing." (*WL* 26–27)

Now, although the seemingly universalizing "people" in his last remark sounds Rousseauistic, the emphasis earlier in the discussion suggests the more Nietzschean sorting out into two types: those whose spontaneous actions we would welcome and those others who are not "fit" to act out in this way. Further, Birkin expects Gerald to be one of the "very few" who could appreciate this argument. While Birkin/Lawrence never unequivocally decides even by the end of the novel whether he is a Rousseauean or Nietzschean on this issue, the very structure of the novel itself, as I hope to show later, presupposes the Nietzschean view.

Whatever our initial potential – and we shall return to this issue – Birkin is thoroughly convinced that by the early twentieth century mankind can be sorted out into two types: the healthy and the unhealthy. A few have managed to maintain the delicate balance of the primal self; many more have not. In both cases, however, one's fate is decided almost exclusively beneath consciousness:

> He [Birkin] was not very much interested any more in personalities and in people – people were all different, but they were all enclosed nowadays in a definite limitation, he said; there were only... two great streams of activity remaining... They acted and reacted involuntarily according to a few great laws, and once the laws, the great principles, were known, people were no longer mystically interesting. (*WL* 296–97)

This is fully consistent with the famous letter to Garnett, but, it is worth mentioning, presents enormous difficulties for the novelist. If there are only two essentially different types of human being and variety is merely the relatively superficial elaboration of derivative character, how is a novelist to engage our interest in his typically well populated fictive world, especially, as is the case here, when that fictive world extends to 500 pages? In the end, it seems, he must rely on our inveterate fascination with character as he parades before us, *Inferno*-style, all the manifestations of souls gone wrong: Hermione, Gerald, Gudrun, Mr. Crich, Halliday and the whole London bohemian set, Loerke, and others. Yet Lawrence's reliance on traditional reader response should not detract from his radical project and the problems it presents. What sort of ethics would be available given a view of the self that is so deeply rooted in the physiological? Can one amend behavior? Does moral suasion serve any purpose as we move involuntarily in attraction and repulsion from one another?

These questions lead inevitably to a consideration of how exactly one falls into the category of healthy or unhealthy and whether the unhealthy can be salvaged. The clearest example of a healthy character is certainly Ursula. Lawrence describes her honorifically with biological metaphor as a plant about to blossom, and her instincts are invariably right as she encounters others. She may not accept Birkin's theoretical disquisitions on selfhood, but like a Wordsworthian child, she lives naturally in a relationship to the world she has no need to thematize. In contrast, we have her sister Gudrun, identified as a *fleur-du-mal*, corrupt and inevitably attracted to corruption. At crucial points in the novel, the sisters are shown side by side in radically different response to an event. When, for example, Gerald brutalizes a mare with his spurs as he forces it toward an oncoming train, Ursula cries out in protest at the cruelty while Gudrun, spellbound in dark understanding, loathes her sister's naked and very different reaction. Why the difference? Lawrence never comments on it and that itself may be his tacit answer. He makes the sisters as close in age as he can – Ursula is twenty-six, Gudrun twenty-five – and shows strained relationships with the parents in both cases, if anything, worse in Ursula's. Almost without question, then, he seems to be going out of his way to discount a developmental difference that would account for Ursula's far healthier nature. This impression is supported when Birkin speculates on how such a limited father, incoherent in thought and feeling, could have possibly produced such a remarkable daughter and concludes "[t]he spirit had not come from any ancestor, it had come out of the unknown. A child is a child of the mystery or it is uncreated" (*WL* 248). His physiology has become metaphysical.

What makes things hard for Lawrence, I think, is that he realizes the tremendously formative effect of childhood connections – how could he, especially, be unaware of this? – but does not want to rely on this sort of explanation by the time of *Women in Love*. If Birkin had been given something akin to Lawrence's own family dynamic and that dynamic were crucial, it is difficult to see how Birkin would have emerged as part of the healthy elect. While as late as *The Rainbow*, we are shown in great detail Ursula's largely dysfunctional relationship with her father, we get none of this background with Birkin. Astonishingly, in the portrait of a protagonist created in the age of Freud, we hear absolutely *nothing* about Birkin's parents or childhood. Lawrence has invested Birkin with all his own prickly sensitivities, in particular his fear of female domination, but gives us no psychological provenance. As a result, Birkin's pronouncements are shorn of almost all autobiographical inflection. He is represented as simply speaking for the age, or more accurately, as the authorized critic of his age.

Given the persistence of this criticism, however, Lawrence is under obligation to offer some explanation of how we reached the current sorry state of affairs. And here the novel become distinctly Nietzschean, for Lawrence wants to show how the age is the product of innately deficient psyches writ large. The prime example is provided by Gerald whose worldly success is due to the fact that he has made the world in his image. From his father he inherited the dilemma of trying to reconcile, on the one hand, a Christianity that teaches equality of soul and rejection of Mammon with, on the other hand, the enormous inequality of wealth he enjoys and the authority that goes with it. Old Mr. Crich's piecemeal charity was his attempt at a solution, but one increasingly perceived by his workers as hypocritical, and according to Lawrence, rightly so. Gerald assumes control of the coal mining company and quickly solves the dilemma by getting rid of one of its elements: he simply jettisons the Christianity and creates a world in which *his* will might be done. The world he fashions is one of pure instrumentality in which "of a man as of a knife: does it cut well. Nothing else mattered" (*WL* 215). In a perfectly consistent way for Lawrence the organicist, Gerald, who abuses animals and tries to dominate women, sees his crowning conquest as that of the earth itself:

> He, the man, could interpose a perfect, changeless, godlike medium between himself and the Matter he had to subjugate. There were two opposites, his will and the resistant Matter of the earth. And between these he could establish the very expression of his will, the incarnation of his power, a great and perfect machine, a system, an activity of pure order, pure mechanical repetition, repetition ad infinitum, hence eternal and infinite ... And Gerald was the God of the machine, Deus ex Machina. (*WL* 220)

This power-questing will take us as far as we can get from the happily functioning will of the healthy that acts as delicately alert responder to the subtleties of the circumambient world.

Any discussion of the properly functioning will forces us once again, though, to return to Lawrence's own ambivalence on the issue of the innate purity of the primal self. There is a great deal of talk in the flotilla of explanatory pieces already discussed – "Education of the People," *Psychoanalysis and the Unconscious*, and *Fantasia of the Unconscious* – about a "mental will" that takes its cue from a falsely idealized notion of the self based on the thin rationalizations that make up our conventional life. Now if this is really to be Lawrence's last word on the subject, it would be possible, at least theoretically, to recognize this error and try to listen instead to the quieter promptings of the primal self. In *Women in Love*, certainly Birkin does seem to talk as if this were possible. Hermione, in particular, he harshly chastises for reliance on the "mental will": "you want to have everything in your own volition, your deliberate voluntary consciousness. You want it all in that loathsome little skull of yours, that ought to be cracked like a nut" (*WL* 36). And, again, perhaps even more bitterly when she confesses to breaking childish habits by force of the same will, he barks: "It is fatal to use the will like that ... disgusting. Such a will is an obscenity" (*WL* 131). But on closer examination is this really the root of the problem? Between these two passages Hermione *has* for the only time in the novel acted spontaneously and nearly killed Birkin with a paperweight. And Birkin himself seems to realize that no one would want to see much more of a spontaneous Hermione: "But he would never, never dare to break her will, and let loose the maelstrom of her subconscious, and see her in her ultimate madness" (*WL* 132). Thus, it seems much more faithful to Lawrence's view to say that the dictates of the mental will, however disconnected from the primal will, are actually necessary for those like Hermione in order to limit the destructiveness that seethes within. Not coincidentally, Gerald is meticulously *comme il faut* in his public persona, though this façade has little in common with his darker, subterranean urgings. The adherence to a non-integral social self and obedience to the will that acts as its agent is symptom, not cause of the problem. Much as the laws of the city are necessary in a Calvinist dispensation to curtail the inevitable evil of the damned, these external impositions serve a similar function in the world of this novel. In the end, Lawrence really must give up the Rousseauean vision of corrupted innocence if his psychology is to cohere.

The Nietzschean alternative of innate deficiency seems further borne out when we examine more carefully Gerald's history. While Lawrence refuses to show us Birkin's childhood, he does allow us a useful glimpse into Gerald's. Gerald's nurse describes him as "a demon if ever there was one, a proper demon, ay at six months old" (*WL* 204). Though Gerald's family is far from ideal with mismatched parents always at odds with one another, it is hard to imagine this could have been decisive at six months. As in the case of the healthy Ursula and Birkin, the unhealthy Gerald's psyche seems to be innate. This impression is only strengthened when we learn that Gerald has pointed a gun, unknowingly loaded, at his brother's head, fired, and killed him. Both Birkin and Ursula are convinced this act is deeply revelatory of the primordial motions of Gerald's soul and not pure accident. Ursula protests that she could not – "instinctively" – pull the trigger of a gun while someone was looking down the barrel (*WL* 42). Gudrun, who, like all the unhealthy characters is uncomfortable with talk about instinctive selves, offers the alternative explanation that Ursula's response is due to a woman's enculturation. Ursula flatly denies this, and almost certainly Lawrence means for us to trust her on this issue. Thus, it appears that Lawrence's Rousseauistic vision of universal benevolence, somehow societally warped, gives way to the Nietzschean view of innate differences that inevitably play themselves out.

Of course, Lawrence is not naïve enough to think that this unhealthy era has no impact whatsoever on the healthy. In fact, at his most despondent, Birkin wonders whether it is possible for *anyone* to maintain his or her psychic equilibrium in such radically skewed times. He offers this gloomy prenuptual analysis to Ursula:

"Aphrodite is born in the first spasm of universal dissolution – then the snakes and swans and lotus – marsh-flowers – and Gudrun and Gerald – born in the process of destructive creation."

"And you and me–?" She asked.

"Probably," he replied. "In part, certainly. Whether we are that in toto, I don't yet know." (*WL* 164)

Certainly Birkin's relationship with the manifestly unhealthy Hermione supplies ample proof that he is implicated in the very dissolution he describes. And although he does manage finally to free himself from this entanglement, he never ceases to crave the unregenerate Gerald's company. Of the minor characters, Mrs. Crich, trapped in the industrial world of her husband with its attendant hypocrisy "like a hawk in a cage . . . had gone almost mad" (*WL* 207). Of the characters that Lawrence portrays as healthy, only Ursula remains relatively unscathed by the surrounding corruption.

While healthy psyches can be tainted, Lawrence gives us no example of the unhealthy progressing toward health. Gudrun is thoroughly incorrigible, as is the grotesque Hermione. Birkin does lecture both Hermione and Gerald, at times almost cruelly, yet this seems intended by Lawrence more to clarify to the reader what precisely has gone wrong with them than to imply that amendment is actually possible. Gerald especially will listen attentively, if condescendingly, to Birkin's admonishments, but can do nothing to alter the circuitry he came with. At most, one could argue that Birkin makes him aware enough of his desperate inward deficiency that he chooses suicide, but that is hardly advanced by Lawrence as a positive change and Birkin is heartbroken by the act. The only indication that the unhealthy sense their own lack and reach out for help is in their unconscious hankering to batten on the positive energy of their opposites: the deeply repressed Hermione seeks Birkin like a drug, Gerald returns again and again to him also though they disagree on almost everything, and Gudrun insists during the water party that Ursula sing so that she can dance to her sister's song. Yet ultimately this connection merely drains the healthy without renewing the unhealthy. Lawrence, with a Calvinistic rigor, deposits the majority of mankind irretrievably in the category of the damned.

The logic of Lawrence's binary psychological typology demands that he show a strong family resemblance among these unhealthy characters. To provide this connection he begins by systematically demonstrating a skewed response to the animal world as he lets us see how each of these characters is compelled to exercise dominance. This pattern begins innocuously enough in the example of Gudrun sculpting "small things, that one can put between one's hands, birds and tiny animals" (*WL* 32). Shortly thereafter, Hermione takes odd delight in the abasement of a male swan defeated in its mating efforts (*WL* 80). But this tendency soon erupts in the already mentioned episode of Gerald's violent abuse of the mare, followed by Gudrun's tormenting and stampeding of the bullocks at the water party, and culminates with Gerald's nearly fatal blow to his sister's pet rabbit. It is this last act that finally binds Gudrun and Gerald together "in mutual hellish recognition" (*WL* 234).

The compact between them is sealed with Gudrun's arbitrary slap across Gerald's face and this sets in motion a sadomasochistic seesaw in which ultimately "one of them must triumph over the other" (*WL* 403). Their first sexual encounter allows Gerald to pour out his corrosive pain while a joyless Gudrun submits, then sleeplessly endures the weight of his slumbering body for hours. In the end, though, it is Gudrun who narrowly prevails as a rejected Gerald, after nearly strangling her to death, chooses to commit suicide in the Alpine wastes. This sexualized violence echoes that of the cast-aside Hermione who seeks "her consummation of voluptuous ecstasy" in bringing down a paperweight with murderous intent on the head of Birkin. These episodes are supplemented by similar behavior among the less central characters, too. Halliday and Minette have an ongoing relationship in which he alternately reveres and degrades her, while she, who "wanted him completely in her power," plays her role to perfection. The cynical artist, Loerke, the novel's most far-gone character, delights in slapping his teenage model, as he proudly announces, "harder than I have ever beat anything in my life" (*WL* 424). Like Freud, Lawrence insists that psychic distortions reveal themselves most readily and destructively in sexual pathologies. Unlike Freud, he does not believe that there is any therapy available.

Thus, Lawrence's theory of the instincts posits them as far more irrational than does Freud's. Freud is interested in the way the body's physiological drives relate to the intentionality of mental life and behavior, and believes somatic energies can be productively rerouted.[19] Only in the case of psychotics, whose ego is so vastly diminished that the therapist has no ally, does Freud claim that nothing can be done. Lawrence, by contrast, finds only a few who can be helped: the innately healthy who may be aided in swimming against the current of dissolution. Birkin's long,

---

[19] Ronald de Sousa, "Norms and the Normal," in *Philosophical Essays on Freud*, ed. Richard Wollheim (Cambridge: Cambridge University Press, 1982), pp. 141–42.

heartbreaking, and ultimately doomed attempt to salvage Gerald is, in effect, evidence of the failure of "the talking cure" for even the most impressive of the unhealthy. Lawrence emerges, then, as far closer to Nietzsche who urges those with superior wills-to-power to become gardeners of the self. For the others he has no advice. If there is a difference between Nietzsche and Lawrence it is in terms of historical optimism. Nietzsche believes that the healthy may in the future contrive the conditions for their own flourishing, something analogous to the age of the old Homeric heroes. Despite some desperate toying with similar ideas in the leadership novels of the early 20's, Lawrence knows in *Women in Love* earlier and *Lady Chatterley's Lover* later that the future much more likely will be Birkin and Ursula in "the chinks" or Mellors and Connie huddled in a diminishing Wragby Wood like an endangered species.

If this reading of Lawrence is correct, then what becomes of our emotional lives? Do we speak of emotions in Lawrence simply because they are the closest approximations we can muster to account for the physiological attraction/repulsion of primal selves? Certainly, Birkin sees love as much smaller and derivative of what he has in mind by emotionless bonding:

> At the very last, one is alone, beyond the influence of love. There is a real impersonal me, that is beyond love, beyond any emotional relationship ... But we want to delude ourselves that love is the root. It isn't. It is only the branches. (*WL* 137)

Aside from the problems for the novel already mentioned in substituting "impersonal" selves for characters, there is the larger problem of the ethical import of a work of literature that seems to sideline emotion. If the detailed charting of emotions that are central to our ethical understanding is what distinguishes literature from philosophy, what are we to do with Lawrence? Must we concede that he is an aberrant outlier, or does he, too, finally rely on the emotions in a way not apparent in the passage above? An avenue of access to these questions is provided by a short essay that Lawrence wrote in 1925 entitled "The Novel and the Feelings." There Lawrence makes a distinction that Eliot had employed between emotions and feelings. Essentially for Lawrence the emotions refer to that part of our affective lives that we feel comfortable with: "Our emotions are our domesticated animals, noble like the horse, timid like the rabbit, but all completely at our service."[20] In opposition to these he places the feelings, those affective elements that baffle and disturb us:

---

[20] Lawrence, "The Novel and the Feelings," in *Phoenix*, p. 756.

And our feelings are the first manifestations within the aboriginal jungle of us. Till now, in sheer terror of ourselves, we have turned our backs on the jungle, fenced it in with an enormous entanglement of barbed wire, and declared it did not exist.[21]

Much like Nietzsche, who tries to waken us to the beast of prey within, Lawrence tries to get us to harken to these darker and more powerful currents. This does not mean that we should succumb to them, but as he more temperately advises, "we have to cultivate our feelings" (here akin to Nietzsche's gardener of the instinctive self). Novels, or at least novels by Lawrence, allow access to this buried self that originally we may need to explore vicariously: "If we can't hear the cries far down in our own forests of dark veins, we can look in the real novels and there listen in ... to the low, calling cries of the characters, as they wander in the dark woods of their destiny."[22] For Lawrence it is not character that is destiny, but primal feeling.

As they occur in *Women in Love*, these jungle cries are typically experienced long before they are fully acknowledged or understood by the characters themselves. The gap in recognition is not surprising since these dark urgings run counter to the image of ourselves we would like to maintain. Lawrence quickly introduces us to what he has in mind. The opening dialogue between the two sisters, ostensibly well disposed toward one another, ends in unexpected internal spasm when Ursula jumps up "as if to escape something, thus betraying the tension of the situation and causing a friction of dislike to go over Gudrun's nerves" (*WL* 5). Yet, there is absolutely no indication that the two are ever consciously aware of any antagonism. Only moments before we are told that "Ursula admired her [Gudrun] with all her soul" (*WL* 4). What catches the reader off guard is that in a conventional novel *this* would be the internal view against which all behavior would be measured. In Lawrence, however, there are feelings that lie beneath the "soul." It will be Ursula especially who is acutely sensitive to these deeper promptings, but be puzzled as to how they should be translated into choice.

Ursula's bewilderment comes about because she first wants to hew her feelings into emotions before responding to them. Lawrence's distinction between these two types of affect is a topic Birkin hammers away at, and Ursula's failure to understand is the source of a great deal of the early tension between the two characters. Nowhere is the friction greater than when they discuss the nature of their attraction to one another:

---

[21] Ibid., p. 757.   [22] Ibid., p. 760.

"There is," he said in a voice of pure abstraction, "a final me which is stark and impersonal and beyond responsibility. So there is a final you. And it is there I would want to meet you – not in the emotional, loving plane – but there beyond, where there is no speech and terms of agreement ... "

Ursula listened to this speech, her mind dumb and almost senseless, what he said was so unexpected and so untoward.

"It is just purely selfish," she said. (*WL* 137–38)

From the Lawrentian viewpoint Ursula is still bound to the all-too-familiar demesne of ego. She has identified herself especially with the fine sensitivity of her emotions and naturally enough is unwilling to concede that they are merely excrescences of a profounder self. But as Freud came to realize, there is no such thing as an unconscious emotion, and Lawrence/Birkin wants Ursula to abandon consciousness.[23]

Only in the tenderness of reconciliation after their most violent exchange does Ursula finally experience what Birkin has been trying to tell her. In truth, his telling has been thoroughly futile, arousing only hostility. Rather, as so often with Lawrence, touch is the gateway to this deeper somatic knowledge. Just prior to making love, in a moment akin to religious rapture, Ursula "unconsciously" runs her hands along Birkin's thighs, releasing "a dark flood of electric passion ... released from the darkest poles of the body and established in perfect circuit" (*WL* 305–6). Perhaps not surprisingly, Ursula, who had always seemed the healthier character, is able to give herself over more completely to the moment than Birkin, who still has twinges of self-consciousness. For her, this episode constitutes a full-fledged conversion experience, and with the zeal of a convert, she becomes the most consistent advocate for primal energies in the remainder of the novel.

We are left, then, to wonder exactly how these intimations of primal being – feelings as opposed to emotions – are factors in our ethical decisions, or even more broadly, how they enter consciousness at all. As T. H. Adamowski succinctly and accurately asserts: "it is better to think of him [Lawrence] as an 'ontological' rather than a 'psychological' novelist. He is not primarily concerned with the variable natures of men and women – their characters or egos or personalities – but with that which makes it *possible* for them to *adopt* such natures."[24] And the path from

---

[23] David Sachs, "On Freud's Doctrine of Emotions," in *Philosophical Essays on Freud*, ed. Wollheim, p. 98.

[24] T. H. Adamowski, "Self/Body/Other: Orality and Ontology in Lawrence," *D.H. Lawrence Review*, Fall 1980 (13), 194. See also Gregory Tague "Metaphysical Consciousness in the Work of D. H. Lawrence" in *D. H. Lawrence Review*, vol. 32–3 (2003–4), 126–38. Tague correctly observes that

ontology to ethics is not one literary critics typically are used to tracing. Matters are made even worse when one must begin from an essentially materialist conception of the self, and such a seemingly eccentric materialism at that.

While Lawrence's primal self bears resemblance to Eliot's immediate experience insofar as both exist apart from ordinary consciousness and are characterized by feeling, the differences are crucial. For Eliot, following Bradley in the idealist tradition, immediate experience is non-relational, i.e., there is no sorting out of subject from object; for Lawrence, ultimately indebted to Darwinian biology (via Nietzsche and Freud), the self is a discrete organism in sharp reaction to its environment. Closest to Lawrence's electromagnetic conception of the self is Freud's early attempt to establish a neuropsychological model in which the discharge of neuronal energy gives rise to the experience of satisfaction, and the blockage of such energy leads to an experience of pain. The organism moves toward situations in which the first occurs and flees situations in which the second occurs.[25] The primordial attraction-repulsion of this view is something that appealed greatly to Lawrence, and it wouldn't take much ingenuity to chart a novel like *Women in Love* as an elaborate minuet of characters coming together and falling apart in biological rhythm.

The problem any neuropsychological model faces, however, is to demonstrate how exactly the purely physiological intersects with the psychological. Darwin had claimed that love, jealously, our aesthetic sense, the development of musical organs (both vocal and instrumental), and qualities of courage and pugnacity were all derivative from the driving force of sexual selection. More familiarly, Freud had argued that friendship was fueled by aim-inhibited sexual energy, and that aggression was traceable to the death instinct. (The pain of frustrated somatic energies leads the organism to seek relief through the ultimate quiescence of a death; eros, except in the case of suicides, manages to bend this desire for destruction outward onto others.) And certainly the arrow of influence can work the other way in Freud when the energy results in hysterical symptoms. Yet, while both Darwin and Freud come close at times to asserting a purely materialistic position, neither is quite comfortable with reducing consciousness to a function of brain. Mind awkwardly resists resolving itself into either the effect or the subjective concomitant of physical states.

---

"Lawrentian characters come to the edge of what one can label *ethical* only after having struggled through stages of bodily and then metaphysical consciousness." He offers a persuasive analysis of how this works in *The Rainbow*.
[25] Frank J. Sulloway, *Freud, Biologist of the Mind* (New York: Basic Books, Inc., 1979), pp. 116–17.

However amateurish Lawrence's terminology might be, he is clearly aware of the problems Darwin and Freud encounter. The very fact that he chooses to call his neurobiological substratum primal *consciousness* indicates as much. But perhaps here a caveat is in order. My purpose is not to present Lawrence as a philosopher of mind who just happened to be a creative artist. Clearly, the only reason to engage with his theories is in order to better understand the art. Were it not for the fiction, no one in his right mind would ever be tempted to open *Fantasia of the Unconscious*. What is fascinating about Lawrence is that he does present a view of the self in his fiction that is genuinely so unlike almost anything else that has preceded him that he threatens Aristotelian assumptions about character, will, choice, and, finally, emotion that I believe must be the ground for literature's ethical import. Unlike the case of, say, Sartre, where we test the creative work for faithfulness to the philosophy, with Lawrence we test the "philosophy" for faithfulness to the creative work. He himself claimed that the explanatory essays were abstractions from the fiction, not manifestos he was trying to imaginatively render. If the abstractions are misleading from time to time, as I believe they are, it is they that must be abandoned. As Lawrence aptly reminded us, "trust the tale, not the teller."

The questions we must ask of his novel, then, are 1) What is the relationship, if any, between primordial feeling and the more familiar realm of emotion? 2) What is the effect of these affects on our ethical lives? 3) Can literature make any difference in our moral responsiveness? With these questions in mind, let us turn to those moments in *Women in Love* where Lawrence indicates by his language that characters are responding to the ebb and flow of their primal selves and see what is taking place. Here, for example, is Gerald in the grip of primal attraction to Minette:

> Minette sat near to Gerald, and she seemed to become soft, subtly to infuse herself into his bones, as if she were passing into his veins like a magnetic darkness, and concentrated at the base of his spine like a fearful source of power. Meanwhile her voice sounded reedy and nonchalant, as she talked indifferently with Birkin and Maxim. (*WL* 65)

No emotion attends this powerful fusion, and Lawrence goes out of his way to indicate the rift between the banal chatter and unconscious force fields. Nor will Gerald or Minette subsequently ever translate this intense feeling into talk of love or even affection. There is simply no emotional yield. This will stand in contrast to the coming together of Birkin and Ursula. The passage quoted earlier in which Ursula establishes connection with

Birkin by running her hands down his thighs concludes in the following way:

> It was the dark fire of electricity that rushed from him to her, and flooded them both with rich peace, satisfaction.
> "My love," she cried, lifting her face to him, her eyes, her mouth open in transport.
> "My love," he answered, bending and kissing her, always kissing her. (*WL* 306)

While the primal bonding of Birkin and Ursula is as purely unconscious as that of Gerald and Minette, it percolates into consciousness, first as a sensation of satisfaction and then in the emotion of love. Birkin had spoken earlier of love being the branch of primal feeling, not the root, but now it is clear that, in a well constituted nature, the organic connection is vital. A brief survey of the unhealthy characters reveals that they are uniformly incapable of love. Gudrun extorts the confession from Gerald that he has never loved and she can supply no evidence from her own life that she has either. Hermione and Loerke are not even candidates. But beyond just the failure to experience love, these characters all seem weirdly estranged from themselves. Hermione, massively repressed, moves with the jerky gait of a zombie; Gudrun, realizing that "inwardly was a bad joke," delights in the suggestive badinage of Loerke; Gerald regards his face in the mirror as if it were a "composition mask" and fears that one day "he would be a purely meaningless babble lapping round a darkness" (*WL* 225). The prevalent emotion of the unhealthy characters is, as in the case of Gerald, fear. This is not a fear that emotionally records the instinctive recoil of the primal self – that would be a positive, organic emotion – but a fear *of* the primal self. When they attend too carefully to primal feeling, Gerald, Hermione, and Gudrun all experience panic attacks.

The healthy individual, then, is one whose emotional life is tightly linked to primal feeling. Given the strongly somatic emphasis in Lawrence, it would probably be most faithful to his intention to see the emotions as the subjective appearance in consciousness of purely physiological activity. Thus, the emotions would be the most reliable guides for a life led in consonance with pure selfhood. Now, admittedly this is a view which grants emotions far less rationality than Aristotle's. In effect, what Lawrence has done is to elevate what Aristotle referred to as the nutritive soul, the involuntary, unconscious bodily basis for life, that part of the soul which is morally irrelevant, into the most morally alert part of the self. In Lawrence, our emotions, untutored (tutoring can only twist them according to the "mental will") record like seismographs the opaque subterranean rumblings of this primal self. Aristotle, it will be recalled, staked everything on the conscious refinement of our emotions. Emotions were shaped according to rational investigation of the good, though they could take on a cognitive life of their own thereafter. Lawrence's bold assertion, quoted earlier, that pure morality is only the instinctive response of the (healthy) primal self would have undoubtedly struck Aristotle as an appeal to a low form of hedonism, a championship of bodily pleasure as the greatest good.

Despite this glaring difference between Aristotle and Lawrence, is it the case that emotions, according to Lawrence, play a similarly crucial role in our ethical lives? If they are epiphenomena of primal feeling, as he indicates in both essays and fiction, do they still retain any cognitive value at all? I think the answer is "yes." While the primal self of healthy individuals may be infallible in its judgments, the judgments themselves are basic: movement toward or away from an object. The ability to get this right is crucial, naturally, for, if we attach ourselves to the wrong objects, not much positive can result whatever subtle adjustments we try to make consciously (Birkin with Hermione). There are times, too, when the primal self moves us away from the sought after object to ensure independence (this seems especially important for the male). In this way, primal consciousness functions in Lawrence like the reason in Aristotle – it alone is capable of establishing the path of a good life. But Lawrence is far too aware of the importance of the fine discriminations of quotidian life to dispense with "mental consciousness" as at best a non-obtrusive redundancy.

Primal consciousness dictates those worthy of our attachment and those unworthy, but we cannot function as pure automata of this primal consciousness. There are decisions that cannot be made solely on the basis of the ebb and flow of primordial energies, though these decisions must be consonant with them. Mental consciousness is required to convert this subterranean dynamic into a specific plan of action. And it is our emotions that are the best representatives of the primal self as it enters consciousness. Only when Ursula and Birkin acknowledge that what they are experiencing is something they can both comfortably call love that they can strike out definitively to forge a new life. Immediately they decide to quit their jobs, get married, and leave England. Never again do they discuss mystical union on an impersonal plane in referring to their relationship using the language of the primal self. The goal of emotional awareness has been reached.

Nevertheless, Lawrence remains near the limit of the case that can be made for literature's ethical significance. His emotions are *in origin* completely irrational, being supervenient on the motions of the primal self. They are linked to no set of beliefs, that which can lend a cognitive element to emotions on the Aristotelian view. Nor are we to tutor them according to the dictates of reason as Aristotle would have us – that is a recipe for pure disaster. Finally, whatever reliability emotions have at all is limited to Lawrence's spiritual aristocrats, and even then only when they have managed with enormous difficulty to slough off the carapace of convention.

But if Lawrence seems to claim far less for the emotions in terms of rationality, he claims far more in terms of perception. Aristotle was aware that on occasion the emotions were truer guides to the ethically salient than the twistings and turnings of deliberative reason. In Lawrence, however, when the emotions are pure reflections of primal consciousness, they are *always* truer guides. Aristotle talks of noble emotions, scrupulously refined through education and habituation, becoming second nature to the virtuous individual; for Lawrence they are linked intuitively to primary nature. Granted, the organic self that Lawrence champions is only available to a select minority, but this sort of exclusivity is far from unknown among advocates of those who are passionately and delicately attuned. Gottfried limits *Tristan* to "noble hearts" and Stendhal dedicates *The Red and the Black* "to the happy few," in both cases soliciting a readership akin to the innately large-souled protagonists. Certainly, if Lawrence didn't believe *any* corrigibility were possible, the steady didacticism of his mature novels would be bewilderingly inappropriate. The healthy must be taught to trust their essential selves as this occluded stratum percolates via emotions into consciousness. If this can be accomplished, an equilibrium is achieved in which our unconscious awareness flows freely into our conscious knowledge. As in the case of Nietzsche and other exponents of authenticity, we may continue to be nervous, though, about Lawrence's belief that the well-organized individual is to be the standard of his own morality. This self-ratification is open to obvious abuse. We may continue to balk, too, at making central what Thomas Nagel would call an instance of "moral luck," the chance inheritance of a disposition that disqualifies some of us a priori from the good life. As Nagel correctly points out, "[t]o Kant this seems incoherent because virtue is enjoined on everyone and therefore in principle must be possible for everyone."[26] Yet, for Lawrence to count as a contributor to our ethical knowledge it is not necessary that we agree with him on all points any more than we are called on to accept everything that

---

[26] Thomas Nagel, "Moral Luck" in *Mortal Questions* (Cambridge: Cambridge University Press, 1979), p. 33.

Plato, Kant, Mill, and others in the philosophic tradition have to say – an impossibility, in any case, given their conflicting views. We need only ask of Lawrence that he enriches our thinking about what it means to lead the ethically alert "good life" and that, at his best, this knowledge is something he could only have conveyed by means of a literary presentation of the densely felt inner life of his characters. Despite the eccentricity of some of his views, this is a standard that Lawrence clearly meets.

CHAPTER 4

# *Epistemology and Ethics in Virginia Woolf*

Like Lawrence, Virginia Woolf poses a severe challenge to the case for literature's ethical significance, since she, too, is dissatisfied with the traditional conception of character that constitutes the basis for Aristotelian agency. Stability of belief, of disposition, and of behavioral response is so important to Aristotle that he is unwilling to count an otherwise praiseworthy act as deserving of approval unless it is performed by someone of steadfastly virtuous character. One cannot be sporadically or haphazardly ethical. In tension with his insistence on coherence and constancy issuing in purposive action, let us juxtapose Mrs. Ramsay from *To the Lighthouse*, speaking almost certainly for Woolf herself here: "our apparitions, the things you know us by, are simply childish. Beneath it is all dark, it is all spreading, it is unfathomably deep; but now and again we rise to the surface and that is what you see us by."[1] The elusive personhood that Mrs. Ramsay refers to as "a wedge-shaped core of darkness" manifests itself most faithfully in impressions and memories linked in the expansive leisure of free association. For Woolf, this privacy of perception merits far more attention than activity in a public sphere where we can only clumsily represent the richness of our inward lives. On such a view, discussion of virtue would seem to be a non-starter. Indeed, it would be hard to see how one could get clear on the interior world of another or, even if that were possible, praise or blame what one found there.

The radical challenge that Woolf presents to an ethically interested criticism is typically overlooked when one starts from *A Room of One's Own* or even Moore's *Principia Ethica*, which she read in 1908. This is by no means to say that feminist concerns were not extremely important to her; they clearly were. And Moore's conclusion to the *Principia* – "that personal affections and aesthetic enjoyments include all the greatest, and

---

[1] Virginia Woolf, *To the Lighthouse* (1927; rpt. Harcourt Brace & Company, 1981), p. 62. Hereafter all references to this work will be indicated in the text by *TL* and page number in parentheses.

by far the greatest, goods we can imagine" – might easily stand as Bloomsbury's credo.[2] Yet to move from either of these texts immediately to Woolf's fictional rendering of interpersonal relations and obligations is to move too quickly and easily. Logically prior and far more foundational for Woolf is the very problem of perception. Is there a mind-independent reality? If so, what sort of access do we have to it? Why should minds select differently from the flood of sensory data that she refers to as "an incessant shower of innumerable atoms."[3] The self for Woolf is thus, most basically, a perceiver. Individuation is inextricably bound up with what we choose to see. In short, Woolf is first an epistemologist.[4] The problem of other minds is a subset of this concern; how we should respond to the possessors of those other minds (ethics) is in large part determined by what we can know of them. While it may seem intuitively misguided to approach the weaver of such exquisitely lyrical fiction via the dense and often ponderous world of epistemological inquiry, such an opinion shortchanges Woolf. Her familiarity with epistemology is, as Ann Banfield has exhaustively demonstrated in *The Phantom Table* (2000), traceable to Bloomsbury's tight connection to Cambridge philosophy that was immersed at the time, especially in the work of Bertrand Russell, in the very issues that would occupy her. Indeed, Banfield goes on to argue, plausibly enough, that Woolf's famous, though unexplained, remark that human character changed "on or about December 1910" is meant to record a shift in epistemological fault lines represented by Fry's First Post-Impressionistic Exhibition that ran from November 1910 through January 1911. According to Fry, Impressionism took to the extreme a representational tendency in Western art, the recording of light and color as it struck the eye, in an attempt to capture "the totality of appearance."[5] By contrast, Post-Impressionism went beyond this data to discover a reality behind, the "geometry" Cézanne reveals in the world of objects. Without abandoning realism, the Post-Impressionists emphasized the vision of the artist to select meaningfully, to discover patterns. For Woolf, this change acknowledged the

---

[2] G. E. Moore, *Principia Ethica* (Cambridge: Cambridge University Press, 1903), p. 189.
[3] Virginia Woolf, "Modern Fiction," in *The Common Reader: First Series* (London: Hogarth Press, 1968), p. 189.
[4] Jaako Hintikka was the first to draw sustained attention to Woolf as epistemologist in "Virginia Woolf and Our Knowledge of the External World," in *Journal of Aesthetics and Art Criticism*, 38 (Fall 1979–80), 5–14. The most extensive discussion can be found in Ann Banfield, *The Phantom Table* (Cambridge: Cambridge University Press, 2000). Most recently, James Harker has highlighted the importance of perception in his "Misperceiving Virginia Woolf," *Journal of Modern Literature*, vol. 34, no. 2 (2011 Winter), (2), 1–21.
[5] Roger Fry, *Vision and Design* (London: Chatto & Windus, 1920), p. 11.

deep subjective contribution to perception, the perceiver as potential *poetes*. The relation of perceiver to world had become *the* question, and one that was getting a new answer. Even subtracting for ironic hyperbole on Woolf's part, this changing conception of the way we see did mark for her a change in the way we view "human character," and, as she will make clear in "Mr. Bennett and Mrs. Brown," in the way this subjectivized character is to be rendered in fiction.

Woolf's interest in these epistemological matters is evident in her first published short story, the oft-anthologized "The Mark on the Wall" (1917). Late in life, looking back on her early years, Woolf strikingly recalls her sense of being a sequestered self that apprehended the world as if through the skin of a grape.[6] This metaphor suggests beautifully not only the vulnerability of ego evident in all her fiction, but also the problematic nature of perception itself as it is filtered through a distorting membrane. "The Mark on the Wall" begins with an expression of this same epistemological uncertainty:

> Perhaps it was the middle of January in the present year that I first looked up and saw the mark on the wall. In order to fix a date it is necessary to remember what one saw. So now I think of the fire; the steady film of yellow light upon the page of my book ... Yes, it must have been the winter time, and we had just finished our tea, for I remember that I was smoking a cigarette when I looked up and saw the mark on the wall for the first time. I looked up through the smoke of my cigarette.[7]

To ascertain even the season, the narrator must recall the most evanescent of impressions, "the steady film of yellow light upon the page." The external world and its distinctions must be indexed to an internal world that is far more vivid. The mark itself is perceived though a cloud of smoke that, much like the grape skin, allows only a gauzy view of what lies outside. Even when the mark is perceived, it serves mainly as a trigger for imaginative speculation:

> How readily our thoughts swarm upon a new object, lifting it a little way, as ants carry a blade of straw so feverishly, and then leave it ... If that mark was made by a nail, it can't have been for a picture, it must have been for a miniature – the miniature of a lady with white powdered curls, powder-dusted cheeks, and lips like red carnations.[8]

---

[6] Virginia Woolf, "A Sketch of the Past," in *Moments of Being*, ed. Jeanne Schulkind, 2nd edition. (New York: Harcourt Brace & Company, 1985), p. 65.
[7] Virginia Woolf, "The Mark on the Wall," in *Monday or Tuesday* (New York: Harcourt Brace & Company, 1921; rpt. Denton and White, 2014), p. 60.
[8] Ibid., p. 60.

To actually get up and inspect the mark to see if it was made by a nail strikes the narrator as an act of epistemological hubris since "ten to one I shouldn't be able to say for certain; because once a thing's done, no one ever knows how it happened." With the gathering of evidence thus being pointless, the narrator concludes that it is far preferable to remain in her chair where she can "sink deeper and deeper, away from the surface, with its hard separate facts." Better to leave the quest for facts to "retired colonels" who poke about the English countryside "examining clods of earth and stone"[9] to determine if a tumulus is the remains of a tomb or an encampment. In the end, these doddering antiquarians never will reach a definitive answer, and much good would it do them even if they could. The story concludes with the appearance of (apparently) the narrator's husband who goes off to buy a newspaper in his male quest for factual tabloids. As he leaves, he identifies the mark on the wall as a snail and the mock-appreciative narrator leaves us to weigh the value of this sparse observation against the elaborate embroidery of her reveries.

Coupled with her rejection of traditional character, this epistemic skepticism that slips quickly into bemused indifference about the true nature of the external world would seem to sideline Woolf as an author who might enhance our ethical awareness. To compound the difficulty, there is an almost omnipresent thread of morbidity that runs through her fiction. The desire to lapse into the recesses of a private world frequently has as its next step a consideration of utter self-dissolution, the quiescence of death. Even in the unthreatening world of "The Mark on the Wall" thoughts of death weave through the narrator's consciousness. The dust on her mantelpiece recalls the destruction of Troy, with "only fragments of pots utterly refusing annihilation." In the imagined debate over the origin of the barrows, the narrator finds the view that they were tombs more temperamentally congenial: "Of the two, I should prefer them to be tombs, desiring melancholy like most English people; and finding it natural at the end of a walk to think of the bones stretched beneath the turf."[10] When she awakes from terrifying dreams at night, she takes solace in her chest of drawers, something that draws her out of an inner world gone sour. Yet, not long thereafter, her thoughts drift to an imaginary storm-toppled tree that provided the wood, and she enters the final experience of the fallen tree itself, returned to the earth. The gravitational tug toward oblivion here and elsewhere in Woolf tends to trivialize human activity as something dubiously worth the pain. The long view of time's expanse and

---

[9] Ibid., pp. 61, 62, 65.  [10] Ibid., p. 65.

the indifference of the universe, both so much part of her speculative repertoire, generate a kind of enervated Dionysianism, an effectless swirl of thought and feeling in the face of individual annihilation.

Woolf's world is thus one of extraordinary fluidity: the flux of time that leaves behind not facts but indefinite "marks" and the free association of characterless selves that ruminate endlessly on these marks as they drift half-willingly toward death. Moreover, language itself is frequently indicted as woefully inadequate to the task of recording the flow of consciousness, and this despite the lyric beauty of Woolf's style that moves the novels in the direction of tone poems. The solitude that nearly all her characters crave is not so much an oasis from the hurly-burly of the external world – the leisurely lives most of her characters lead are far from harried – but retreat into the solipsism of private theater. There the authenticity of being is ratified to an audience of one. Woolf's choice of the mark on the wall as her subject functions as a deliberate exaggeration of the humble, domestic ordinariness of Cézanne's bowls and apples. But it is in this very exaggeration that we can see what will be the central problem of Woolf's fiction. Perceptively, Woolf observed of Cézanne's apples that the longer you looked at them the heavier they seemed to get. Her remark is faithful to Cézanne's announced purpose of "grappling directly with objects," nowhere more evident than in the dense "thereness" of the apples.[11] Yet Woolf's mark has none of this weightiness; it serves instead as *occasion* for imaginative speculation rather than as something infused with that speculation. The very triviality of the mark serves to keep the world at arm's length as something not entirely worthy of our attention. Admittedly, were Woolf to fully acquiesce in such radical self-enclosure, it would be hard to salvage much of value ethically from the delicate gossamer of her fictional worlds.[12] But, as she begins the period of her mature and most enduring novels, she holds out hope that these discrete centers of consciousness, perceiving so differently, can be connected at some level. Writing in her diary while working on *Mrs. Dalloway* (tentatively entitled *The Hours*), she touches briefly on her intersubjective goal:

> I have no time to describe my plans. I should say a good deal about The Hours, & my discovery; how I dig out beautiful caves behind my characters; I think that gives exactly what I want; humanity, humour, depth.

---

[11] Quoted in Julian Barnes, "The Secrets of Cézanne," *TLS* (December 19, 2012)
[12] Among recent critics, Lee Oser is most keenly aware of this problem as the central one in evaluating Woolf's introspective world: "a realm of disembodied freedom, where the spirit navigates an opalescent atmosphere, unstained by earthly creatures." See his chapter "Virginia Woolf: Antigone Triumphant," in *The Ethics of Modernism* (Cambridge: Cambridge University Press, 2007).

> The idea is that the caves shall connect, & each comes to daylight at the present moment[13]

However promising, this is certainly cryptic enough, and we will need to determine what Woolf might have meant and how this new method plays itself out in her major novels in order to decide whether she can provide enough communal ground for meaningful interpersonal relations to take place.

If her major novels can be said to be "about" anything, it would be precisely this problem of intersubjectivity. Her characters not only exemplify the difficulties of the struggle to connect with one another, but thematize the issue for us in the free indirect discourse that Woolf handles so subtly. In this way, less stridently than Lawrence, but no less persistently, Woolf allows radical manifesto to seep into her novels. Here, for example, is Peter Walsh's recollection of Clarissa Dalloway grappling with the dissatisfaction of "not knowing people; not being known" as she rides the bus:

> she felt herself everywhere; not "here, here, here"; and she tapped the back of the seat; but everywhere. She waved her hand, going up Shaftesbury Avenue. She was all that. So that to know her, or any one, one must seek out the people who completed them; even the places. Odd affinities she had with people she had never spoken to, some woman in the street, some man behind a counter – even trees, or barns. It ended in a transcendental theory which, with her horror of death, allowed her to believe, or say that she believed (for all her skepticism), that since our apparitions, the part of us which appears, are so momentary compared with the other, the unseen part of us, which spreads wide, the unseen might survive, be recovered somehow attached to this person or that, or even haunting certain places after death ... perhaps – perhaps.[14]

Such theories – even when, as here, a report of another's views – are always offered meditatively, privately, so that we do not get the questioning and debate we find in Lawrence. Nor do we get competing private visions. Those whom we feel sure would reject Clarissa's theories – Drs. Holmes and Bradshaw – are granted no inner monologue whatsoever. Thus, debate remains implicit, and foreclosed, for we are led throughout the novel to dislike both medical men precisely for their insensitivity to the inner life of

---

[13] *The Diary of Virginia Woolf: Volume Two 1920–1924*, ed. Anne Oliver Bell (New York: Harcourt Brace Jovanovitch), p. 263 (August 30, 1923).
[14] Virginia Woolf, *Mrs. Dalloway* (New York: Harcourt Brace Jovanovitch, 1985), pp. 231–32. Hereafter references to this work will be indicated in the text by *MD* and page number in parentheses.

their patients. If anything at all seems definite in *Mrs. Dalloway*, it would be that, despite the occasional satire, Clarissa's metaphysical speculations are not far from Woolf's.

At only a slight remove is the related theory of Peter Walsh. Lamenting the fact that other minds are always occluded, he sees human beings as something akin to sea creatures who lead a mysterious submarine life, surfacing only grudgingly out of necessity:

> For this is the truth about our soul, he thought, our self, who fish-like inhabits deep seas and plies among obscurities threading her way between the boles of giant weeds, over sun-flickered spaces and on and on into gloom, cold, deep, inscrutable; suddenly she shoots to the surface and sports on the wind-wrinkled waves; that is, has a positive need to brush, scrape, kindle herself, gossiping. (*MD* 244)

In both passages there is an expressed need for others, but these others may be total strangers (according to Clarissa) or objects of gossip whom we "brush" (according to Peter). It is precisely this extraordinarily etiolated sense of community that gives Woolf's novels their quintessential strangeness. We pass almost as phantoms *through* one another, leaving at most some residual trace. Peter, for example, spies an attractive young woman in Trafalgar Square and follows her for blocks to her residence off Great Portsmouth Street. Though she is completely unaware of him, her presence "shed on him a light which connected them, which singled him out," or so he believes. The surrounding traffic, like a sympathetic chorus, seems to whisper to him the intimate name by which he secretly addresses himself. Nor are we to view this hallucinated vision as in any way eccentric, even if compensatory; it is all in the soul-work of a day.

The narrator ratifies such visions by seeming to participate in them – perhaps even create them – herself. Shortly after Peter's episode with the mystery woman, he hears the indistinct singing of a beggar woman outside the Regent's Park tube station. Without being told whether it is Peter's perception or the narrator's, we are informed that the voice was that "of an ancient spring sprouting from the earth ... from a tall quivering shape like a funnel, like a rusty pump" only to metamorphose one more time into an ageless figure, lamenting for millions of years her lost love in unintelligible syllables that flow like a river down Marylebone Street leaving a damp stain in their path" (*MD* 122–23). Peter presses a coin into the woman's hand, so obviously he has reacted to the song, but we have no way of knowing if the vision is free indirect discourse with no markers or the narrator's own view. In either case, this is not an unreliable vision, nor is the old woman, for

Woolf, merely symbolic; she has an enduring metaphysical identity. When Peter gives her the coin, we are meant to believe that he has somehow become part of her and thereby will share in her immortality.

Even in the relationship between Peter and Clarissa where there are genuinely shared and poignant memories, Woolf will use the narrative voice in an extremely unusual way to heighten the connection. When Peter calls on Clarissa in the morning, her slip of the tongue calls to mind for both that he had been her rejected suitor. The narrator quickly likens Peter's grief to the moon (something he almost certainly would not have the emotional distance to do, under the circumstances) and then places that moon above an imaginary terrace upon which Peter and Clarissa sit:

> [Peter] was overcome with his own grief, which rose like a moon looked at from a terrace, ghastly beautiful with light from the sunken day. I was more unhappy than I've ever been since, he thought. And as if *in truth* [italics mine] he were sitting there on the terrace he edged a little towards Clarissa; put his hand out; raised it; let it fall. There above them it hung, that moon. She too seemed to be sitting with him on the terrace, in the moonlight. (*MD* 62–63)

Strikingly, the characters literally seem to inhabit the metaphorical world of the narrator. As James Naremore points out, this technique, which obscures the difference between authorial voice and the thoughts of characters, is especially appropriate for Woolf's overall view that "there is no clear boundary between the 'inside' and the 'outside.'"[15] Coalescence is permissible everywhere. Yet, however appropriate the technique, however masterfully executed, we are caught up in a sleight-of-hand. Characters are held together in soul-mixing intimacies more by the gossamer of verbal artifice rather than any demonstrated reciprocity that could justify such intensity. In the passage quoted above, for example, it is never made clear that Clarissa is emotionally participating in the grief, and if so, how. Too often we feel that Woolf has willed this degree of intersubjectivity rather than motivated it.

Connection is implied, too, as the narrative voice insinuates itself into different consciousnesses with scarcely a pause. Early in the novel, Clarissa, waiting on a street corner, is spotted by her neighbor. We enter first his mind: "A charming woman, Scrope Purvis thought her (knowing her as one does know people who live next door to one in Westminster); a touch of the bird about her" (*MD* 4). Following a slight transition, made even

---

[15] James Naremore, *The World without a Self: Virginia Woolf and the Novel* (New Haven: Yale University Press, 1973), p. 103.

smoother by the fact that the narrator picks up the bird image – "There she perched, never seeing him, waiting to cross, very upright" – we glide into Clarissa's mind: "For having lived in Westminster – how many years now? over twenty – one feels even in the midst of traffic, or waking at night, Clarissa was positive, a particular hush, or solemnity" (*MD* 4). Purvis does not bother to greet his neighbor and she is unaware of him, yet the repetition of the word "Westminster" (even though the narrator supplies it for Purvis) is meant to convey minds in communion. Here, dubiously large dividends are paid on negligible personal investment.

Woolf herself was at least aware that style may be masking deficiencies of feeling, but rejects the suspicion. In June of 1923 she notes in her diary: "But now what do I feel about *my* writing? – this book, that is The Hours, if that's its name? One must write from deep feeling, said Dostoevsky. And do I? Or do I fabricate with words, loving them as I do? No I think not."[16] But what is really at stake is not whether she is fully engaged with her work, but the degree to which her characters are engaged with each other, given the claims she makes for their connection. Indeed, one could argue that it is precisely because Woolf has deposited so much of herself in the novel that the characters have too little independent life. Long ago, James Hafley astutely observed that, unlike Joyce, Woolf is "always present in her novels ... Beneath the diverse points of view presented to the reader there is the impersonal narrator – the central intelligence – of which, in and after *Mrs. Dalloway* the reader is never allowed to become immediately aware, but which extends the idea of a common impulse beneath diversity."[17] As we move from consciousness to consciousness, contents will vary, but the meditative voice is always the same: that of the narrator.[18] Because of the uniformity of tone, a tone that bears us along with its lyricism, we are made to *feel* that characters share a common life rather than shown what that life might be.

In two instances, however, Woolf does try to show a sense of public community. In the first of these, a royal limousine passes slowly and "everyone looked at the motor car" as each speculates about who might be the passenger: queen, prince, or prime minister. A surge of unifying patriotism runs through the crowd as the car wends its way toward Buckingham Palace. Yet later in the novel when we actually see the prime minister at Clarissa's party, he looks so nondescript that Peter

---

[16] *Diary, vol. 2* (June 19, 1923), p. 248.
[17] James Hafley, *The Glass Roof: Virginia Woolf as Novelist* (New York: Russell and Russell, Inc. 1963), p. 74.
[18] Naremore, *The World Without a Self*, p. 90.

imagines him selling biscuits in a shop. The significance of the car with its mystery celebrity is further undercut when attention is completely diverted by the sudden appearance of a skywriting airplane, tracing letters that disperse into wispy clouds. Trying to make sense of these letters, transfixed onlookers combine them into "glaxo," "creemo," and "toffee." The scene cleverly underscores Woolf's belief in the referential inadequacy of language, but, more importantly, allows her to shift with more justification than usual from one consciousness to another since all are riveted on the same event. Yet, except for the phantasmagorical reaction of the insane Septimus Warren Smith, these consciousnesses contain nothing of the richness we encounter when minds meander in isolated reverie. Compounded of patriotism and commercialism, a common culture holds, in the end, little of comparative worth.

Indeed, the very fact that Septimus' response is so purely personal and idiosyncratic is meant to justify the disproportionate attention Woolf lavishes on his visions. His is the consciousness that it will be especially worth connecting with. And in the boldest strategy of the novel, Woolf tries to establish a deep bond between her heroine Clarissa and Septimus, though Clarissa has never met him. The attempted link is made even more difficult since the range of experience in the two minds is so vastly different: Septimus is a shell-shocked soldier haunted by the death of his closest friend on the battlefield; Clarissa is a West End hostess, haunted by her failure to be invited to lunch at Lady Bruton's. If Woolf can convince us that Clarissa is the secret sharer of Septimus' hallucinated agonies, she will have gone a long way to demonstrating the effectiveness of her announced method of tunneling between "caves."

Because Woolf places so little importance on whatever might be shared in our common response to external circumstance, she will try instead to superimpose Septimus' emotional life onto Clarissa's.[19] (We know from the introduction to the Modern Library edition that Septimus was only added in a later draft and took on the suicide originally intended for Clarissa.)[20] And certainly both characters are convinced that their emotional lives define them, though Septimus, who feels most intensely,

---

[19] Jean Guiget, *Virginia Woolf and Her Works*, trans. by Jean Stewart (New York: Harcourt Brace & World, Inc., 1965), p. 234.
[20] Quoted in David Daiches, *Virginia Woolf* (Norfolk, Conn: New Directions, 1963), p. 75. In the preface that was written three years after the novel and occurred only in the first Modern Library Edition of 1928, Woolf informs us that "in the first version Septimus, who later is intended to be her double, had no existence; and that Mrs. Dalloway was originally to kill herself at the end of the party."

believes he is losing the power to feel (*MD* 131). Since these two characters have no shared life as ordinarily understood, Woolf chooses to elevate crucial affective moments to a kind of ecstasy, radiant to others. The oscillating waves of euphoria and depression are steeper in Septimus, thus he is more naturally the emitter of such energy. Here, for example, is Septimus' reaction to the skywriting airplane:

> So, thought Septimus, looking up, they are signaling to me. Not indeed in actual words; that is, he could not read the language yet; but it was plain enough, this beauty, this exquisite beauty, and tears filled his eyes as he looked at the smoke words languishing and melting in the sky and bestowing upon him in their inexhaustible charity and laughing goodness one shape after another of unimaginable beauty and signaling their intention to provide him for nothing, for ever, for looking merely, with beauty, more beauty! Tears ran down his cheeks. (*MD* 31)

Given that later on the same day Septimus will be hounded to a death that is presented as a sacrifice, critics have justifiably seen this revelation as intended to call to mind the passion of Christ. In confirmation of this association, shortly thereafter Clarissa returns home "like a nun" who "felt blessed and purified." She slowly ascends to her attic chamber, her "virginity ... clinging to her like a sheet" and recalls moments in her life when she was overwhelmed with the charm and beauty of certain women:

> It was a sudden revelation, a tinge like a blush which one tried to check and then, as it spread, one yielded to its expansion, and rushed to the farthest verge and there quivered and felt the world come closer, swollen with some astonishing significance, some pressure of rapture, which split its thin skin and gushed and poured with an extraordinary alleviation over the cracks and sores! Then, for that moment, she had seen an illumination; a match burning in a crocus. (*MD* 47)

Though neither Clarissa nor Woolf herself was Christian, the religious allusions are meant to heighten the experience's importance for us and justify by association the quasi-mysticism that gathers up the two moments into one. Generally – and generously – critics have been willing to accept the notion that there is some sort of interpenetration of such moments, one even extravagantly detecting in all this the "communion of saints."[21]

The crucial test of relationship between Septimus and Clarissa will come, however, with his actual suicide and how, if at all, it might be a shared experience. Woolf begins on the very first page of the novel to prepare us for

---

[21] See Suzette Henke, "The Communion of Saints," in *New Feminist Essays on Virginia Woolf*, ed. Jane Marcus (Lincoln: University of Nebraska Press, 1981), 125–47.

this affiliation. Here is Clarissa's first remembrance, triggered by a squeaky door hinge:

> What a lark! What a plunge! For so it had always seemed to her, when with a little squeak of the hinges, which she could hear now, she had burst open the French windows and plunged at Bourton into the open air. How fresh, how calm, stiller than this of course, the air was in the early morning; like the flap of a wave; the kiss of a wave; chill and sharp and yet (for a girl of eighteen as she then was) solemn, feeling as she did, standing there at the open window, that something awful was about to happen. (*MD* 3)

This first glimpse inside Clarissa is clearly meant to parallel our last glimpse inside Septimus as, in flight from Dr. Holmes, he casts about for the best means of suicide, one by one rejecting a knife, gas fire, and razors:

> There remained only the window, the large Bloomsbury-lodging house window, the tiresome, the troublesome, and rather melodramatic business of opening the window and throwing himself out. It was their idea of tragedy, not his or Rezia's (for she was with him). Holmes and Bradshaw like that sort of thing. (He sat on the sill.) But he would wait till the very last moment. He did not want to die. Life was good. The sun hot. Only human beings – what did *they* want? Coming down the staircase opposite an old man stopped and stared at him. Holmes was at the door. "I'll give it you!" he cried, and flung himself vigorously, violently down on to Mrs. Filmer's area railings. (*MD* 226)

Literary foreshadowing, though, is hardly sufficient to show how the timid, fearful Clarissa who "plunges" by merely opening a window can seriously be thought of as vicarious participant in the gruesome suicide of a mind-seared veteran. We are an awfully long way here from Marlow's earned participation in the life of Kurtz, whom he travels months to find, comprehend, and then haul out of the heart of darkness. As so often in this novel, rhetorical devices cajole us into making connections that have no real substance.

Let us see, though, to be fair, what Clarissa herself makes of the suicide when she learns of it. At first indignant that Dr. Bradshaw should dampen the mood of her party with such news, she then begins to work through the death imaginatively:

> A thing there was that mattered; a thing, wreathed about with chatter, defaced, obscured in her own life, let drop every day in corruption, lies, chatter. This he had preserved. Death was defiance. Death was an attempt to communicate; people feeling the impossibility of reaching the centre which, mystically, evaded them; closeness drew apart; rapture faded, one was alone. There was an embrace in death.

> But this young man who had killed himself – had he plunged holding his treasure?
>
> ...
>
> She felt somehow very like him – the young man who had killed himself. She felt glad he had done it; thrown it away. The clock was striking. The leaden circles dissolved in the air. He made her feel the beauty; made her feel the fun. But she must go back [to her party]. (*MD* 280–84)

Joyce has taught us that people much humbler and more ordinary than Clarissa are capable of epiphanies that illuminate the status of their soul, so Woolf is certainly justified in granting such a moment to her heroine, whose intuitive powers have been on display beforehand. The difficulty arises insofar as Clarissa uses Septimus' suicide as a moment in her own psychodrama. Has she not taken his experience rather than accepted his (completely unintended) "gift" to her, as sympathetic critics have fashioned what is going on?[22] Her very construal of the event seems to belie what we know Septimus was going through. As Deborah Guth has persuasively noted:

> Septimus expresses none of the exalted self-affirmation that Clarissa sees in his death. There is no treasure, no mystical embrace, no joyous communication or lyrical prose-musing. Instead there is the terror of the hunted beast, the short, spasmodic thoughts of panic that focus almost exclusively on the menial trappings of daily life – the breadknife, the gas fire, and the razor which must help him to escape.[23]

Simply put, Clarissa – who cannot even bother to distinguish the Armenians, destroyed in the century's first genocide, from the Albanians, and admits she cares nothing about either – is too deeply immersed in her private world to "double" this war-ravaged soldier in any serious way.

Woolf, to her credit, does satirize the comfortably sequestered Clarissa, who "always had the feeling that it was very, very dangerous to live even one day" (*MD* 11). And we are meant to chide her naïve self-indulgence

---

[22] Molly Hite offers a subtle analysis of the lack of tonal cues that would normally allow us to evaluate more confidently scenes like this. She attributes the divergent readings to this authorial ambiguity. While she acknowledges this ambiguity likely reflects Woolf's own conflicted evaluation of Clarissa and Septimus, she sees this "tonal labyrinth" as providing a positive opportunity for readers to work out their own ethical response. Hite never indicates whether she thinks this degree of freedom of the reader was intended by Woolf, for it is worth mentioning that if a reader chooses to exercise her interpretive carte blanche by rejecting the depth of Clarissa's connection to Septimus, Woolf's intersubjective purpose in the novel is badly damaged. See Molly Hite, "Tonal Cues and Uncertain Values: Affect and Ethics in *Mrs. Dalloway*," *Narrative*, vol. 18, no. 3 (October 2010), 249–75.

[23] Deborah Guth, "'What a Lark! What a Plunge!': Fiction as Self-Evasion in *Mrs. Dalloway*," *Modern Language Review*, vol. 84, no. 1 (January 1989), 19–20.

when she vainly wonders if her attention to her roses might not help the Armenians/Albanians. Yet despite this occasional deprecation of her heroine, there is far too much at stake for Woolf in the unified experience of Septimus and Clarissa for *that* to be part of the satire. The difficulty Woolf faces is that the external world of "facts" is the province of men such as her limited husband, fatuous Hugh Whitbread, and the faintly ridiculous prime minister, yet it is in that world of facts that Armenians are massacred, some of whom presumably had inner lives of their own. Her solution is to allow Clarissa access to the larger world by letting her expropriate Septimus' intense emotional response to his traumatic participation in that world. But this does not solve in any convincing way the problem of other minds, nor does it get us very far in establishing the nature of ethical intercourse.[24] In her next novel, *To the Lighthouse*, Woolf makes a much better attempt at addressing both these issues.

Once again, Woolf will highlight the importance of felt time over chronological time by describing in detail the inward life of characters on two single days, separated by the rapid passage of ten years. But wisely she limits the cast of characters to the Ramsays and their houseguests on an island off the coast of Scotland. Thus, she begins with a sense of community rather than having to will it into being as in *Mrs. Dalloway*'s London. Further, she seems much more at home with the peculiarity of her worldview and jettisons what she now refers to as "the desperate accompaniment of madness" employed in the previous novel.[25] Finally, she changes the flow of energy: whereas earlier she had concentrated on the way Mrs. Dalloway had absorbed disparate experiences, now she focuses on the way Mrs. Ramsay's influence permeates the other characters.[26]

Despite all these advances, the obstacles to knowing other minds recur, though now integrated far more convincingly into the text. On the novel's first page, James Ramsay, inwardly aglow at the prospect his mother holds out of going to the lighthouse, sits cutting out pictures from a catalogue:

> [He] ... endowed the picture of a refrigerator, as his mother spoke, with heavenly bliss. It was fringed with joy. The wheelbarrow, the lawnmower,

---

[24] For a very different view, see Jessica Berman, "Ethical Folds: Ethics, Aesthetics, Woolf," in *Modern Fiction Studies*, 50.1 (Spring 2004), 151–72. Berman believes that Clarissa's feeling of disgrace at the death of Septimus signals "the moment of ethical awareness" in which Clarissa is made aware that "Septimus's shell shock is everyone's shell shock; his war death engages us all in the confrontation with death and our responsibility for it."

[25] *Diary, vol. 3* (November 23, 1926), p. 117.

[26] Jean Guiguet, *Virginia Woolf and her Works* (New York: Harcourt, Brace & World, 1965), p. 253.

the sound of poplar trees ... all these were so coloured and distinguished in his mind that he had already his private code, his secret language, though he appeared the image of stark and uncompromising severity ... so that his mother watching him guide his scissors neatly round the refrigerator, imagined him all red and ermine on the Bench. (*TL* 3–4)

If even a mother – and one as extraordinarily sensitive as Mrs. Ramsay – cannot deduce the feelings of her child from observation of his appearance, what hope is there for anyone else? Actions prove equally nonindicative. Shortly after the scene with James, Mrs. Ramsay walks into town with the prickly graduate student Charles Tansley. Suddenly struck with her extraordinary beauty, though she is fifty and the mother of eight, he envisions her "with stars in her eyes and veils in her hair, with cyclamen and wild violets ... stepping through fields of flowers and taking to her breast buds that had broken and lambs that had fallen" (*TL* 14). The result: "He took her bag." From this simple act it would be impossible to deduce anything like the elaborate fantasy that inspired it, and indeed Mrs. Ramsay, turning instead to say goodbye to a friend, seems almost oblivious of anything special. Finally, words are once again portrayed as clumsy communicative tools. Even the simplest message reverberates in unpredictable ways. Mrs. Ramsay, after telling her daughter Cam to ask the cook if the guests have arrived, reflects: "The words seemed to be dropped into a well, where, if the waters were clear, they were also so extraordinarily distorting that, even as they descended, one saw them twisting about to make Heaven knows what pattern on the floor of the child's mind" (*TL* 54). Thus, the signs that novelists traditionally rely on to indicate character – appearance, action, words – are uniformly inefficacious in Woolf's world without character.

The difficulty of ever getting clear about other minds is exacerbated insofar as the dense network of memory and personal association makes shared perception virtually impossible. So instantaneously does perception trigger private thoughts and feelings that there seems to be almost no common world. When Lily and William Bankes stand side by side, gazing together at the sand dunes across the bay, she ruminates on the endurance of the landscape and the transitoriness of human life; he recalls an incident from the past involving a brood of chickens when he knew that his friendship with Mr. Ramsay was altered forever. Perception of things near-at-hand where there is more competition for our attention is worse yet. Each of us dispositionally picks out radically different sets of things (a phenomenon that Woolf will explore exhaustively in *The Waves*). Lily, with her painterly eye, notices color everywhere. Mr. Ramsay, absorbed in abstraction, amazes even his wife with his obliviousness to the circumambient object world: "Indeed he seemed to her sometimes made differently from other people, born blind, deaf, and dumb, to the ordinary things, but to the extraordinary things with an eye like an eagle's. His understanding often astonished her. But did he notice the flowers? No. Did he notice the view? No" (*TL* 70). When Lily tries for a moment to imagine the world the way Mr. Ramsay perceives it the results are comical. Told that his epistemological investigations involve thinking of objects when they are not present, she tries to "see" the outline of a sparse kitchen table in the fork of a pear tree: "And with a painful effort of concentration, she focused her mind, not upon the silver-bossed bark of the tree, or upon its fish-shaped leaves, but upon a phantom kitchen table ... which stuck there, its four legs in the air" (*TL* 23). Acutely aware that such differences in vision may cause others to regard her own view as eccentric, Lily is especially apprehensive about showing her painting, and imagines it eventually relegated to an attic.

Male characters such as Mr. Ramsay and Charles Tansley address the problem of other minds in career-enhancing dissertations and books on "subject and object and the nature of reality," while the female characters lament our mutual opacity in quieter, more personal terms. Wistfully, Mrs. Ramsay reflects on how we bustle through the world cut off from even those closest: "She took a look at life, for she had a clear sense of it there, something real, something private, which she shared neither with her children nor with her husband" (*TL* 59). Lily conceives the mystery of Mrs. Ramsay as akin to "tablets bearing sacred inscriptions, which if one could spell them out, would teach one everything, but they would never be offered openly, never made public" (*TL* 51). Unable to decipher these hieroglyphics, Lily wonders if she might not be able to simply fuse with Mrs. Ramsay "like waters poured into one jar, inextricably the same, one with the object one adored." But this proves just as futile as the more rational quest for knowledge. As she sits, intimately leaning her head on Mrs. Ramsay's knee, nothing happens.

Characters are, most of the time, quite content to remain in isolation, however. Mr. Ramsay enjoys the self-dramatizing view of himself as lone adventurer pushing back the boundaries of darkness as he strides back and forth on the terrace, lost in contemplation: "He was safe, he was restored to his privacy" (*TL* 33). His parody, Charles Tansley, generally incapable of even rudimentary social interaction, seeks welcome refuge in his room where his dissertation awaits. Less sociable yet is Augustus Carmichael, shrouded in an opium trance, speaking to no one. Whereas Mr. Ramsay and Charles occasionally need to be stroked by Mrs. Ramsay, Augustus wants absolutely nothing from her. In response to her simple offer to pick up something for him in town, "he shrank away from her . . . making off to some corner where he did acrostics endlessly" (*TL* 42). Though hurt by his rebuff, Mrs. Ramsay, who lends whatever coherence there is to this group of isolatoes, must do so with a massive expenditure of energy and relishes those moments when

> She could be herself, by herself. And that was what now she often felt the need of – to think; well, not even to think. To be silent; to be alone. All the being and doing, expansive, glittering, vocal, evaporated; and one shrunk, with a sense of solemnity, to being oneself, a wedge-shaped core of darkness. (*TL* 62)

At this point the question is unavoidably raised whether social life, including the circle of one's own family, is so far removed from authenticity of being that to participate in it is an exercise in self-alienation.

Not only, then, is the difficulty in knowing others virtually insurmountable, but the very attempt to do so may also involve a prohibitively high cost. Yet, sporadically Woolf's characters do make the attempt and we must ask why. On the most obvious level, they all need the ratification of others – the men most desperately, but the women, too. Mr. Ramsay needs to know his work matters; Charles Tansley needs to be perpetually assured that he has transcended his working class origins; Mrs. Ramsay needs to be recognized as maternal caregiver (she is filled with self-doubt when Augustus wants nothing from her); and, finally, Lily needs to prove that women, or at least this woman, can paint. Yet these insecurities, recognizable enough and sufficient to supply motivation in most novels, are too weak as they stand to do so in the world Woolf has envisioned. Why would her characters care this deeply about public perception if the persona that is perceived bears such scant resemblance to the reality beneath? Something more has to be at stake.

When we look again into the interior of those characters to whom we are given access, we discover that there, underlying the variety of social concerns, is a persistent, common anxiety: the fear that nothing can be rescued from the inexorable march of time, that they will leave no trace behind. Mr. Ramsay shudders to think that his modest contribution to philosophy will be absorbed in a more profound thinker's work that in turn will itself be absorbed. He tries to buoy himself up by determining that the antiquated Sir Walter Scott can still give pleasure. But finally he is reduced to the perverse satisfaction of imagining that even Shakespeare, centuries hence, will be forgotten. Mrs. Ramsay is oddly disturbed by the possibility that her old friend Carrie Manning may never have thought of her during their ten-year absence, and more pessimistically than her husband "felt this thing she called life terrible, hostile, and quick to pounce on you if you gave it a chance" (*TL* 60). Lily, in a passage already mentioned, sees human endeavor dwarfed by the immutable sand dunes. Closest to Woolf herself, she wavers between yielding to oblivion – "why not accept this, be content with this, acquiesce and resign?" – and the desire to arrest the flow of time by giving form to the moment of her vision (*TL* 142). However, by the time she finally does complete her painting of the Ramsay family, the family itself has already begun to disintegrate, for Mrs. Ramsay and two of her children have died in the intervening decade. Dissatisfied with the category of "novel" to describe *To the Lighthouse*, Woolf wonders whether "elegy" might not be a more appropriate designation.[27] And given that her characters share her obsession with the passage of time and inevitable loss, it is a reasonable choice.

The fear of being totally effaced is what ultimately motivates Woolf's characters to seek the company of others. Grudgingly, almost like individuals in Locke's state of nature, they are driven together for sheer self-preservation. If we return to the scene where Lily and William Bankes look with such different eyes at the sand dunes, we find that there is a common element: both are struck with a sense of loss – she for the passing of all life; he, more particularly, for the passing of his friendship with Mr. Ramsay. Yet the scene had begun with a moment of mutual uplift. Both enjoyed briefly a "common hilarity" at the sight of a racing sailboat. Abruptly, however, the boat "stopped: shriveled; let its sails drop down; and then, with a natural instinct to complete the picture, after this swift movement, both of them looked at the dunes far away, and instead of merriment felt come over them some sadness" (*TL* 20). This awareness of the arc of life provides an omnipresent filter for vision in Woolf's world. Human endeavor, almost inevitably, seems to call to mind by "natural instinct" its termination.

This common perception, however bleak, does have the power, though, to bring us momentarily together. In the justly famous dinner party scene, just as the evening is about to unravel disastrously, Mrs. Ramsay calls for the candles to be lit. By sudden contrast, the night outside appears to course by the window, reflecting a world "in which things wavered and vanished, waterily." Inside, huddled together "[s]ome change at once went

[27] *Diary* (June 27, 1925), p. 34.

*Epistemology and Ethics in Virginia Woolf*

through them all ... and they were all conscious of making a party together in a hollow, on an island; had their common cause against that fluidity out there" (*TL* 97). This change in consciousness is reflected brilliantly in Woolf's subtle intermingling of direct, indirect, and free indirect discourse. In the following passage, worth quoting at length, partitions between thought, speech, and, ultimately, Mr. Bankes and Mrs. Ramsay themselves slowly dissolve:

> "It is a triumph," said Mr. Bankes, laying his knife down for a moment. He had eaten attentively. It was rich; it was tender. It was perfectly cooked. How did she manage these things in the depth of the country? he asked her. She was a wonderful woman. All his love, all his reverence, had returned; and she knew it.
> "It is a French recipe of my grandmother's," said Mrs. Ramsay, speaking with a ring of great pleasure in her voice. Of course it was French. What passes for cookery in England is an abomination (they agreed). It is putting cabbages in water. It is roasting meat till it is like leather. It is cutting off the delicious skins of vegetables. "In which," said Mr. Bankes, "all the virtue of the vegetable is contained." And the waste, said Mrs. Ramsay. (*TL* 101–2)

Does Bankes think or actually say that Mrs. Ramsay is a wonderful woman? Is the sentence that follows about the return of his love an observation of the narrator, confirmed by Mrs. Ramsay's thought, or all Mrs. Ramsay's thought? Does Bankes think or say that the food was French? In the next sentence, whatever difference in expression may have taken place, only the single common observation that English food is an abomination is recorded: they seem to speak with one voice. Are the examples that follow spoken by Bankes (the food faddist) mutual observations, alternating comments? We simply don't know. And finally, Mrs. Ramsay completes Bankes' remarks about the skins of vegetables. Here, unlike what was too often the case in *Mrs. Dalloway*, technique grows out of the event rather than substituting for it.[28]

Woolf, as one might expect, places far more value on the *memory* of significant events than the events themselves. We can impress ourselves on the memories of others for better or worse, and it matters greatly which. At last, in this distinction between better and worse, Woolf emerges from a world of cloistral selves to join a more familiar ethical universe where behavior is assessable. When, for example, Mr. Ramsay truthfully but

---

[28] Erich Auerbach was the first to draw attention to this kind of indeterminacy as a hallmark of Woolf's prose. See "The Brown Stocking," in *Mimesis* (1946; translated by Willard Trask (Princeton: Princeton University Press, 1968). Hafley directed attention to the subtle use of this technique in the exchange between Mrs. Ramsay and Mr. Bankes. See Hafley, *The Glass Roof*, pp. 90–91.

brutally tells the expectantly joyful James that, given the wind, a trip to the lighthouse will be impossible, Mrs. Ramsay notes ruefully that her son "will remember that all his life." Indeed, ten years later when we see him again on the novel's last day, he is still smoldering with resentment. We feel certain, too, that Lily will never forget Tansley's cruel jibe about women not being able to write or paint. (It is still haunting her, as did James' remembrance, on the last day we see her.) More benignly, Mrs. Ramsay reflects with pleasure at the end of her unifying dinner party that the guests "would . . . however long they lived, come back to this night; this moon; this wind; this house: and to her too. It flattered her . . . to think how, wound about in their hearts, however long they lived, she would be woven" (*TL* 113). This is not just trivial vanity on her part. Denied the continuation of personal identity in any conventional religious sense, Woolf's characters can only hope to endure in the memories of those who knew them. Given the amazing ability for memories to generate almost endless threads of association, Woolf suggests that they will be passed on in however attenuated form, partaking of a kind of immortality.

This regenerative power can be seen most clearly in the aftermath of Mrs. Ramsay's death. Lily, returning to the island along with the remaining family members and Augustus Carmichael, is suddenly moved to take up her unfinished painting of the Ramsay family begun ten years before. The success of the painting is dependent on Lily's ability to recover and understand her memories of the Ramsays. In a reference to Woolf's technique of "tunnelling," inaugurated in *Mrs. Dalloway*, Lily is described as "tunnelling her way into her picture, into the past."[29] Woolf's second attempt to employ this method may be judged, then, by the viability of Lily's efforts. Incapable of understanding the dynamic between Mr. and Mrs. Ramsay, a frustrated Lily at first resorts to diminishing Mrs. Ramsay by calling to mind her failure as a matchmaker. In a disingenuous half-truth, she assures herself that in any event "the dead are at our mercy." Yet, as the later juxtaposition of Lily's pain at Mrs. Ramsay's absence to that of a fish with a piece cut out of its side makes graphically clear, she is at least as much at the mercy of the dead. Aware of her own evasion, Lily finally tries to enter with imaginative sympathy into the life Mrs. Ramsay must have led with husband. With intense concentration, "all her faculties in a trance, frozen over superficially but moving underneath with extreme speed," she

---

[29] John Batchelor, *Virginia Woolf: The Major Novels* (New York: Cambridge University Press, 1991), p. 104.

manages to recreate the emotional rhythms of Mrs. Ramsay as she moved in attraction and repulsion from Mr. Ramsay (*TL* 201). At the end of a lengthy reverie compounded of actual memories and emotionally charged extrapolations, Lily's intensity is rewarded when Mrs. Ramsay, summoned back by her cry, appears before her, knitting the stocking she had intended for the lighthouse boy.

We are, then, essentially to be identified with the emotional current of our life. It is this that holds together the "incessant shower of innumerable atoms" that bombard our consciousness. The rise and fall of Woolf's lyricism is intended to record the moment-to-moment rhythms of this life that lies beneath doing, even thinking, for as Lily finally realizes "[i]t was one's body feeling, not one's mind" that constitutes the basis of personal identity (*TL* 178). This identity endures when it can impress itself on the affective life of those nearest to us. It is not simply a passive reception, however. Lily is only able to inhabit the emotional life of Mrs. Ramsay after she has struggled to feel sympathy for the demanding, intimidating Mr. Ramsay. Work is required: enlargement of emotional range. When Lily allows herself to respond to Mr. Ramsay's humbly kneeling to tie her boot – the triggering event is, as almost always in Woolf, insignificant – she begins to earn access to the interior life of Mrs. Ramsay. Unlike the rather glib appropriation of Septimus by Mrs. Dalloway, here Lily's quest to understand Mrs. Ramsay has been deeply personal and arduous. When, at the end, everything comes together in her "vision," we are persuaded that the vision has been earned.

Earned, too, is the understanding between Mr. and Mrs. Ramsay. Once again, though, this is not a knowledge of the other's mind. In a passage already cited, Mrs. Ramsay expressed bewilderment at her husband's mode of thought that could deal with the most abstract issues, yet be oblivious to the flowers that occupy her. For his part, Mr. Ramsay cannot fathom the way women in general, and his wife in particular, conceive of the world: "women are always like that; the vagueness of their minds is hopeless; it was a thing he had never been able to understand; but so it was. It had been so with her – his wife" (*TL* 167). Mrs. Ramsay's inability to connect barometer readings to weather patterns so frustrates her husband that he ends up cursing her. Later, seeing him frowning for reasons she can't deduce at the dinner that means so much to her, she wonders in despair how she could ever have felt the slightest emotion for him. Yet even in such a discordant moment, they are able to communicate their feelings rapidly, precisely and silently:

> He hated people wallowing in food. He hated everything dragging on for hours like this. But he had controlled himself, Mr. Ramsay would have her observe, disgusting though the sight was. But why show it so plainly, Mrs. Ramsay demanded (they looked at each other down the long table sending these questions and answers across, each knowing exactly what the other felt.) (*TL* 96)

It is this ability to respond to the feelings of the other, even though the given set of events does not call forth anything like similar feelings in both, that yield moments of extraordinary grace and delicacy:

> She was lovely, lovelier now than ever he thought. But he could not speak to her. He could not interrupt her. He wanted urgently to speak to her now that James was gone and she was alone at last. But he resolved, no; he would not interrupt her. She was aloof from him now in her beauty, in her sadness. He would let her be, and he passed her without a word, though it hurt him that she should look so distant, and he could not reach her, he could do nothing to help her. And again he would have passed her without a word had she not, at that very moment, given him of her own free will what she knew he would never ask, and called to him and taken the green shawl off the picture frame, and gone to him. For he wished, she knew, to protect her. (*TL* 65)

Such a moment shows a profound respect for the otherness of the partner. He refuses to invade a privacy he will never really understand; she, in return, leaves that privacy to offer him exactly what she feels that he desires, though his desire does not reflect her own. To achieve this level of intimacy one must be the kind of person who can, at least temporarily, grant the obscure world of the other a primacy over one's own internal world that in Woolf threatens to become coterminous with reality itself. In the end, knowledge of another is not so much an epistemological problem as an ethical one.[30]

Achieved over the lifetime of a marriage, this intimacy endures for Mr. Ramsay as productive memory after the death of his wife. Less dramatic than the *éclat* of Lily's retrieval, the quiet remembrance of his wife's desires and emotions leads Mr. Ramsay to take the ten-years-deferred trip to the lighthouse. He arrives, ambassador of his wife's wish to give, bearing a present for the lighthouse family. Whatever his parcel consists of it is clearly not the long useless boy's stockings knitted by Mrs. Ramsay, but something of his own devising. The memory of

---

[30] Martha Nussbaum, "The Window: Knowledge of Other Minds in Virginia Woolf's *To the Lighthouse*," *New Literary History*, 26 (1995), 732.

Mrs. Ramsay endures, then, not as a museum piece, but as something incorporated and personalized by those closest to her. Her posthumous presence generates one final, rarer act of giving in her husband when he finally brings himself to praise his alienated son for steering the boat well. The reconciliation that ensues, inspired by Mrs. Ramsay, also bears Mr. Ramsay's signature, for his estimation of James' seamanship is understood to be true, not mere courteous consolation. The Oedipal James, who has struggled to sort out his relationship to his father, needs, like Lily, "an image to cool and detach and round off his feeling in concrete shape" (*TL* 185). His first attempt to capture this feeling yields only a childishly lopsided view of his father's connection to him as purely destructive, a wheel indifferently crushing a foot. Like Lily who had originally rejected Mr. Ramsay, James must work much harder than this. With a painful honesty reminiscent of his father, James concedes "that he had come to feel, quite often lately, when his father said something or did something which surprised the others, there were two pairs of footprints only; his own and his father's. They alone knew each other" (*TL* 184–85). In this effort to see more comprehensively and magnanimously, he has earned the gift his father – and mother – bestow. When Mr. Ramsay stands in the bow of the boat "very straight and tall" bearing his parcel as they arrive at the lighthouse, James has his image, compounded of his father's forthright frankness and his mother's generosity.

Woolf's use of an omniscient narrator with access to inner lives invisible to others allows her to avoid the problem faced by those philosophers who try to establish an impenetrable essence behind the realm of phenomena: how can we reasonably posit a thing-in-itself whose very definition entails that nothing can be known about it? But if this is to be more than a purely artistic solution, she must grant – even if just on extraordinarily rare occasion – a similar insight to her characters. In *To the Lighthouse* she is willing to do this as those characters prepared to listen hard and long enough to the emotional rhythms of those closest can finally hear them – indeed, feel them in their own pulse. Yet, by the time of *The Waves* (1931), Woolf has, by her own admission, abandoned interest in creating character, giving us instead minimally fleshed out viewpoints with names.[31] No longer does her omniscient narrator glide gracefully from interior to interior facilitating a sense of intersubjective feeling, but serves as static recorder of disparate soliloquies issuing from the self-absorbed

---

[31] *Diary, vol. 4* (October 5, 1931), p. 47.

consciousnesses of Cartesian egos. The result is something that can hardly be called a novel.

Woolf herself was aware that she had transcended a genre and cast about for a description of what she was attempting. Her definitions tend to mix genres – "a play-poem" – or absorb them all: "a new kind of play, prose yet poetry, a novel and a play."[32] Perhaps most faithful to the finished product, however, is the definition that avoids locating the book as a genre at all, choosing rather to call it "an abstract mystical eyeless book."[33] What makes Woolf's project especially hard for an early-twenty-first-century audience to appreciate is that we are saturated with attempts to demonstrate the subjectivity of objectivity, whereas her concern, conversely, was to explore the objectivity of subjectivity. In this regard she is far closer to her contemporaries like Lawrence, who sought a systematic account of pure individuality, and Eliot, who tried to provide in his poetry objective correlatives to link isolated centers of consciousness. More radically conceived than *To the Lighthouse*, in which Woolf had established a commonality despite vast differences in her characters, *The Waves* ambitiously tries to reach a substratum beneath difference, a metaphysics of self.

The book begins with the first of nine descriptive passages that periodically trace the sun on its arc from sunrise to sunset. The career of the sun on a single day will correspond to the lives of the six characters as they rise from childhood to maturity and then descend into old age, the vast discrepancy of time in the parallel structure underscoring once again the ephemerality of human life that preoccupies Woolf. In the first of these passages the sun sorts out the sea from the sky, an echo of Genesis, but in Woolf's indifferent universe no God is implied. It is against this backdrop that we are introduced to the six main characters who appear in sparse phenomenological reduction:

> "I see a ring," said Bernard, "hanging above me. It quivers and hangs in a loop of light."
> "I see a slab of pale yellow," said Susan, "spreading away until it meets a purple stripe."
> "I hear a sound," said Rhoda, "cheep, chirp; cheep, chirp; going up and down."
> "I see a globe," said Neville, "hanging down in a drop against the enormous flanks of some hill."

[32] Virginia Woolf, *A Writer's Diary*, ed. Leonard Woolf (New York: Harcourt, Brace and Company, 1954), p. 103.
[33] *Diary, vol. 3* (November 7, 1928), p. 203.

"I see a crimson tassel," said Jinny, twisted with gold threads."
"I hear something stamping," said Louis. "A great beast's foot is chained. It stamps, and stamps, and stamps."[34]

While each of these declarations is marked by "said," fairly obviously this highly stylized speech is not that of nursery school children. We are immediately puzzled by both the artificiality of the serial observations and the level of diction. Compounding the uncertainly is the fact that these speeches engender no response. Even when there is an imperative – as in Rhoda's "Look at the table-cloth, flying white along the table" – that might seem to imply an audience, no one reacts to the call. The imperative apparently indicates nothing more than an enthusiasm connected to the perception. But if these statements are not uttered outwardly, it scarcely helps to view them as interior monologue, for the terse, ordered expression, both here and also later when the observations become more complex, has nothing of the uncensored messiness we expect of this technique. Who, then, is speaking, and what relation does the speaker have to the characters in whose mouths the speech is placed? So central are these questions that Guiguet can claim without exaggeration that "to define that voice is to solve the whole problem of *The Waves*."[35]

An ingenious suggestion advanced by Hafley is that we are dealing with an unusually poeticized form of free indirect discourse.[36] As practiced by Flaubert and George Eliot, among others, this technique allows the narrator to articulate the thoughts and feelings of a character in ways beyond the capacity of that character. The difficulty with this view, however, is that the observations themselves, after the stilted childhood ones mentioned above, rarely, if ever, seem to need this outside assistance. Even Susan, arguably the dullest of the bunch, is never given an insight of which we feel she would be intellectually or psychologically incapable. Further, as a number of critics have rightly remarked, the narrative voice has a sameness of tone that makes no effort to accommodate itself to differences in character. This voice is characterized by a distanced self-consciousness even in moments of emotional turmoil for the character whose inner life it purports to record:

> "Through the chink in the hedge," said Susan, "I saw her kiss him. I raised my head from my flower-pot and looked through a chink in the hedge. I saw her kiss him. I saw them, Jinny and Louis, kissing. Now I will wrap my agony inside my pocket handkerchief. It shall be screwed tight into a ball." (*W* 9)

---

[34] Virginia Woolf, *The Waves* (London: Hogarth Press, 1963), p. 6. Hereafter all references to this work will be indicated in the text by *W* plus page number in parentheses.
[35] Guiguet, p. 284.  [36] Hafley, *The Glass Roof*, p. 108.

As a result of this aloofness we do not have the sense of a narrative voice intent on revealing the rich lives of independent characters, but a voice for whom the characters serve as a series of exploratory feelers. J. W. Graham is closest to the mark when he observes of Woolf's characters: "They are not meant to be 'human beings' but figures who act out the dilemma of consciousness for its own enlightenment."[37] Much like Fichte's God who creates the world so that he might know himself in differentiated multiplicity, Woolf's voice deposits itself in character as an act of reflective self-awareness.

The absorption in moment-to-moment phenomenology is heightened by Woolf's frequent use of the pure present. In a traditional novel, the effect of breathless immediacy this creates would render a mundane event like the following ridiculous: "Yes, I hold Gray's *Elegy* in one hand; with the other I scoop out the bottom crumpet, that has absorbed all the butter and sticks to the bottom of the plate" (*W* 60). But Woolf's use of the present tense is intended to rivet attention, not on the event, but on the mind that perceives (or as the phenomenologists would more accurately say "intends") the event. By any ordinary standard, this book is plotless, or if one can speak of plot, it would consist in the unfolding career of consciousness. The use of the present tense serves a second purpose, related to Woolf's cosmic concerns. It underscores the ephemerality of all occurrences. No sooner have they been mentioned, then they have been replaced. This lends the book an odd sort of weightlessness, for as Graham observes, this technique "seems to rob them [actions] of their psychological substance, their felt duration *as actions*."[38] As a result, characters learn very little *about* the world and we are left with a sense that almost any sequence of experiences would have sufficed as well.

Because of this lack of forward-driving narrative, as the characters grow older the voice grows in weariness, at times oddly surfeited by the events it must survey. Here is Neville, dismayed by the company in a third-class railway coach, envisioning his future:

> They will drive me in October to take refuge in one of the universities, where I shall become a don; and go with schoolmasters to Greece; and lecture on the ruins of the Parthenon. It would be better to breed horses and live in one of those red villas than to run in and out of the skulls of Sophocles

---

[37] J. W. Graham, "The Point of View in *The Waves*: Some Services of Style," *University of Toronto Quarterly*, vol. xxxix (1969–70), 206.
[38] Graham, "The Point of View in *The Waves*," p. 195.

and Euripides like a maggot, with a high-minded wife, one of those University women. That, however, will be my fate. I shall suffer. (*W 51*)

This is not to say that the six lives themselves are not variegated, for they are. Susan marries, has children, and lives on a farm; Jinny, effortlessly beckoning men, is a fashionable party-girl; Rhoda, with the exaggerated sense of the danger of life that recurs in Woolf's female characters, commits suicide; Neville fulfills his prediction of an academic future, though minus the wife, for he discovers his own homosexuality; Louis, the Australian outsider, establishes himself as a business executive in the City of London; and Bernard, the youthful creator of fictions, ends up a failed novelist. In each of these cases, the solemnity of response is not so much because great expectations have not been fulfilled, but because to have expectations at all is to suggest that anything matters terribly much. Thus, the thread that connects all these lives is one of ontological disappointment as middle-age progresses, and this disappointment tends to justify the univocally understated voice of the narrative consciousness that reaches awareness through them.

The other common element that ties these six figures together is their uniform attraction to the shadowy Percival whom they meet at school. Granted no soliloquies whatsoever, Percival is even less a character than his admirers, serving much in the same way that the army officer does for Doestoevky's Underground Man: a foil to hyperconsciousness. Athletic, robust, ever at ease, and generally indifferent to his entourage, he embodies an unquestioning sense of self, that which eludes, in varying degrees, the other six. The painfully self-aware Neville, for example, remains enthralled for a lifetime with the image of Percival when he nonchalantly "flicks his hand to the back of his neck" (*W* 26). Though Woolf is fonder of dealing in patterns of imagery than outright symbols, Percival fairly clearly represents the possibility of unreflective consciousness, a kind of prelapsarian innocence. It would be difficult to see the nature of his appeal otherwise, since he rarely appears and has scant interaction with the group that treats him almost iconically. At the farewell dinner party for Percival, who is about to embark for India, Neville speaks for all in claiming "But without Percival there is no solidity. We are silhouettes, hollow phantoms moving mistily without a background" (*W* 87). And when Bernard adds "sitting here we love each other and believe in our own endurance" we are reminded, in pared down, abstract form, of Mrs. Ramsay's dinner that performed a similar function for the nerve-worn guests. Once again the concerns are familiar: personal identity and the passage of time that threatens to trivialize human endeavor. Now, however, this is virtually all that these figures address as they seem to move in blank, indeterminate space. The events of their lives, sketchily presented, serve almost exclusively as occasions to reflect on one's ontological status.

Yet, when one ceases to try to fit *The Waves* into the conventions of a novel, the developmental progress becomes fairly apparent. We are at first presented with consciousness as it is flooded with perception. On the book's first page, already quoted above, Bernard sees a ring, Susan sees a slab of yellow, Rhoda hears a sound, and so on. Shortly thereafter consciousness becomes aware of its own attachment to body. The following episode retains its importance for Bernard throughout his life:

> Mrs. Constable, girt in a bath-towel, takes her lemon-coloured sponge and soaks it in water; it turns chocolate-brown; it drips; and holding it high above me, shivering beneath her, she squeezes it. Water pours down the runnel of my spine. Bright arrows of sensation shoot on either side. I am covered with warm flesh ... Rich and heavy sensations form on the roof of my mind. (*W* 19)

Certainty soon extends to an awareness of oneself as separate from others. Bernard, looking back, remembers the moment he first came to this realization: "It was Susan who cried, that day when I was in the tool house with Neville; and I felt my indifference melt. Neville did not melt. 'Therefore,' I said 'I am myself and not Neville,' a wonderful discovery" (*W* 170). (What is peculiar to Woolf is that this is not just a one-time recognition. We find Bernard, at twenty-one, still struggling with primary narcissism: "I am not part of the street – no, I observe the street"). (*W* 82) But the crucial moment for consciousness is when it becomes aware of its own mortality. It dawns on Neville, strikingly, in a Wordsworthian spot of time when he hears of a man who had his throat cut:

> The apple-tree leaves became fixed in the sky; the moon glared; I was unable to lift my foot up the stair. He was found in the gutter. His blood gurgled down the gutter. I shall call this stricture, this rigidity, "death among the apple-trees" for ever ... the ripple of my life was unavailing ... we are doomed all of us by the apple trees, by the immitigable tree which we cannot pass. (*W* 17–18)

It is only the figure of Percival – whose consciousness is never revealed – whom we must assume lives in unruffled indifference to his own inevitable demise. This, of course, is the source of his fascination for the others.

The book's pivotal point occurs when, with a grim irony, he falls from a horse in India at twenty-four and dies. The reaction of the others is extreme. For Neville, the "lights of the world have gone out" and he finds himself before the immitigable tree once again (*W* 107). Stricken, Bernard laments that the center of his life is now "empty." Rhoda, "alone in a hostile world," sees the human face as "hideous" as she begins her downward spiral toward suicide (*W* 113). The last half of the book is given over to the ways in which consciousness tries to cope with the now unavoidable and pressing awareness of its own incipient annihilation.

During the course of this evolution, there are the crises of identity, familiar from Woolf's earlier fiction, but now presented as if consciousness were periodically uneasy in its local manifestations. Because the issue is presented more as a philosophical problem – how is consciousness related to its corporeal instantiation – than a psychological instability, the effect is typically one of detached curiosity. In this distanced way, Louis questions the nature of the coherence of perceptions: "What is the solution, I ask myself, and the bridge? How can I reduce these dazzling, these dancing apparitions to one line capable of linking all in one" (*W* 155). Bernard wonders what the connection is between his work-a-day self and the mind that feels itself separate enough to pose the question: "When I say to myself, 'Bernard,' who comes?" (*W* 58). And, in a Sartrean moment, he observes "To be myself (I note) I need the illumination of other people's eyes, and therefore cannot be entirely sure what is my self" (*W* 83). Susan has difficulty sorting herself out from circumambient nature: "But who am I, who lean on this gate and watch my setter nose in a circle? I think sometimes (I am not twenty yet) I am not a woman, but the light that falls on this gate, on this ground. I am the seasons, I think sometimes, January, May, November; the mud, the mist, the dawn" (*W* 70–71). Jinny, whose "body seems to live a life of its own," is disconcerted whenever she views herself in other than a full-length mirror. And poor Rhoda whose consciousness feels as vulnerable and exposed as a brain in a jar, translates this anxiety as "identity failed me." The oddness of what is going on here should not be overlooked. Literature presents us with no lack of characters who question their identity, but Woolf's creations are not asking merely *who* they are, but *how* they are.

It is left to Bernard, a creator of narratives like Woolf, to reassemble the scattered consciousnesses of his friends within himself, and offer a summation of their collective experience. He has available to him – and perhaps this is what motivates Woolf's use of the word "mystical" to describe the book – not only his observations of the others, but their internal, private experience as well. From an early age, the others have foreseen that Bernard would be the shaper of their histories: "Let him describe what we have all seen so that it becomes a sequence" (*W* 27). In a forty-page soliloquy, Bernard attempts to do just that. More precisely, his is the struggle of consciousness as it goes from believing it is everything to fearing that, cosmically considered, it may be nothing. The dark undercurrent of *To the Lighthouse* is here starkly foregrounded.

The story that Bernard unfolds is one of oscillation between two perspectives, with the intervals between the two becoming shorter as time goes on. On the one hand there is the easy lapse into habituation as "Tuesday follows Monday; then comes Wednesday. The mind grows rings; the identity becomes robust; pain is absorbed in growth" (*W* 182–83). On the other hand, there are those glimpses into the abyss when one conceives of oneself as "forgotten, minute, in a ditch." In such moments, as Bernard says, "[o]f story, of design, I do not see a trace then" (*W* 169). From this perspective, to make the effort to shape one's life into an autobiography seems futile, for "what is the use of painfully elaborating these consecutive sentences when what one needs is nothing consecutive but a bark, a groan?" (*W* 178). Percival's death marks a watershed; thereafter the Apollonian veil of life-maintaining illusion becomes harder to preserve.[39] Bernard is never able to transmute the loss into consolatory art: "No lullaby has ever occurred to me capable of singing him to rest" (*W* 172). Even the notion that "I am not one person, I am many people," familiar enough from Woolf's earlier work, now seems tossed off and relatively uninspiring since we are essentially talking about facets of consciousness not rounded characters trying to bridge the space between themselves (*W* 196).

Because of the shift in focus from intersubjectivity to consciousness confronting its own demise, the transcendental moment that Woolf always relies on to justify existence is now no longer one of union with others, but of pure clairvoyance. The vision comes unexpectedly, though it has been amply prepared for: "one day as I leant over a gate that led into a field, the rhythm stopped; the rhymes and the hummings. The nonsense and the poetry. A space was cleared in my mind. I saw through the thick leaves of habit" (*W* 201). The resisting self that had always anchored him in mundanity "made no answer ... threw up no opposition." Almost immediately the body falls away: "Now it was done with. I had no more appetites

---

[39] Susan Dick, "I Remembered, I Forgotten: Bernard's Final Soliloquy in *The Waves*," *Modern Language Studies*, vol. 13, no. 3 (Summer 1983), 44.

to glut ... no more sharp teeth and clutching hands or desire" (*W* 202). Bernard gropes his way toward pure impersonality of perception: "How can I proceed now, I said, without a self, weightless and visionless, through a world weightless without illusion?" (*W* 202–3). At long last Bernard the phrasemaker is nearly at a loss for words, for "how describe the world seen without a self?" (*W* 205). Indexed to no self, Bernard's consciousness is distilled to pure perception and becomes indistinguishable from the detached viewpoint of the interludes.[40] Woolf here remarkably tries to do what Descartes thought impossible: to give us thought without a thinker.

This ecstatic view from nowhere cannot last forever, though, and in the last pages of the book, Woolf tries to show how Bernard integrates the vision as he reassumes identity. At first, the discrepancy between nearly limitless power of mind "unconfined and capable of being everywhere on the verge of things" and the decrepitude of his body is more than he can assimilate (*W* 207). The decaying physical world looms up as a sordid den where we fill our mouths "with the bodies of dead birds." Though neither Bernard, nor Woolf herself, is prepared to ratify the holiness of nature and its countless, minute wonders as does Tolstoy's Levin, nevertheless Bernard opts to fight "unyielding" against death. Hovering tantalizingly between embrace and abdication of self, this final affirmation faithfully records the ambivalence of Woolf's own dual tendencies to want to burrow into the labyrinth of self and to seek escape from it.

Suzette Henke has placed this confrontation between consciousness and the fact of its own demise in a Heideggerian context of Dasein's quest to achieve authenticity by accepting life as a being-toward-death.[41] But this raises the question of whether we can properly speak of anything like a recognizable Heideggerian being-in-the-world when Woolf has chosen to give us consciousness with only the merest sketch of character. If one wishes to locate her work in the phenomenological tradition – and I believe this is, indeed, helpful – her creation looks much closer to Husserl's self-enclosed phenomenology as the "science of the essence of consciousness" with the world bracketed than to Heidegger's ontologically denser phenomenology that entails intimately inhabiting a world of hammers and shoes as well as being-with-others. A major difference, and one crucial for determining whether *The Waves* can properly be said to address ethical

---

[40] Avrom Fleishman, *Virginia Woolf: A Critical Reading* (Baltimore: Johns Hopkins University Press, 1975), p. 162.
[41] See Suzette Henke, "Virginia Woolf's *The Waves*: A Phenomenological Reading," *Neophilologus*, vol. 73, no. 3 (July 1989), 461–72.

concerns whatsoever, is that Heidegger's view allows room for ethics whereas Husserl's pointedly does not. Consistent with her Heideggerian reading, Henke stresses the importance of *The Waves'* communal moments, the farewell dinner for Percival and a subsequent reunion many years later. These she likens to "what Heidegger calls 'concernful Being-with-one-another,' a unitive vision of solidarity and communion that ushers in a sense of triumph."[42] This claim would have been true for *To the Lighthouse*, but it is far less convincing here. Who in this book ever really *cares* for another in the way the Ramsays do for each other, or Lily for Mrs. Ramsay? The only candidate for this kind of concern would be the group's attachment to the colorless, speechless Percival, the least substantial human representation of them all. Significantly, at the book's end Bernard narrates his vision to an anonymous stranger who shares his table at dinner, and we never learn of his reaction. It simply would not matter. In the end, neither the appeal of the world nor those in it is offered as motivation for Bernard's resistance to death. There is simply a naked will to continue. This is at once the most abstract, deeply personal, and solipsistic of Woolf's works.

Because *The Waves* is an extended piece of prose fiction, some critics have chosen to see it as a novel.[43] Yet Woolf herself, in her oft-quoted manifesto "Mr. Bennett and Mrs. Brown," insists "that all novels, that is to say, deal with character, and that it is to express character . . . that the form of the novels . . . has been evolved" and this book, as I hope to have shown, contains nothing that we can comfortably call characters.[44] The very fact that this work defies classification by genre (however loose and inadequate definitions may be) is itself an indication of its anomalous nature. It slips between the cracks not because it is a troublesome hybrid, as Woolf at times suggested, but because it is *sui generis*. All genres are marked by *attachments*, a *philia* for something specific in the world outside the self, even if that world be defined largely negatively as in satire. But this is not true of *The Waves*. Emotions are portrayed, but these are almost exclusively self-referential: anxiety over loss of identity and fear of death. Even the courage of Bernard's resistance to death is bloodless. As such it is impossible to see it as a ground clearing for engagement with others – the distance is too great, the desire to bridge it too small. In this oddly transcendent

---

[42] Henke, "Virginia Woolf's *The Waves*," p. 464.
[43] John Batchelor in particular emphasizes *The Waves*' continuity with the tradition of the novel. See his *Virginia Woolf: The Major Novels*, pp. 114–31.
[44] Virginia Woolf, "Mrs. Bennett and Mrs. Brown," in Virginia Woolf, *Collected Essays, vol. 1* (New York: Harcourt, Brace & World, 1967), p. 324.

work, which takes the impersonal tendencies of modernism to their extreme, we drift far beyond Nussbaum's Jamesian engagements. Virginia Woolf's stark vision has left almost no room for Apollo, the god of illusion, the god of mattering, who, among other functions, leads us to believe that ethics make a difference.

CHAPTER 5

# *George Bernard Shaw: History as Cosmic Comedy*

While Woolf, Lawrence, and Eliot present a challenge to any ethical theory based on the emotional refinements of character insofar as these authors reduce character to a function of a metaphysically prior interiority, Shaw presents an opposite challenge insofar as he tends to flatten character as something incidental to the exterior purposes of historical evolution. It is largely because of this difference that literary history has had a notoriously bad time accounting for Shaw. Born before all the great modernists, he produced his major works concurrently with theirs, outlived most of them, and wrote his last plays shortly before *Waiting for Godot*. Yet, in his concerns, in the cast and quality of his mind, he often seemed to modernist writers to be an irrelevant outsider. Virginia Woolf lumped him with the externally oriented Edwardians like Galsworthy, Wells, and Bennett, whom she denigrates for caring more about the furniture of a character's flat than the furniture of her mind.[1] Eliot can only credit him for sleight-of-hand in "conceal[ing] from his readers and audiences the shallowness of his own thought" and finds his "posturing glibness" not to merit even the dignity of contrast with the grander wisdom of a Coleridge or John Henry Newman.[2] In the same vein, the ever blunter Pound dismisses him summarily as "profoundly trivial." Lawrence, reacting against a perceived lack of passion, calls for rebellion: "I'm sure we are sick of the rather bony, bloodless drama we get nowadays – it is time for a reaction against Shaw." Less specifically, though just as crucially, his narrator in *Lady Chatterley's Lover* laments "[o]urs is a tragic age, so we refuse to take it tragically," rendering Shaw, whose creative gifts were essentially comedic, especially

---

[1] Letter from Virginia Woolf to Janet Case, May 21, 1922 in *The Letters of Virginia Woolf*, ed. by Nigel Nicholson and Joanne Trautmann, 6 vols (London: Hogarth Press, 1975–80; II: 1912–1922), p. 529, quoted in Ruth Livesey, "Socialism in Bloomsbury and the Political Aesthetics of the 1880s," *Yearbook of English Studies*, vol. 37, no. 1 (January 2007), 126.
[2] T. S. Eliot, "The Literature of Politics," in *To Criticize the Critic and Other Writing* (New York: Farrar, Straus & Giroux, 1965), p. 143.

culpable.[3] Worse, this comedic spirit bubbled over in the effervescence of fecundity – more and more of the wrong thing – causing his countryman Yeats to envision him in a nightmare as a perpetually smiling sewing machine. With remarkable unanimity, then, his canonized peers found him to be a facile avoider of the problems of his time, someone radically unlike themselves.

If, as Lionel Trilling argued, "[n]othing is more characteristic of modern literature than its discovery and canonization of the primal, non-ethical energies" traceable to Nietzsche's Dionysian, then the modernist consensus about Shaw's irrelevance would seem to be confirmed.[4] As even the sympathetic critic Robert Brustein concedes, "Shaw can look for a moment into the bottomless pit, but it is not long before he is whistling up his spirits again. His messianic rebellion is his last refuge, his Utopian idealism his last escape, from the tragic impasse of modern existence."[5] Like his contemporaries, Shaw had read Nietzsche, and he openly acknowledges him as a kindred spirit, but the Nietzsche he responds to is not the one that inspires Lawrence or Yeats. For Shaw, as *Man and Superman* makes clear, Nietzsche is valuable insofar as he is an evolutionary ameliorist. Shaw is far more concerned with what he calls "the Life Force" that will escort us from man to superman than he is with the enormous effort any such superman must exert to marshal, without renouncing, his own dark drives, and forge a morality based on the Will to Power. As a result, nothing could be further from Nietzsche's view of tragedy as growing out of a Dionysian vision of "the terror and horror of existence" than Shaw's socialist take: "the only real tragedy in life is the being used by personally minded men for purposes which you recognize to be base."[6] This view of the tragic is borne out in the announced intention behind *Mrs. Warren's Profession*, the most accomplished of Shaw's early plays. As he points out in the preface, the play was written "to draw attention to the truth that prostitution is caused, not by female depravity and male licentiousness, but simply by underpaying, undervaluing, and overworking women so shamefully that the poorest of them are forced to resort to prostitution to keep body and soul together."[7] The abyss for Shaw is a shameful pothole left by faulty social engineering.

---

[3] D. H. Lawrence, *The Letters of D. H. Lawrence*, ed. James T. Bouton and George J. Zytaruk (Cambridge: Cambridge University Press, 1979), letter to Edward Garnett, p. 509.
[4] Lionel Trilling, "On the Modern Element in Modern Literature," *Partisan Review* Jan/Feb 1961, 25.
[5] Robert Brustein, "Bernard Shaw: The Face Behind the Mask," in *G. B. Shaw: A Collection of Critical Essays*, ed. R. J. Kaufmann (Englewood Cliffs: Prentice Hall, 1965), p. 102.
[6] Bernard Shaw, "Epistle Dedicatory," in *Man and Superman* (Baltimore: Penguin, 1969), p. 32.
[7] Bernard Shaw, *Mrs. Warren's Profession in Complete Plays with Prefaces* (New York: Dodd, Mead & Co., 1963), vol. 3, p. 3.

In effect, then, Shaw is far closer in outlook to Socrates, whom Nietzsche accused of destroying Attic tragedy by taking "it to be his duty to correct existence," than he is to anything resembling the Dionysian.[8] For Socrates, as for Shaw, virtue equals knowledge; vice equals ignorance. It would be impossible to *know* the good and not to do it, unless one were mad, since the good is what brings us happiness. Dionysian tragedy is thus translated into miscognitions that leave us less happy than we ought to be. Yet, luckily, these miscognitions are dialectically corrigible, occasioning both the Socratic dialogues of Plato, purely cerebral dramas, and the ongoing clash and refinement of opinion in Shaw's plays. In his lengthy analysis of the theater of Ibsen that serves as a manifesto for his own art, Shaw notes: "The discussion conquered Europe in Ibsen's *Doll's House*; and now the serious playwright recognizes in the discussion not only the main test of his highest powers, but also the real centre of his play's interest."[9] And again: "In the new plays, the drama arises through a conflict of unsettled ideals rather than through vulgar attachments, rapacities, generosities, resentments, ambitions, misunderstandings, oddities, and so forth as to which no moral question is raised."[10] Both Socrates and Shaw are intent on *talking* Dionysus to death.

Consistent with their existential optimism, both Socrates and Shaw inhabit selves with virtually no subterranean depths. Nietzsche records with astonishment that the instincts in Socrates manifest themselves only as a sporadic whisper on those rare occasions when his prodigious intellect seemed to founder.[11] Shaw, born within a few weeks of Freud, managed to live ninety-four years without anything resembling a Viennese unconscious, and his characters are similarly untroubled. Although Freud was too topical not to find his way into Shaw's plays, psychoanalysis merely provides one more subject for witty repartee. One's *opinion* of Freud serves to reveal character, but the theories themselves do not. As Brustein accurately observes: "in the century of Freud, they [Shaw's characters] are totally free from any real anguish, suffering, or neurosis. The Shavian soul is generally a sunlit soul – empty of menace, without fatality."[12] Even less congenial to Shaw's historical meliorism than the tentacular sexuality that warps behavior is the innate aggression that Freud posits. Unfavorable

---

[8] Friedrich Nietzsche, *The Birth of Tragedy* in the *Birth of Tragedy and the Case of Wagner*, trans. Walter Kaufmann (New York: Vintage, 1967), p. 87.
[9] George Bernard Shaw, "The Quintessence of Ibsenism," in *Major Critical Essays* (London: Constable and Company, Ltd, 1947), p. 135.
[10] Ibid., p. 139.   [11] Nietzsche, *Birth of Tragedy*, p. 88.
[12] Brustein, "Bernard Shaw: The Face Behind the Mask," p. 102–3.

social conditions simply cannot be the product of unalterably vulpine natures: "It is quite useless to declare that all men are born free if you deny that they are born good."[13] Both Socrates and Shaw refuse compromise with Dionysian irrationalism, whether metaphysical, psychological, or political. They create solely in the service of Apollo.

The problem that Shaw presents, then, for a theory of literature's ethical significance based on the exploration and refinement of emotions, is that he seems to be almost constitutionally incapable of acknowledging the power of deep-seated affect to shape lives. In this respect, we are an awfully long way from Aristotle's view of tragedy as the catharsis of fear and pity. Of course, it might be reasonably objected that Shaw essentially creates in a comic mode even when he treats the material of tragedy, as in *St. Joan*, and therefore is freed from the necessity of tragic pathos. But one must still demonstrate what sort of role emotions play in his work. If a theory of literature cannot account for a comic vision, then it is a non-starter to begin with. Are emotions in Shavian drama simply of use as rhetorical coloration – a petulant rebuttal, an embarrassed confession – or is there something more at stake?

Unfortunately, very little has been preserved of Aristotle's comments on comedy in the *Poetics*. The sketchy observations we do have, however, indicate that he made no distinction between tragedy and comedy in terms of their function of universalization, as opposed to the particularization of history. If there is any difference between the two modes of drama, it is that comedy tends to reduce character to a dominant obsession. As Butcher neatly observes: "Whereas comedy tends to merge the individual in the type, tragedy manifests the type through the individual."[14] Thus, one might more properly speak of a comic flaw than a tragic one. Ben Jonson would later refer to this ruling passion as a "humor," and Molière would make monomania the focal point of his greatest comedies: *Le Malade Imaginare, Le Misanthrope, L'Avare, Tartuffe*. The lightness or darkness of comedy is determined by how much harm emanates from the illusion of the "humorous" character. If the illusion is largely self-contained we are allowed to focus on the ridiculous element; the more it jeopardizes others and the closer it veers to bringing about the danger it threatens, the darker the comedy. The ridiculous moves us not just to laugh at, but also to sympathize with a character so much entangled in his own foible. We enjoy a sense of superiority mixed with the intuition that we ourselves may not be immune, in lesser degree, to something analogous. Sympathy is harder to

---

[13] George Bernard Shaw, preface to *Major Barbara*, p. 37 (Baltimore: Penguin Books, 1968), p. 37.
[14] S. H. Butcher, *Aristotle's Theory of Poetry and the Fine Arts* (New York: Dover, 1951), p. 388.

evoke in the darkest comedies, often called "problem plays" for this very reason. Yet even in such cases, as in *Measure for Measure*, these plays will supply us with a ludicrous minor character who bears distinct resemblance to his more sinister double. Thus, we can grant our sympathy and laughter to Elbow, whose verbal ineptitude makes justice all but impossible, yet withhold it from the calculating Angelo, who attempts to twist justice to further his own sexual cravings. And the comic resolution in which imminent death is avoided, though no thanks to Angelo, allows for traditional forgiveness even in his case. The emotional axis of comedy ranges, then, from sympathy to indignation. The generic expectation of restored harmony at the end of comedy prevents sympathy and indignation from being driven to pity and fear.

In his magisterial study of literary typology, *Anatomy of Criticism*, Northrop Frye sees literature, at its most fundamental, as the expression of desire in conflict with a recalcitrant world. Prior even to generic conventions, Frye abstracts four "narrative structures" each representing a particular accommodation of the world to our wishes. Tragedy, for example, "is a vision of what does happen and must be accepted. To this extent it is a moral and plausible displacement of the bitter resentments that humanity feels against all obstacles to its desires."[15] Conversely, comedy records desire (typically the love of a young couple) overcoming obstacles (typically the blocking prejudices of the older generation). Generally the comic obstacles and resolution are social, but they can ascend to the metaphysical, as in Dante's *Divine Comedy*. By analogy with the seasonal cycle of flourishing and decay, Frye associates comedy with springtime. (Romance, which achieves fulfillment only by fancifully abridging the ordinary laws of nature, is associated with summer, presumably as a time of maximum lushness.) Both the romantic and vernal connections Frye posits are faithful to comedy's origins in fertility ritual. Shakespeare's romantic comedies, which show the transformation of a crabbed society by the triumphant ethos of "the green world" of sylvan lovers, become paradigmatic for Frye. The vitality of young love has a mandate that supersedes the repressive edicts of a geriatric society. Frye's definition of comedy, more far-reaching than Aristotle's or Jonson's, concurs with theirs in locating the source of frustration in the exaggeration of characters imprisoned in their own delusions, but goes beyond theirs by highlighting the countervailing passion that overcomes the dominant absurdity.

---

[15] Northrop Frye, *Anatomy of Criticism* (New York: Atheneum, 1968), p. 157.

A comic playwright, then, may concentrate on either the delusion or the liberation from delusion. Molière's theater of obsession is an example of the first, Shakespeare's romantic comedy an example of the second. In either case, however, it is passion that drives the discourse. The obsessed character – Alceste or Argon in Molière, Angelo or Shylock in Shakespeare – speaks eloquently, and often with great subtlety, but precisely in order to justify his passion. Heightened rhetoric is compelled by the need to defend the absurd. Theirs is the casuistry of misguided attachments. The romantic lovers, too, are moved to eloquence in proclaiming the depth of their love or the virtues of the loved one. Poetic excess is virtually a requirement to establish a lover's *bona fides*. As the cynical Jacques says in *As You Like It*, the enraptured youth is expected to sigh "a woeful ballad/Made to his mistress' eyebrow" (II.vii.148–49). Even when we are almost completely sympathetic to the lovers, we remain certain that the object of praise cannot deserve *those* words. In both kinds of comedy, the verbal flourishes draw our attention to emotional misjudgments. To put it in Aristotelian terms, the speaker betrays the fact that he or she does not feel toward an object in the right degree. The comic effect resides in the gap between what ought to have been felt and what is felt. Comedy, just as tragedy, works primarily to calibrate our emotional understanding.

Clearly, then, to achieve its effect comedy must rely heavily on constancy of character, whether it be the obsessive, defined by his monomania, or the young lovers, as the embodiment of irrepressible eroticism. This constancy can be readily seen in non-dramatic comedy as well. Orwell remarks that Dickens' comic genius resides in his ability to have his comic figures behave in the same grotesque fashion yet one more time even as we believe he could not possibly make them do so again. Television's endless string of sit-coms relies almost purely on a similar typology of characters. We expect to see the same characters doing the same kinds of things week after week. Periodically one of the characters will resolve to reform, but by the end of the half-hour inevitably relapses into his old self, much to the delight of the audience. The attempt has merely refreshed our sense of the impossibility of any alteration.

In Shaw's theater, by contrast, ideas are what are absurd, not the characters who hold them. In drawing a distinction between Molière and himself, Shaw sees Molière as a satirist who pillories individuals yet never establishes any *necessary* connection between their deficiencies and the profession of which the caricature is supposed to be representative. Of *Tartuffe* he complains, "his satire on clericalism achieves nothing more than a warning that a priest may be a scoundrel, which no intelligent Catholic has ever doubted."[16] He sees this same sort of non-explanatory lampooning in Dickens' treatment of the revivalist preacher Stiggins in *Pickwick Papers*. Clearly Dickens means to rouse us to share his antipathy by means of the ridiculousness of the portrayal, but, as Shaw protests "[d]runkenness or unctuous windbaggery occur among Free Church ministers just as they occur among atheist lecturers: there is no organic connection in either case."[17] Because, for Shaw, ideas are not a function of character (and here he departs most radically from Nietzsche) but amenable to rational persuasion, his theater is committed to ironizing intellectual error, not satirizing the character who espouses the error. For this reason, as he says, his stage presents no villains or buffoons. In fact, he goes out of his way to show that in areas of life unrelated to the erroneous opinion a misguided character is often admirable. The vivesector is not cruel outside the laboratory; the slumlord is an impeccable family man.

Simply put, Shaw is not terribly interested in character, if we take character in the Aristotelian sense of a fixed intertwining of beliefs, emotions, and dispositions that has become, through habituation, a virtual second nature – and it is this indifference on Shaw's part that represents his chief challenge to a theory such as Nussbaum's. His dramatis personae tend to be highly malleable holders of opinion. In fact, the chief comic device of Shaw is to chart the reversal(s) of opinions during the course of events. Major Barbara, for example, begins by idealistically believing that the Salvation Army can nourish the bodies and souls of the London underclass without resorting to the lucre of morally dubious businessmen like her father, only to recognize in the end that his money is acceptable since it results from his courageous attempt to avoid the sin of poverty. The debate that swirls around this play has to do with the validity of this position, not with the character of Barbara herself. We may discuss endlessly why Hamlet delays, but we have no interest in what there was in the character of Barbara that made her change her mind. As Shaw's remarks on Molière and Dickens make clear, he regards the indexing of a belief to the holder of the belief an illegitimate *ad hominem* argument. There is no logical, or even psychological, reason why someone different might not have maintained the same original position or changed her mind in exactly the same way.

---

[16] Shaw, private correspondence with Archibald Henderson, quoted in Henderson, *George Bernard Shaw: Man of the Century* (New York: Appleton-Century-Crofts, Inc., 1956), p. 740.
[17] Ibid., p. 740.

In the preface to *Man and Superman*, designated as *A Comedy and a Philosophy*, Shaw asserts "As for me, what I have always wanted is a pit of philosophers; and this is a play for such a pit."[18] To address this intended audience Shaw provides, as he does with almost all his major twentieth-century plays, a contextualizing preface of more than thirty pages. This prosaic directive is supplemented in *Man and Superman* by "The Revolutionist's Handbook," a fifty-page compendium of Shavian wisdom, appended after the conclusion of the play. Further, inserted into the center of the play is a lengthy debate among Don Juan and three interlocutors that Shaw refers to as "a Shavio-Socratic dialogue," smuggled in as (a pointedly non-Freudian) dream sequence. Rarely has a major writer so little trusted his own art, made so many concessions to making sure his audience gets the dialectic right. Here, then, is a theater of such tightly controlled ethical didacticism that Plato himself might have approved. As a result, we are left to consider what exactly the artistic representation of contending positions adds to our ethical awareness. Are his plays anything more than animated prefaces? Has he so reduced the importance of character that it makes little sense to even ask how the emotional lives of his personages might be contributors to their evaluative judgments? His marked preference for the allegorizing Bunyan over the "utterly bewildered" Shakespeare, who "has much to shew and nothing to teach," confirms the relevance of these questions.[19]

In order to begin to answer such questions, one must inevitably try to come to terms with Shaw's commitment to the concept of a Life Force, for he places his art in its service. The sources – Hegel, Marx, Butler, Darwin, Nietzsche, Schopenhauer, and Bergson, to name only the most prominent – are fairly transparent; the results, less so. What can at least be said with certainty is that Shaw's overall intention was to restore to the evolutionary theories of Hegel and Marx the teleology of which Darwinism threatened to rob them. From Schopenhauer, Bergson, and especially Nietzsche he learned that the world was Will and that this Will had a purpose. From Butler, whom he lavishly overpraised as a luminary of the last half of the nineteenth century, he found a way to biologize this Will by seeing it working as a genetic memory from generation to generation. Evolution was not propelled by the adaptive selection of certain random variations, but by an ongoing process of transmittable, often purely somatic, intelligence. The fetus "knows" how to generate its organs. Crucially, for Butler, this meant that "birth has been made too much

---

[18] Shaw, preface to *Man and Superman*, p. 28.   [19] Ibid., pp. 30–31.

of." The individual should more properly be seen as part of a biological continuum. Even more radically, Butler concludes that "in reality [there is] nothing but one single creature, of which the component members are but, as it were, blood corpuscles or individual cells."[20] Though Shaw never couched his notion of the Life Force in terms quite so dismissive of the individual, his Marxist background had prepared him for the idea that history uses us for its purposes.

Content with this dynamic, Shaw needed only to supply the telos itself. What precisely does the Life Force want? To help frame an answer, he reaches back for an idea familiar in Hegelianism. For Hegel the absolute, or *Geist*, seeks to understand itself in a process of unfolding that takes it through its objective manifestation in Nature en route to the reflective human mind. Only when this reflective mind ascends to the exercise of pure reason does the absolute come to recognize itself as the transcendental reality behind the swirl of variety and contradiction. In *Back to Methuselah* (1921), the Hegelian influence is evident when Shaw has our *Ureltern* Lilith explain that the Life Force wants "redemption from the flesh to the vortex freed from matter, to the whirlpool of pure intelligence." Or, as Don Juan puts it more prosaically in *Man and Superman*, "my brain is the organ by which Nature strives to understand itself." Showing a flair for adaptation himself, Shaw has thus managed to use the Will from Nietzsche and Schopenhauer in order to motivate the cool Hegelian quest for pure knowledge. Life *desires* to *know* itself.

Not only does the intentionality of the Life Force allow Shaw to avoid the randomness of Darwinian biology, it also allows him to avoid the rigid determinism of the Marxist model in which history inexorably proceeds from economic stage to economic stage.[21] Because the Life Force must ultimately rely on the eccentricity of human intelligence to discover and fulfill its purposes, it moves in fits and starts and often (as in the modern age, Shaw believed) seems to stagnate altogether. The very fact that Shaw had identified this force with a Will seems to imply that a groping forward rather than a focused progression more faithfully describes its evolutionary career. Indeed, the misguided divagations of this force are what constitutes

---

[20] Samuel Butler, *Life and Habit* (Charleston: BiblioLife, 2008), p. 87. Quoted in *The Encyclopedia of Philosophy* (New York: Collier-Macmillan, 1967), ed. Paul Edwards, vol. 1, entry on Samuel Butler, by Elmer Sprague, p. 435.

[21] See Garret Griffith *Socialism and Superior Brains* (London: Routledge, 1993) for the best discussion of the sources behind Shaw's vitalism and the inherent tensions created by this patchwork philosophy. Pages 125–38 are especially useful in this regard, and I am indebted to them for the discussion in this paragraph.

evil for Shaw.[22] Much like Augustine, he views evil as a shadow-casting non-entity: it is the unilluminated gap between what we ought to seek and what we do seek. We stray off course, and benighted confidence in these cul-de-sacs crystallizes as the false idealizations of a society. Again, we are not bad by nature; we are merely trapped in delusions.

Shaw's insistence on a benevolent cosmic force that we so frequently, though not perversely, misconstrue presupposes that it does not communicate its wishes transparently. While this force is the metaphysical justification for our ethical lives – we are under obligation to advance its purposes – it does not make manifest our duties and responsibilities in anything like Mosaic tablets or even Lockean natural law. Rather, in a passage that sounds surprisingly Lawrentian, Shaw concedes that there may be realms of being inaccessible to intellect: "The unconscious self is the real genius. Your breathing goes wrong the moment your conscious self meddles with it. Except during the nine months before he draws his first breath, no man manages his affairs as well as a tree does."[23] Only those who attend to these unconscious whisperings can advance evolution: "The reasonable man adapts himself to the world: the unreasonable one persists in trying to adapt the world to himself. Therefore all progress depends on the unreasonable man."[24] Yet, however much Shaw needs to posit an unconscious to hold together his patchwork philosophy, it is a realm in which he feels distinctly uncomfortable. As Griffith observes, "his vitalism brought him few insights into the irrational recesses of the human psyche." Much like Freud's and Lawrence's unconscious, Shaw's, too, directs our sexual matings, yet his lacks their searing compulsions. In *Man and Superman*, when Jack Tanner finally is forced to acknowledge that his long-time flirtation with Ann is due not to the attractions of her witty banter, but a response to the promptings of the Life Force, he reacts with all the surprise and anguish of a man who has just lost a devilishly well-played hand of cards. At such moments, the Life Force has scarcely more *gravitas* than the fairies in *Midsummer Night's Dream*, a quasi-divine vehicle for bringing about the resolution of romantic comedy.

Further, the Life Force's preoccupation with breeding raises the inevitable question: What precisely is it breeding for? We realize that it seeks to become fully self-aware, but how exactly is that to be accomplished? Shaw certainly does not make things easy for himself insofar as his notion of Creative Evolution borrows heavily from the politically incompatible

---

[22] Alfred Turco, Jr., *Shaw's Moral Vision* (Ithaca: Cornell University Press, 1976), p. 171.
[23] Shaw, "The Revolutionist's Handbook," in *Man and Superman*, p. 260.    [24] Ibid., p. 260.

visions of Marx and Nietzsche. Did the Life Force that pulsed through all of us seek to reproduce this commonality in egalitarian social relations? Or did the very idea of evolutionary progress presuppose the ultimate reign of supermen? In the end, Shaw's gift for assimilation allows him to forge an ingenious compromise. The Life Force, possessed of "a mystic will to equality," strives to bring about a socialist distribution of wealth, but it seeks this equality only in order to push further. As Edwin Pettet rightly observes: "Equality of income emerged not as a goal in itself, but as a means of equalizing intellectual opportunity and intermarriageability."[25] Thus, socialism 1) ensures that intellectual energy is not wasted in the need to provide the bare necessities of sustenance, and 2) by eradicating class considerations, gives mating an unrestricted pool from which to choose, theoretically accelerating utopian eugenics. What this unlimited biological matrix should ideally produce, however, is a quantum leap forward: "you must admit that unless we are replaced by a more highly evolved animal – in short by the Superman – the world must remain a den of dangerous animals."[26] In the end, it seems socialism provides a platform for the generation of superior specimens, antennae of the Life Force. Griffith adds, "Shaw's claim was that if the race did not improve under such conditions, then it was simply unimprovable."[27] In considering this far-off and bleakest of all scenarios, Shaw betrays a hint of the apocalyptic despair that more regularly haunted his post–World War I contemporaries. Should we fail to achieve the purpose of the Life Force, then we would forfeit the right to exist as a species. Just for a moment Shaw allows himself to glimpse Birkin's non-human future, returned to grass and rabbits.

While Shaw's neo-Lamarckianism contains much that is preposterous, it is hardly to be distinguished in this regard from Lawrence's electrical circuitry or Yeats' gyres and phases of the moon. Just as critics have uniformly discounted the truth value of Lawrence's and Yeats' far-fetched speculations and concentrated instead on what such concoctions allowed them to accomplish, so we should extend the same courtesy to Shaw. In doing so, we can see that these metaphysical notions allowed him to move beyond a thinly conceived, though well-intentioned, socialism to deeper, almost Aristotelian inquiries into the proper function of a human being. The purely rationalistic utilitarianism that characterized Shaw's

---

[25] Edwin Burr Pettet, "Shaw's Socialist Life Force," in *Educational Theater Journal*, vol. 3, no. 2 (May 1951), 113–14.
[26] Shaw, "The Revolutionists Handbook," p. 242.
[27] Griffith, *Socialism and Superior Brains*, p. 120.

thought through the mid-nineties begins to give way to a rounder conception of the self as possessed of a will that responded to sub-rational intimations. These intimations urge alignment of the personal will with that of the Life Force. As a result, our purpose is not to increase the sum of personal happinesses, but to advance the cause of Life. In stressing the obedience of the individual will to cosmic intention, Shaw can give vent to a deeply engrained Protestant voluntarism that energizes his moral vision in a way that Millian calculus never quite could. Shaw can finally move to interiority. Having disdained Freudian explorations of the psyche, he finds his way within by means of the quasi-religious belief in souls harkening to the whispers of the Life Force. This is not by any means to say that what Shaw finds there approximates the dark intensities of his contemporaries; it doesn't. He remains too much the rational optimist for that. But the move inward allows Shaw to ally himself with Modernism in its preoccupation with salvation. To rely on Lionel Trilling one more time:

> [Modern literature] asks us if we are content with ourselves, if we are saved or damned – more than with anything else, our literature is concerned with salvation. No literature has ever been so intensely spiritual as ours. I do not venture to call it religious, but certainly it has the special intensity of concern with the spiritual life which Hegel noted when he spoke of the great modern phenomenon of the secularization of spirituality.[28]

The "special intensity" of which Trilling speaks erupts in Shaw's twentieth-century plays in moments when the acceleration or retardation of the species hangs in the balance. It is only then that he allows himself to grant the emotions primacy and power.

Because the fate of the species will demand the forfeiting of an elevated soul's personal happiness, Shaw's finest works of the twentieth century present us with a theater of sacrifice, bringing him closer to drama's ritualistic origins than has ordinarily been recognized. This is adumbrated early in the century in the figure of Barbara in *Major Barbara* who must violate her religious sensibilities in order to wage war on poverty rather than sin. But it is only the experience of WWI, the numbing spectacle of the waste of a generation, that causes Shaw to shift attention from the cosmic comedy that requires the sacrifice to the passion of the affected individuals. Both Ellie in *Heartbreak House* and Joan in *St. Joan* must suffer for the sake of the future, and Shaw does not minimize the cost. It is against this background of self-sacrifice that we can instructively read his

---

[28] Trilling, "On the Modern Element in Modern Literature," p. 15.

complaints about Shakespearian tragedy. Shakespeare, according to Shaw, engages us in the fate of tragic heroes whose *agon* is essentially personal, even though it inevitably spills over to the kingdom. Macbeth, Hamlet, and Lear are the creations of "the fashionable author who would see nothing in the world but personal aims and the tragedy of their disappointment."[29] Because Shakespeare can envision no larger framework for his tragic heroes, their suffering strikes Shaw as a purely arbitrary, trumped-up spectacle. Such tragedies are philosophically undermotivated. To underscore this point, Shaw, demonstrating his penchant for provocative reversals of received opinion, claims: "The plays in which these figures [Hamlet, Macbeth, Richard III, and Iago] appear could be changed into comedies without altering a hair of their beards."[30] The omnipresent possibility of comedy swallowing up tragedy is, of course, more relevant to Shaw's creations than Shakespeare's, for, in the end, Shaw's eschatology must render all pure tragedy otiose. What he will offer us instead, in *Heartbreak House* and *St. Joan*, are a fantasia and a chronicle with tragic scenes, and it is to these two plays that we now turn.

In the preface to *Heartbreak House*, Shaw makes a concerted effort to account for the carnage of WWI by adopting a God's-eye view of historical evolution. Coolly he observes, in a subsection entitled "Nature's Long Credits": "Nature's way of dealing with unhealthy conditions is unfortunately not one that compels us to conduct a solvent hygiene on a cash basis. She demoralizes us with long credits and reckless overdrafts, and then pulls us up cruelly with catastrophic bankruptcies."[31] Eventually, the Life Force reorients us by punishing egregious deviations. While there is little doubt that Shaw, the philosopher of history, believes this to be an adequate explanation for 15,000,000 deaths, Shaw, neighbor to so much suffering, knows that more, other, needs to be said. Just as Augustine's theory of evil as a privation seems too tepid to account for the chronicle of human savagery and the massive pain it leaves in its wake, so, too, does Shaw's theory of a self-correcting Life Force. The result of his awareness of this inadequacy is a play that is far more highly charged and tortured than the preface prepares us for. In much the same way that Eliot's magisterial tone in the extended footnotes to *The Waste Land* jars with the spiritual anguish of the poem, Shaw's preface and the opening fussy stage direction sit uneasily with the emotional turmoil of the play itself.

---

[29] Shaw, Preface to *Man and Superman*, p. 31.   [30] Shaw, *Quintessence of Ibsenism*, p. 141.
[31] Shaw, "Heartbreak House and Horseback Hall," Preface to *Heartbreak House* (Baltimore: Penguin, 1970), p. 11.

Shaw claimed that *Heartbreak House* "began with an atmosphere and does not contain a word that was foreseen before it was written."[32] This lack of deliberation is all to the good since for once he seems to be trying to catch up with his characters rather than presenting them in calculatedly didactic combination. The play has an astonishing number of entrances and exits, almost as if the characters were trying to outrun the theories that would ensnare them if they lingered too long. They are in flight, not just from their creator, but also from each other, and most especially from themselves. Thus, just beneath the comic whirlwind of comings and goings, the audience senses pure panic. Depressed sometimes into despair, heightened at other times into hilarity, the electricity of panic galvanizes all the major characters, making this Shaw's most emotionally charged play to this point – and his best. At long last, we have characters who are more than simply their ideas, or to put it even more precisely, the ideas they do have are in large part shaped by an affective response to the world.

The play's very first line – the nurse's ejaculation "God bless us!" – signals the febrile tone to follow while at the same time introducing the thematic fear of salvation's loss that causes nerves to be high-strung. In such an atmosphere, rational assessment proves again and again to be misleading. Captain Shotover assumes Ellie is a pirate's daughter; Lady Utterword assumes she is one of her nieces; later, Hesione introduces her to her own father. While Shaw takes full advantage of the great comic potential of these misrecognitions, for the first time the comedy of confusion is closer to the existential flounderings of Beckett's stage than the witty effervescence of Wilde's. The inability of the other characters to get clear on just who Ellie is turns out to be a refraction of their own shifting self-identity. In earlier Shaw, where the self amounts to little more than the sum of one's opinions, lability indicates the virtue of open-mindedness; in the world of *Heartbreak House*, where self begins to approximate Aristotelian character, it is a sign of failure. Now opinions typically serve as camouflages. With the possible exception of Captain Shotover, all the characters are fabulists. The theatricality of their self-presentation is often dazzling, especially in the case of the boundlessly charming Hector and Hesione Hushabye, but there is a bass note of Kierkegaardian despair at betrayal of one's soul, a sound not heard so plangently in Shaw before. This concern with tortured subjectivity places Shaw squarely in the company of his fellow modernists. No longer does he seem like Yeats' endlessly smiling sewing machine.

---

[32] Henderson, *George Bernard Shaw: Man of the Century*, p. 625.

That something here is different – and more enduring – in Shaw is indicated by an advance in the way he resolves his ongoing *agon* with Shakespeare. Prior to this, he had made no secret of the fact that he regarded Shakespeare as scarcely worth the rivalry: "With the single exception of Homer, there is no eminent writer, not even Sir Walter Scott, whom I can despise so entirely as I despise Shakespeare when I measure my mind against his."[33] As he revealed to Archibald Henderson, *Caesar and Cleopatra* (1899) was conceived as a rectification of Shakespeare's unforgiveable liberties: "Shakespeare's Caesar is the *reduction ad absurdum* of the real Julius Caesar ... My Caesar is a simple return to nature and history."[34] Shakespeare's Caesar offends against both naturalism, the ordinary warts-and-all Caesar, as well as the very order of things insofar as Shakespeare fails to see the Roman's true purpose in history. Bound to the outmoded notion of a Great Chain of Being, Shakespeare asks us to concern ourselves with the inner turmoil of characters who threaten or defend that order. Yet, according to Shaw, the resultant high mimetic emotion, decked out in poetic language, can only serve to distract us from cool, hard-headed, and, most importantly, *progressive* analysis. In *Heartbreak House*, once again, Shaw attempts to rewrite Shakespeare. The eighty-year-old Shotover, a querulous eminence in decay with three daughter figures, the elder two betrayers, the youngest faithful, make the parallel clear. The storm scene of *King Lear* becomes the typhoon Shotover had to endure; Albany's apocalyptic "fall and cease" is literalized in the threatening bombers at the end of Shaw's play, and so on. All of this has been remarked on frequently. But what is new here is that for the first time desires seem to generate misguided notions, rather than follow from them – and this is the far greater acknowledgment of Shakespeare's theater.[35]

Along with this tacit concession to Shakespeare, Shaw imports a heavy dose of classical allusion to mythological darknesses. As Stanley Weintraub notes, we have not only the obvious Hector, but also Hesione (in the first draft Hecuba), Ariadne, and Ellie (a diminutive of Helen).[36] Hesione was the mythic queen of Asia saved from the jaws of a ravening sea monster by

---

[33] "Blaming the Bard" in *The Collected Works of Bernard Shaw* (New York: William Wise, 1931), vol. 24, p. 205.
[34] Quoted in Henderson, *George Bernard Shaw: Man of the Century*, p. 556.
[35] For a contrarian opinion see Sonya Freeman Loftis, "Shakespeare, Shotover, Surrogation: 'Blaming the Bard' in *Heartbreak House*," in *Shaw: The Annual of Bernard Shaw Studies*, vol. 29 (2009), 50–65. Loftis sees Ellie's interest in Shakespeare as a negative sign of her obsession with father figures representing "worn out ideals and a dying culture."
[36] Stanley Weintraub, "Shaw's Troy: *Heartbreak House* and Euripides *Trojan Women*," in *Shaw: The Annual of Bernard Shaw Studies*, vol. 29, no. 1 (2009), 42.

Heracles; Ariadne the rescuer of Theseus from the Minotaur; and, of course, Helen and Hector, respectively precipitator of the Trojan War and its heroic victim. While Shaw seems to struggle against his own darkening vision by bestowing the ridiculous surname of Hushabye on Hector and Hesione, a choice reminiscent of the Vainloves and Sneerwells of Restoration comedy of manners, this should not disguise the fact that the Greek names are all borrowed from "mythic figures who lived lives intensified by meaningful confrontation with death."[37] This reliance on Greek mythology to organize our response to the modern world anticipates by a few years Eliot's identification of the use of mythic parallels as the future of modern literature: "It is simply a way of controlling, or ordering of giving a shape and significance to the immense panorama of futility and anarchy which is contemporary history."[38] By looking to the past in this way, rather than to an upwardly evolving future, Shaw shifts his attention to universal emotional patterns of response. Perceptively, Weintraub notes that the lamentations of Hecuba in Euripides' *The Trojan Women* becomes a norm against which the final ecstasy of Hermione and Ellie is to be measured:

MRS HUSHABYE But what a glorious experience! I hope they'll come again tomorrow night
ELLIE (radiant at the prospect) Oh, I hope so.[39]

Unlike Eliot, Shaw here does not use the past for relentless castigation of the present – how could he, without abandoning his political vision entirely? – but rather to add a substratum of emotional depth, heretofore lacking in his work. Thus, Hecuba is not invoked to show the inferiority of Hesione and Ellie, but to show the similarity. Let me follow once more Weintraub's subtle commentary on the Greek sources. Among the speeches of the grieving Hecuba, bereft of both son and grandson, he singles out the following:

> Had thou fallen fighting [she tells the dead grandson in her arms]
> … hadst thou known
> Strong youth and love and all the majesty
> Of godlike kings, then had we spoken of thee
> As of one blessed.[40]

[37] Dennis Leary, "*Heartbreak House*: A Dramatic Epic," in *The Independent Shavian: The Journal of the Bernard Shaw Society*, vol. 37, no. 1–2 (1999), 7.
[38] T. S. Eliot, "Ulysses, Order, and Myth," *Dial* 75 (November 1923), 483.
[39] Shaw, *Heartbreak House*, p. 160. Hereafter all citations from the play will be indicated in the text by page numbers from this edition.
[40] Quoted in Weintraub, "Shaw's Troy," 47.

Hecuba is still committed to the warrior ethic that has cost her such painful loss. Her glorification of war is echoed in the rapturous comments of Hesione and Ellie quoted above. Yet Shaw's postwar audience, many of whom, as he mentions in the preface, were caught up in jingoistic propaganda, must, like Hecuba, try to make sense of that *and* the furious carnage. Hesione and Ellie, Hecubas-in-waiting, serve as sources of dramatic irony, and an irony that deeply implicates the audience as well. By the end of the play, it is hard to imagine that many of the viewers are speculating about an impersonal Life Force's long-term goals.

To reach this point, though, Shaw must move beyond his instinctive tendency to regard emotion as the result of a comedic misjudgment, the occasion for corrective raillery. In Act One, for example, we find Shaw in this earlier mode in the following exchange between Ellie, suddenly bitterly disillusioned about Hector, and Hesione:

> ELLIE I am not damning him: I am damning myself for being such a fool. [*Rising*] How could I let myself be taken in so? [*She begins prowling to and fro, her bloom gone, looking curiously older and harder*].
> MRS HUSHABYE [*cheerfully*] Why not pettikins? Very few young women can resist Hector. I couldn't when I was your age. He is really rather splendid, you know.
> ELLIE [*turning on her*] Splendid! Yes: splendid looking, of course. But how can you love a liar?
> MRS HUSHABYE I don't know. But you can, fortunately. Otherwise there wouldn't be much love in the world. (71–72)

The last exchange would not have been out of place in *The Importance of Being Earnest*, but, as the play unfolds, Shaw allows the raw nakedness of emotion to have the final word. In a later conversation between the two women, Ellie takes Hesione to task for just such attempts to contextualize her suffering with a glib worldliness. In response, Hesione drops the bantering façade to reveal, surprisingly, anguished currents of feeling of her own:

> But I warn you that when I am neither coaxing and kissing nor laughing, I am just wondering how much longer I can stand living in this cruel, damnable world. You object to the siren: well, I drop the siren. You want to rest your wounded bosom against a grindstone. Well [*folding her arms*], here is the grindstone. (107–8)

Shaw means for us to concur with Ellie's succinct assessment of Hesione's interior revelation: "Thats [sic] better."

This exploration of emotional interiors shows up most strikingly in an uncanny, almost surrealistic, outburst of self-revelation that occurs toward the end of Act One. Perhaps relying on his background as a keen appreciator and critic of music, Shaw follows the operatic convention of having strong emotion demand song, as the prose of his play gives way to poetic choral chant. In the following passage, we can see anguished emotion straining toward music in this way:

CAPTAIN SHOTOVER [raising a strange wail in the darkness]
    What a house! What a daughter!
MRS HUSHABYE [raving] What a father!
HECTOR [following suit] What a husband!
CAPTAIN SHOTOVER Is there no thunder in heaven?
HECTOR Is there no beauty, no bravery, on earth?
MRS HUSHABYE What do men want? They have their food, their firesides, their clothes mended, and our love at the end of the day. Why are they not satisfied? Why do they envy us the pain with which we bring them into the world, and make strange dangers and torments for themselves to be even with us?
CAPTAIN SHOTOVER [weirdly chanting]
    I built a house for my daughters, and opened the doors thereof, That men might come for their choosing, and their betters spring from their love; But of them married a numskull;
HECTOR [taking up the rhythm]
    The other a liar wed;
MRS HUSHABYE [completing the stanza]
    And now she must lie beside him, even as she made her bed. (90)

Here Shaw comes close to the Nietzsche of *The Birth of Tragedy* who sees music as an expression of primordial, Dionysian truths, nearly unendurable. It is against this backdrop that the pathetically thin, Apollonian fluting of Randall's *Keep the Homefires Burning* that concludes the play must be evaluated.

The nakedness of these revelations, their unsweetened self-knowledge, moves Shaw as close to Shakespeare as he has ever been, for they are, in effect, Shakespearean asides. Compare, for example, Edmund's articulation of his true nature:

> A credulous father, and a brother noble,
> Whose nature is so far from doing harms
> That he suspects none; on whose foolish honesty
> My practices ride easy. I see the business.
> Let me, if not by birth, have lands by wit;
> All with me's meet that I can fashion fit. (I.ii. 172–77)

to Hesione's self-assessment, spoken to no one in particular, as

> A sluttish female, trying to stave off a double chin and an elderly spread, vainly wooing a born soldier of freedom. (152)

Edmund's cynicism is certainly deeper and more startling than Hesione's, but given Shaw's view of human nature, this is the nearest approximation of which he is capable and a huge advance in his exploration of the stains of desire. Admittedly, Mangan is more crassly and harmfully manipulative than Hesione, but his confessions are extorted from him under cross-examination, and are more indicative of sheer ignorance than inner compulsion. When he admits – indeed, boasts – of the way he sabotages other government officials' plans so that they will not be promoted ahead of him, the vast self-deception trumps the self-revelation in a way it does not with Hesione. As the bullying, fraudulent capitalist he owes more to Dickens' Bounderby than to Edmund or Iago.

But the very creation of Boss Mangan and Shotover's efforts to lay his soul bare to reveal the canker echo Lear's relentless quest to account for evil. Driven to the brink of madness by filial duplicity and ingratitude, Lear demands: "Then let them anatomize Regan. See what breeds/about her heart. Is there any cause in nature that makes/these hard hearts?" (III. vi. 74–76). Shakespeare never provides him with a clear-cut answer, for it seems we have arrived at the sheer, brute fact of evil, no further explanation possible than that it is so. This view, for Shaw, would be indicative of Shakespeare's fatalism, one of his chief failures, but in his own play, Shaw comes as close as he dares to this possibility. The anatomization of Mangan by the inhabitants of Heartbreak House leaves Hesione genuinely surprised to discover he is indeed a recognizable human being: "It comes to me suddenly that you are a real person: that you had a mother, like anyone else ... And you have a heart, Alfy, a whimpering little heart, but a real one" (112–13). This vestigial humanity allows Shaw, in keeping with his claim that his stage presents no outright villains, to extend a brief moment of sympathy for Mangan, something Shakespeare never does with Regan or Goneril. Yet, Hesione's recognition that Mangan does have *some* feeling sounds like Shaw's belated reminder to himself that this must be so. Toward the end of the play when Mangan, in grotesque parody of Lear, threatens to strip off his clothes, the others "in consternation" dissuade him, finding the prospect of his physical nakedness no more appealing than his moral nakedness. Though there is comedy here, and the scene is usually played that way, it is brittle and not good-natured. A few moments later, Mangan is blown sky high by dynamite, along with the thief and extortionist Billie Dunn. While Shaw clearly believes this to be a necessary purging akin to the deaths of Edmund, Goneril, and Regan, the problem of evil is no more solved thereby than it is in *King Lear*. The most we can say, in both cases, is that evil feeds on itself, consuming its most vicious agents. At this point, it is hard to believe that Shaw himself is emotionally satisfied by the explanation offered in his preface of a disgruntled Life Force.

This is not, admittedly, the first time that the emotional turmoil of a play goes far beyond the announced agenda of his didactic preface, but it is by far the most disturbing. Perhaps the chief earlier instance of a play surprising us in this way is *Mrs. Warren's Profession*. In the preface to that play, as has been already noted, Shaw announces that the play was written to expose the evils of a laissez-faire capitalism that drives one-pence-an-hour working girls to resort to prostitution. And while this, indeed, is the originating cause of the play's tension between mother and daughter, that tension is far more richly textured than a single-issue conflict would demand. A mother's need for the love of her daughter, her desire to steer the younger life according to her compensatory expectations, are balanced against the daughter's response to the way the mother's love for her has manifested itself, complicated by the natural pull toward independence. Students – and especially female students – typically are more fully engaged with these universal emotional currents between mother and daughter than with the sociological issues that lie behind them. This is not to say that the two foci can or should be divorced. Charles Berst sorts these out as "moral allegory" and "[psychological] realism," but then appropriately points out that "the two levels act as sounding-boards for each other, creating the greater depth and reality of a synthesis."[41] At the play's end, Vivie rejects her mother's plea for filial connection since it seems to her the final and most seductive threat to her own integrity. In terms of the moral allegory, one could argue that she triumphs. Yet, when we last see her, hunched over her account books, having jettisoned both her mother and her lover Frank, it is hard not to regard her as a tragic figure, her independence purchased at the cost of total emotional isolation, the only incandescence that of her desk lamp. Shaw's instincts here are as subtle and sure as they were to be again twenty years later in *Heartbreak House*. In both cases, one is reminded of Lawrence's famous admonition to trust the tale, not the teller. Luckily, too, theatergoers experience the plays without the prefaces.

---

[41] Charles Berst, "Propaganda and Art in Mrs. Warren's Profession," *ELH*, vol. 33, no. 3 (September 1966), 390–404, at 397.

Any discussion of Shaw's portrayal of emotional intensity inevitably leads to his treatment of sexuality. Shaw himself freely admitted that "[t]he suggestion, gratification, and education of sexual emotion is one of the main uses and glories of the theatre."[42] And while there have been a line of critics who believe that sexuality permeates Shaw's plays, most notably Louis Crompton, who asserts that "no playwright has dramatized the naked power of the sex impulse more directly or with more respect," this claim is driven to extravagance as a rebuttal to the long tradition of those who conversely find him to be "bloodless" and "passionless."[43] Those who take Shaw to task point out that he got a great deal of mileage out of shocking late Victorian and Edwardian audiences by merely *talking* about sexuality and he relied on this frisson too heavily and too long. The snappy reversal of sexual/connubial convention is a staple of Shaw's witty comedic genius.

MANGAN Suppose I go straight to Mrs. Hushabye and tell her that you're in love with her husband.
ELLIE She knows it.
MANGAN You told her!!!
ELLIE She told me.
MANGAN [Clutching at his bursting temples] Oh, this is a crazy house. Or else I'm going clean off my chump. Is she making a swap with you – she to have your husband and you to have hers?
ELLIE Well, you don't want us both do you? (97)

While this exchange remains delightfully humorous, as the shock value steadily evaporated, too much was lost. This criticism should not be dismissed as a supercilious ratification of modern mores. One need only compare the witty banter of a Lubitsch film or its darker manifestation in the repartee of film noir to see what is ultimately missing in Shaw: not sexuality, but eroticism. Even if we stick, more fairly, to stage comedy, we can see the difference between Shakespeare's sexual fencing and Shaw's. The obvious forebears of Shaw's Ellie here or Ann Whitefield in *Man and Superman* earlier are the verbally gifted Beatrice of *Much Ado About Nothing* and Rosalind of *As You Like It* who overmatch their male counterparts.[44] The Shakespeare heroines' desires, we are made to feel,

---

[42] Shaw, letter in *The Times* (November 8, 1913), in *Bernard Shaw: Agitations, Letters to the Press, 1875–1950*, ed. Dan H. Laurence and James Rambeau (New York: Ungar, 1985), p. 154.
[43] See Michael W. Pharand, "Introduction: Dionysian Shaw," in *Shaw: The Annual of Bernard Shaw Studies*, vol. 24 (2004), 2.
[44] Bloom cites the connection in *Shakespeare: The Invention of the Human* (New York: Riverhead Books, 1998), pp. 196 and 202.

percolate into the effervescence of wit; the wit of Shaw's heroines draws comparatively little of its energy from erotic heat. Wit in Shaw substitutes for erotic heat, without being occasioned by it.

Shaw's avoidance of eroticism constitutes one more reversal of conventional expectation. Thus, he gives us *Caesar and Cleopatra*, but Caesar is more intimate in his conversations with the Sphinx than he is with Cleopatra, whom he treats as a spoiled Eliza Doolittle. To minimize any sexual tension he reduces Cleopatra's age from twenty-one to sixteen and has her repeatedly remark on how old Caesar appears. Under such circumstances, Caesarion is never dreamed of. The Cleopatra of grand passion is acknowledged only in her fascination with Mark Antony whom, at the end, Caesar promises to send her, as if to provide material for a lesser play that Shakespeare could busy himself with. Likewise, in *Mrs. Warren's Profession*, Vivie learns to her horror that her mother has persisted in the business of prostitution long after there was any pressing financial need, but we get no clear account of what part raw desire played in this decision. Too, we discover that Vivie and Frank very likely have the same father, but this revelation is never developed, serving more to reveal a clergyman's hypocrisy than incestuous Byronic transgression. One need only compare Mrs. Warren with her obvious forebear Moll Flanders to see the foreclosed possibilities. Moll, like Mrs. Warren, avoids poverty by a turn to prostitution, but Defoe makes no secret of the fact that his heroine's choice is made easier by her strong sexual desire. Along the way, Moll unwittingly marries her brother, who, distraught at the news, attempts suicide and lives a broken man thereafter. Even the far from scrupulous Moll is moved to physical revulsion. Defoe the Puritan clearly sees these darknesses as manifestations of Original Sin, something Shaw, though the author of *Plays for Puritans*, refuses to inherit. For Shaw, it is in large part the false *belief* in both the overwhelming force of eroticism, with its attendant desires, and the incorrigibility of that force that has given rise to misguided idealisms meant to curtail this imagined power. These idealisms, in turn, generate the strident moral conventions that make the voice of the Life Force inaudible to us.

Between *Heartbreak House* and *St. Joan*, Shaw endeavors to get behind these very conventions by providing his religion of Creative Evolution with its own foundational mythology in the play he regards as a "World Classic," *Back to Methuselah* (1921). The play begins with a rewriting of Genesis, here devoid of a diabolically inspired serpent or respondent human taint that might be identified with Original Sin. Thus, there is no Fall in Shaw's account, but neither is there any blissful Edenic sexuality.

(Eve instinctively reacts with a spasm of disgust to hear that it is the only means to procreation). In the Adam and Eve scenes of *Methuselah*, the crux of the discussion between Adam and Eve, later joined by Cain, is the status of voices heard variously by the three. Are they internal projections or genuine intimations from without to those fit to bear witness? And if from without, what is their source? Why do the various characters respond as they do? These are not just epistemological puzzles, but involve moral issues as well – indeed, moral issues more importantly, for these voices appeal to the will more directly than to the purely rational faculty. How our ancestors respond becomes the quintessential instance of the Kantian moral imperative for they actually are, quite literally, choosing for mankind. We learn, too, of the existential considerations that inflect these decisions: Adam's fearful discovery of death replaces his earlier anxiety about being locked in selfhood for eternity; Eve comes to understand her role as procreator and takes solace in contemplation of her yet unborn progeny; Cain desires to distance himself from the soil worked by his father and to glory over all other men, in a restless spirit of violent competitiveness. While Shaw does here recognize the importance of our inward lives, he does little more than sketch a range of emotional reactions to Being-Towards-Death.

Indeed, Shaw abandons almost all pretense to character as he distills (if that is the right word for a nearly 250-page play) his belief in Creative Evolution into a series of debates stretching from Adam and Eve to the year 31,920. This is as close to a pure imitation of Platonic dialogue that theater can offer. As Shaw makes clear in his preface when he criticizes his earlier attempt at dramatizing the workings of the Life Force, in *Man and Superman*, for its comic extravagance, any concession to theatricality could only serve as a distraction. The devaluation of art's ability to contribute to human well-being becomes thematic in the last section of the play when the ancients of the future confine art to the infancy of their citizens, which in the accelerated experiential world of the future would be until age four. As in the *Republic*, art is regarded as an image, psychologically revealing perhaps, but adding nothing to true knowledge:

THE SHE-ANCIENT Yes, child: art is the magic mirror you make to reflect your invisible dreams in visible pictures . . . But we who are older use neither glass mirrors nor works of art. We have a direct sense of life. When you gain this you will put aside your mirrors and statues, your toys and your dolls.[45]

---

[45] Bernard Shaw, *Back to Methuselah (Revised Edition with a Postscript)* (New York & London: Oxford University Press, 1947), p. 233.

One could, of course, object that this speech should be read ironically since Shaw makes it part of his own work of art, until one remembers that the She-Ancient's speech is set thirty-one millennia in the future, a time when the race is approaching the telos of pure thought, unencumbered by body. At such time, mind will come to know itself and the world without the help of even an allegorizing art. In anticipation of such time, the play is a fleshed out preface, with as little actual flesh as possible. Here, then, is art almost completely in service to what we might loosely call "philosophy," and the result is, despite a few salvageable moments, an utter dramatic failure, moving one critic to observe "[t]he preface is, for once, a better piece of writing than the play."[46] Whatever the most fruitful relationship of art to philosophy may be, one of this degree of subordination is clearly not the answer.

Shaw does much better embodying his ideas when he creates his most fully realized character, St. Joan, communicant with voices of her own. Though there are mystical elements in Joan as Shaw portrays her, he chooses not to regard her as the culmination of the rich tradition of medieval mysticism, but rather as a proto-Protestant, "the supremacy of private judgment for the individual being the quintessence of Protestantism."[47] This allows him to cast her as an anticipator of historical unfolding and makes her a precursor of Shaw's own Protestant background and frequent iconoclasm. No doubt, too, the ever-explaining Shaw was not entirely comfortable with mystic ineffability. Finally, and most importantly, by tapping into the strongly voluntaristic Protestant tradition, Shaw allows himself to explore the fluctuations of will, a more intimate realm than the taking up and discarding of opinions that typified most of his earlier work. History, of course, must remain the protagonist – the play is designated a chronicle – but, as in *Heartbreak House*, Shaw is now willing to examine seriously the personal cost of sacrifice. In terms of the demands history presents us with, the more Shaw sounds like the humanistic Camus, the less like Sartre, for whom an imagined future justifies the means to get there, the better a playwright he becomes. One can see clearly the change in the difference between his treatment of two of his hero/martyrs: Caesar and Joan. While the audience is aware that the historical changes initiated by Caesar will result in his assassination, that impending event casts virtually no shadow in *Caesar and Cleopatra*. Indeed, the fact that Shakespeare makes it

---

[46] Homer E. Woodbridge, *G. B. Shaw: Creative Artist* (Carbondale: Southern Illinois Press, 1963), p. 111.
[47] Bernard Shaw, *St. Joan* (Baltimore: Penguin, 1969), p. 29.

central to his *Julius Caesar* is essentially why Shaw dismisses the play as trivially personal, a mistaken concentration on the sufferings of the man rather than on his long-lasting effect on the course of history. In *St. Joan*, however, Joan's ecstasies and doubts, tribulations and ultimate martyrdom command Shaw's attention and respect. It is a good sign that Shaw has tilted the play so far toward the tragedy of Joan that he feels the need to append an epilogue to remind us of the importance of the historical aftermath.[48]

The move inward is best seen in the play's obsession with the reality and status of Joan's voices and visions. Virtually everyone in the play – and Shaw himself, at length in the preface – stakes out an opinion. Baudricourt claims "the girl is mad," a deifier of her own imagination. The skeptical, but more sympathetic Dunois tells Joan "I should think you were a bit cracked if I hadn't noticed that you give me very sensible reasons for what you do, though I hear you telling others you are only obeying Madame Saint Catherine" (103).[49] The Archbishop detects, not madness, but a perverse willfulness, the voice of pride. It is only a short step from there to Cauchon's belief that the voices she hears come from the inspirer of sin, Satan. As if a parody of this, the undereducated chaplain, in an excess of nationalistic casuistry, claims that Joan is clearly a witch since the voices spoke to her in French rather than English. Conversely, it briefly crosses Ladvenu's mind "that saints have said as much," anticipating the later view of the Catholic Church. When the newly coronated Charles protests that if the voices were from God, they should come to him, Joan responds "They do come to you; but you do not hear them. You have not sat in the field in the evening listening for them" (106). But, along with the others, even Joan seems to be misreading things here, for her view is considerably more democratic than Shaw's. The definitive view that he presents in the preface is that "[t]here are people in the world whose imagination is so vivid that when they have an idea it comes to them as an audible voice, sometimes uttered by a visible figure" (13). This sort of heightened experience is the mark of certain geniuses: "Socrates, Luther, Swedenborg, Blake saw visions and heard voices just as Saint Francis and Saint Joan did" (103). Shaw, like Kierkegaard before him, is honest enough to admit that such visions have also appeared to the criminally insane, and that he needs to provide some criterion for sorting out the St. Joans from the Jim Joneses of the world.

---

[48] Edmund Wilson goes so far as to claim "Saint Joan ... was the first genuine tragedy that Shaw has written." "Bernard Shaw at Eighty," in *George Bernard Shaw: A Critical Survey*, ed. Louis Kronenberger (New York: World Publishing Co., 1953), p. 146. Quoted in Sylvan Barnet, "Bernard Shaw on Tragedy" *PMLA*, vol. 71, no. 5 (December 1956), 897.

[49] Shaw, *Saint Joan*.

Kierkegaard had tried to distinguish Abraham's willingness to kill Isaac at the behest of revelatory voices from a case of psychopathology by assuming that Abraham recognizes that the "teleological suspension of the ethical" is a scary thing, inspiring fear and trembling. The more rationalistic Shaw is moved to no similarly anguished meditation, concluding instead, confidently and succinctly: "The test of sanity is not the normality of the method but the reasonableness of the discovery" (14). The clairvoyance of revelation is reason working with intense speed and accuracy. And what it perceives is what the Life Force intends.

Because Shaw has passed authoritative judgment on Joan's voices before the play has gotten underway, he creates a situation of extreme dramatic irony: the author and the play's readers conspire over the heads of the various characters, who operate in ignorance. Yet Shaw refuses to condemn them for their ignorance. Even the subsequently vilified Cauchon he defends by insisting that, according to his lights, he operated quite literally in good faith. "There are no villains in the piece," Shaw reminds us, for it is "what normally innocent people do that concerns us" (44). Thus, Shaw remains completely committed to the notion that ignorance does not arise from the bias of desire and associated emotion, but solely from understandable, if at times dreadfully unfortunate, miscognition. But the corollary of this position is that the inner lives of those who fail to comprehend Joan's voices are of no interest. They are mouthpieces in the dialectic of history. As if in compensation for robbing them of their affective life, Shaw grants them an impossible awareness of the historical implications of their positions. Indeed, the fact that he has deprived them of the one makes the granting of the other almost mandatory if the audience is to understand them at all: "But it is the business of the stage to make its figures more intelligible to themselves than they would be in real life; for by no other means can they be made intelligible to the audience" (45). With this in mind, Shaw makes Lemaître and Cauchon uncannily aware of the consequences of what they do for the Inquisition and the Church, and similarly Warwick in terms of feudalism. Even more abstractly, they are prone to pronounce on the nature of hierarchy, individualism, and nationalism with the perspicacity we might expect of Thucydides or Machiavelli. Shaw allows himself this "sacrifice of verisimilitude" in order that "the things I represent these three exponents of the drama as saying are the things they actually would have said if they had known what they were really doing" (45). If their opinions are what is to matter most about them, it is important to Shaw that they not be trivially or casually wrong.

Of course, strictly speaking, Joan gets the voices wrong as well insofar as she attributes them to the Christian god or his ambassador St. Catherine. But Shaw has never been much concerned about that kind of misidentification; he values Bunyan over Shakespeare, for example, essentially because he espouses a teleological view of life, even though the teleology is committedly Christian.[50] Certainly, Shaw would have had few earlier figures to champion if he had insisted that they be Lamarckian evolutionists *avant la lettre*. And, moreover, like the unfolding of the Hegelian *Geist*, the Life Force only reveals itself gradually, he believed. This doctrinal indifference allows Shaw to devote himself to the psychology of Joan. In doing so, he creates his most thoroughly developed *character*, a protagonist whose emotional responses are steadily crucial to her apprehension of the world. We are invited to examine, and ourselves be moved by, the internal nature of Joan's virtue. Max Beerbohm, writing of Shaw's earlier attempts at tragedy, complained that he was incapable of tragic emotion for he lacked the ability "to see into their [his characters'] hearts, and show us what he had seen there. He must be able to create human beings."[51] With the creation of Joan, Shaw has overcome this inability. At long last it makes sense to consider, following Aristotle, whether one of Shaw's figures feels the right emotion, to the right degree, at the right time. It is this new affective intensity that causes Thomas Mann to refer to *St. Joan* as the "most fervent" of Shaw's plays.

We should not underestimate the difficulty of what Shaw has attempted in this play, for he insists on showing us both the illiterate, naïve farm girl and the charismatic visionary, something much harder to do than Eliot's homogenous portrayal of the aloof, rarified Beckett. Joan's hybrid nature and the misprisions it occasions are amenable to comic as well as tragic treatment, and Shaw struggles, generally successfully, to get the tone right. He is careful to ensure that the comedy Joan's simplicity generates is never at her expense. Thus, for example, she mistakenly assumes that the cynical archbishop is an elevated soul, causing much merriment in those who know him all too well, and later she takes a pretentious duchess for the queen, but in both cases those who inspire the error are deflated thereby, not Joan. Because Joan's naïveté in such instances is believably consistent with the pure simplicity of her visions and the subsequent heartfelt plain speaking of her answers to the inquisitors, we have no trouble imagining

---

[50] Barnet, "Bernard Shaw on Tragedy," p. 891.
[51] Max Beerbohm, *Around Theatres* (London: Davis, rpt. 1953), p. 193. Quoted in Barnet, "Bernard Shaw on Tragedy," pp. 894–95.

Joan as a coherent character. In this regard, Shaw is far more successful than he was in the creation of an ordinary side to Caesar, evidenced only in the Roman's inability to pronounce the name of Cleopatra's nurse, Ftatateeta.

In between the comedy of ordinariness and the cosmic comedy of Joan's redemption, Shaw is able to show us Joan the tragic heroine. The temptation to have done otherwise was considerable. The riveting trial of the historical Joan is something Shaw read carefully and that had a natural appeal to his dialectical imagination. Yet, he avoids making the sheer clash of opinion the focus of the inquisition. It is not just *that* Joan believes or *what* she believes, but *how* she believes that touches us most deeply. In his essay "A Dialogue on Dramatic Poetry," after one of the discussants associates poetry with the expression of intense emotion, Eliot has another assert that "Shaw is precocious, but poetically immature."[52] The complaint is not that Shaw writes in prose, but that the intensity of feeling is underdeveloped. This is not to say that Shaw lacked such feeling, but that he lacked the ability to express the feeling: "Shaw has a great deal of poetry, but all stillborn." This is a bald summary of what, I hope in more nuanced, qualified fashion, I have been arguing has vitiated much of Shaw's work. But it is not true of *St. Joan*. Homer Woodbridge rightly claimed that "the magnificent climactic scene of Joan's trial [is] probably the greatest scene Shaw has written."[53] And the centerpiece of that scene is Joan's expressed preference for death rather than the life imprisonment offered in return for her recantation:

> You think that life is nothing but not being stone dead. It is not the bread and water I fear: I can live on bread: when have I asked for more? It is no hardship to drink water if the water be clean. Bread has no sorrow for me, and water no affliction. But to shut me from the light of the sky and the sight of the fields and flowers; to chain my feet so that I can never again ride with the soldiers nor climb the hills; to make me breathe foul damp darkness, and keep from me everything that brings me back to the love of God when your wickedness and foolishness tempt me to hate Him: all this is worse than the furnace in the Bible that was heated seven times. I could do without my warhorse; I could drag about in a skirt; I could let the banners and the trumpets and the knights and soldiers pass me and leave me behind as they leave the other women, if only I could still hear the wind in the trees, the larks in the sunshine, the young lambs crying through the healthy frost, and the blessed church bells that send my angel voices floating to me on the

---

[52] T. S. Eliot, *Selected Essays* (New York: Harcourt, Brace, 1932), p. 38.
[53] Woodbridge, *G. B. Shaw: Creative Artist*, p. 120.

wind. But without these things I cannot live; and by your wanting to take them away from me, or from any human creature, I know that your counsel is of the devil, and that mine is of God. (137–38)

At long last we have the poetic Shaw whose absence Eliot regretted, a Shaw who shows us how the felt life matters.

While some may argue that the controversial epilogue, at times reluctantly performed, undercuts the very real human Passion of Joan by allowing her spirit back on stage to learn of her canonization, it would be fairer to say that Shaw has contextualized her suffering rather than diminished it.[54] A fair analogy might be the pathos that is invoked by Pietàs, made exquisite, but not undercut, by the knowledge that what they represent is not the final word. Moreover, Shaw has not ended his play with Joan triumphant, as he might have, but with Joan in anguish. When she advances the possibility of her own resurrection and return, only to be rejected once again by those who betrayed her, she cries out, in the play's last lines: "O God that madest this beautiful earth, when will it be ready to receive Thy saints? How long, O Lord, how long?" This is tonally consistent with the Joan we have just seen in scene six, not a reversal. To be sure, Shaw is well aware of the delicate bifocal vision that Joan warrants. In the preface, he expresses it epigrammatically: "the angels may weep at the murder, but the gods laugh at the murderers" (p. 44). I think it would be fair to say that Shaw has invested so much in the suffering of Joan that he has ranged himself on the side of the angels.

That this angelic Shaw puts in too few appearances over the course of his career, though, constitutes his main challenge to the richly emotive-cognitive parsings of Nussbaum. Shaw's is essentially a theater without *necessity*, either tragic or comedic. He adamantly refuses to accept the metaphysics of tragedy: that human desire will perpetually be too large or too wrong to find fulfillment in a recalcitrant world. Neither is he willing to admit the primordial driving force of either Shakespearean comedy, an irrepressible erotic energy, or Molièrean comedy, the

---

[54] T. R. Henn remains the most eloquent spokesman for this view. See "The Shavian Machine," in *G. B. Shaw: Collection of Critical Essays*, pp. 168–69. Stanley Weintraub recounts a farcical series of events at the Canadian Shaw Festival when the management cut the entire Epilogue, only to have the Shaw Estate trustees demand its restoration. Put out, the management inserted an interval and a note in the program that the audience was free to leave. The actors had to perform the Epilogue in street clothes reading from scripts. The audience stayed, and cheered. See "Shaw for the Here and Now," in *The Annual of Bernard Shaw Studies*, vol. 25 (2005), 16–17.

"humor" that imprisons the absurd character. Shaw is impatient with internal explanation of events. Character must not determine fate. It is on this basis that he castigates both Shakespeare and Molière for relying on a false necessity. Yet, it is precisely this inevitability that Aristotle had insisted is the hallmark of tragedy and, insofar as we can deduce from his hints, of comedy as well. Character makes the unfolding of events seem to follow an internal logic. Freed of the confusions of accident and vicissitudes, the paradigmatic quality of drama allows it to join philosophy as universal in distinction from the particularities of history. Yet Shaw, in opposition, aligns his drama with history. Caesar, for example, is of interest to him chiefly because Shaw believes the Roman's *ideas* will be ratified in the long expanse of time. It is for the same reason that Shaw labels *Saint Joan* a chronicle and has her appear in an epilogue twenty-five years after her death, her canonization foretold, but herself still too dangerous for the times. Because of Shaw's eschatological preoccupation, the terminus of his later plays is always an unperformed, implied act to be played out in the distant future. That this violates Aristotle's insistence on the unity of plot with a distinct beginning, middle, and end might seem a trivial observation unless one realizes that this unity is itself the product of the inexorable unfolding of character.

Clearly, then, Shaw has managed to create a theater that has largely eluded the net of Nussbaum's Aristotelian-inspired criticism. Yet what is less clear is how much that indicates a flaw in her views (or in their extension to drama), how much in Shaw's dramaturgy. For it is precisely the plays, or parts of plays, that are most amenable to her views that are the best things he has written. Thus, in *Mrs. Warren's Profession*, it is the naked exchanges and emotional rawness in the scenes between Vivie and her mother that keep sending us back to that play – not the exposé of prostitution or the hypocrisy of philandering clergymen. In *Heartbreak House*, despite the obvious charm of the badinage, it is the panic and despair that lies beneath the wit that we respond to and that makes this play one of his two most rewarding. Finally, in *St. Joan*, the other of these two plays, we are riveted by the *character* of Joan moving from faith to recantation and back to faith, rather than her role as harbinger of nationalistic, feminist, or Protestant ideas. This is not by any means to say that it is only when Shaw forgets his commitment to Creative Evolution and the promise of a future that he becomes permanent, but, rather, only when he shows us the inner turmoil of those who are its agents and convinces us that that turmoil ought to matter. Or, to place things in the wider classical context, Shaw only achieves his greatest success when he abandons his

Platonic suspicion of the emotional life as at best a distraction, at worst a danger, and remembers, as Aristotle would remind us, that a nuanced exploration of these emotions is what the theater ought to offer us, for they are deeply implicated in the ethical life, about which Shaw himself was so steadily and often courageously concerned.

# *Conclusion*

The idea for this book originated in a simple academic observation: teachers of literature almost invariably devote a good part of classroom discussion to parsing the ethical implications of the text before them, whether it be an analysis of character and plot in a novel or the affective alignments of the lyric poet; yet, the formal and systematic study of ethics is to be found in departments of philosophy. Was anything of value taking place in the literature classroom that was not being done in a far more sophisticated way simultaneously down the hall in the philosophy classroom? Was the attentive reading of literature little more than Plato for the people – and a Plato that Plato would have strongly disapproved of? This question became more timely with the welcome "ethical turn" in literary studies, that might more properly have been designated a "return." Yet, even then, literary scholars tended to look instinctively and generally unfruitfully to Derrida and Foucault, house philosophers of the preceding age, to lead them forward. Concurrently and more promisingly, moral philosophers sympathetic to the contributions of literature and deeply conversant in the long history of ethics – here I am thinking of, among others, Currie, Carroll, and especially Nussbaum – began to explore cross-fertilization from the other direction.

Two foundational claims that are presented in Nussbaum's work seemed to me compelling: 1) emotions are evaluative and play an indispensable role in our ethical lives; 2) literature, with its nuanced treatment of emotional crosscurrents, is uniquely positioned to refine, at least potentially, these emotional responses, and in so doing, enhance our moral intelligence in ways that philosophy does not. Nussbaum, however, had limited her claim for literature's ethical importance solely to the novel, and almost all recent discussion (pro or con) has followed her in that regard. In this book I have attempted to expand the case to the other two major genres: poetry and drama. In doing so, I have had to demonstrate, especially in the case of poetry, that the dense particularity of the novel was not necessary to a refinement of ethical awareness. The sparse elegance of Eliot's objective correlative can engage us in ways at least as significant and bring us just as readily to the shared emotional life that Nussbaum rightly values as central to our ethical commitments. In the chapter on Shaw, I have addressed the way that comedy, a mode that Nussbaum deliberately avoids, and tragedy, even in the talkative, Socratic theater of ideas, can be accommodated to her theory of the importance of the cognitive-evaluative nature of emotion.[1] I do discuss the novel as well, but mainly in order to set boundaries to the inclusiveness of Nussbaum's position. She had excluded only heavily didactic novels, or those otherwise lacking in subtle discrimination. I have attempted to show that there are highly accomplished novels – by canonized authors such as Woolf and Lawrence – that, insofar as they question the Aristotelian idea of character on which Nussbaum relies, test and even lie outside the range of works that can serve to recalibrate our emotional lives in ethically enhancing ways. Thus, the book is intended both to support the case for literature's ethical importance based on a cognitive-evaluative view of emotions, and to reconfigure the topography of works that have the potential to do this.

Admittedly, the present study leaves unaddressed the pertinent concern of sorting out what literature does in this regard from biography, a narrative form that explores character, and at its best, in highly nuanced ways. At least a few cursory observations are therefore in order. Biography will highlight in a life those crucial moments when moral decisions must be made and try to recreate the external and internal pressures that led to those decisions. Thus, as with the novel, we are invited to examine an alternate life in great detail. Yet two distinctions are pertinent here. Biography is a special form of history and, as Aristotle famously remarked, this is a different sort of thing from poetry (as expansively defined), for history tells us what *did happen*, not what, in a pattern of moral abstraction, *ought to have happened*. The messiness of contingent events can bear us along and away from this pattern. Too, as Wolfgang Iser pointed out, the structure of the novel relies on four perspectives: "that of the narrator, that of the characters, that of the plot, and that marked out for the reader."[2] It is the last of these especially, the meaning-soliciting call to the reader, that is far more developed in the novel than in biography. As we read a good novel, the demanding hermeneutics of a deeply engaged moment-to-moment revision of understanding lies near the center of sense-making in a way that

---

[1] See Martha Nussbaum, *Love's Knowledge* (Oxford: Oxford University Press, 1990), p. 46.
[2] See chapter 2 of *The Act of Reading* for a full discussion of how these perspectives interact.

is not true of biography. More simply put, the author of biography, serving as narrative voice, does far more work for us.

Deserving of a book (or several) unto itself would be the sorting out of our emotional repertoire. Faced with the welter of competing lists of what counts as an emotion, there has been an understandable attempt to get at "basic emotions."[3] But, aside from the fact that there is substantial disagreement on what these basic emotions might be, there is not even agreement on what the term "basic" indicates. In evolutionary biology, neurology, and at times in psychology, "basic" is reserved for those emotions that seem to be "hard-wired" and what is left over are seen as compound or derivative emotions, giving us a kind of affective atomic theory. In distinction to this, when philosophers talk about basic emotions quite often they are making evaluative judgments: these are the emotions that are essential to a life of rich communal living, basic in the sense of being central to *eudaimonia*. They are the ones that must be carefully tutored. In talking about literature's contribution to our ethical awareness, I have generally relied on this way of regarding emotions, though I know more and other needs to be said in terms of physiology, including pancultural facial expressions, and the findings of brain science. It is a welcome sign that philosophers are now becoming more willing to leave the gated community of *a priori*-ville and converse with their neighboring disciplines. In this regard, I would draw attention to Kristján Kristjánnsson's *The Self and Its Emotions* (2010),[4] at the intersection of moral philosophy, psychology, and education theory, as among the best of recent interdisciplinary attempts and one that helped clarify a number of issues.

While the definition of basic emotions and the set of things this might include are various, those who concern themselves with literary emotions frequently place empathy at or near the center. It is this capacity to enter into the mind of others that literature at its best enlarges and refines, they would argue. One might object that the term empathy, a translation of the German *Einfühlung*, is only about a century old, so the vast majority of great literature was written and read with no awareness of it; yet this would be a hasty conclusion. To take just one example, and an extreme one at that, Keats remarks in his famous letter to Benjamin Bailey that "if a Sparrow come before my Window I take part in its existence [sic] and pick about the Gravel." So, it seems clear that the experience of empathy

---

[3] Robert C. Solomon, "Back to Basics: On the Very Idea of 'Basic Emotions,'" in *Journal for the Theory of Social Behavior*, vol. 32, no. 2 (2002), 115–44.
[4] Kristján Kristjánsson, *The Self and Its Emotions* (Cambridge: Cambridge University Press, 2010).

did not rely on its naming. Nevertheless, there are problems with making the cultivation of empathy indispensable to literature's contributions. The first of these is that there needs to be a clearer sorting out of what the dynamics of self and other is in empathy. The definitional problem that dogs almost all discussion of emotion is particularly pronounced with empathy, often used haphazardly to overlap with pity, sympathy, compassion, etc. Even if we could agree on something like "the adoption of another's perspective, both in terms of thoughts and feelings," do we project *ourselves* into the other and try to imagine what it would be like if *we* were in her shoes? Or do we undertake the more strenuous attempt and try to imagine what it is like for the other to be in her own shoes?[5] If the latter, does this entail a kind of arrogance: the presumption that we actually *could* know? Are we seduced into this assumption because the novelist can give us infallible access to the interior of characters' minds, a knowledge unavailable in real life? Would that impossibly obtained fictional knowledge make the reading experience untranslatable into everyday practical interactions?[6] Even more fundamentally, how necessary is empathy to the model of virtue ethics that Aristotle and Nussbaum support?[7] Certainly, it is quite possible to sympathize without empathizing, and conversely it is quite possible to empathize without sympathizing. A good fictional example of the latter would be the case of Humbert Humbert, whose mind we inhabit for three hundred pages, yet (I think I am speaking for the vast majority of readers) do not extend sympathy. Nor, strictly speaking, is empathy required for indignation, grief, fear, shame or any number of responses that we might list as emotive. In terms of the present study, one can ask more starkly whether or not empathy plays any *necessary* role, either constitutive or motivational, in moral judgment. Jesse Prinz, who most emphatically argues that it does not, adds to this the problem that empathy can easily cause us to overvalue those near and dear to us and, also, to respond more fully to individual cases than to morally pressing situations

---

[5] Peter Goldie, *The Emotions: A Philosophical Exploration* (Oxford: Clarendon Press, 2000), pp. 194–205.
[6] Among literary critics, Suzanne Keen is the most pointed critic of the empathy–altruism connection. See her *Empathy and the Novel* (Oxford: Oxford University Press, 2007).
[7] In a fascinating psychological study by Ariel Knafo et al., "Empathy in Early Childhood," in *Values, Empathy and Fairness across Social Barriers* (New York Academy of Science, 1167, 2009), 103–14, the experimenters conclude that children's affective knowledge did not correspond with their empathy: "For example, Machiavellianism is higher for children characterized by low empathy but high affective perspective-taking ability" (p. 112). Perhaps this accounts for the water-board torturer who is fully aware of the emotional distress he is causing.

involving larger numbers.[8] In such instances, then, empathy could lead to moral obtuseness. (This scenario, of course, has its all-too-familiar obverse: those who readily embrace worthwhile causes while treating those in their immediate orbit shabbily.) In response to Prinz, attempts to rescue empathy have tried to build in a degree of impartiality so that we do not simply vicariously take up the inner life of the other person but do so in the normative context of what ought to have been the proper response in such a situation. This adjustment, or "emotion regulation" can be explicit, requiring a conscious effort to adjust, or implicit, the result of ingrained habit.[9] If we accept this view, especially in the mode of implicit regulation, we are returned to something very close to Aristotle's idea of virtue entailing as a kind of second nature the ability to feel at the right time, toward the right object or person, in just the right degree. Thus, we can imagine what it must be like to feel the jealousy of an Othello without, even temporarily, participating in that jealousy because we simultaneously recognize it to be based on a false belief, and excessive even if it were not. But the distancing this presupposes is greater in art, for even in the case of the justified and appropriate fear of Desdemona when her fate becomes apparent, we can fear *for* her without fearing *as* her. We respond to her as the most exquisitely poignant of objective correlatives – a term warmer, as I hope to have shown, than it sounds. And this measured response would be in keeping with Aristotle's insistence on emotional appropriateness. In the end, then, I would argue that the reader's response ought to be more spectatorial, one more of third-party understanding based on a regulated emotional response, than the tight identification that empathy as a kind of mirroring seems to encourage. This is not to deny that empathy has value, and its exercise generally intended as an act of generous expansion, but merely to point out that the case I have been making ought not to succeed or fail on the basis of literature's ability to cultivate this one capacity.

Finally, and inevitably, one must face the question of the practical consequences of the reading experience, if indeed it does enhance our moral understanding. Does a sensitive and engaged reading of *Paradise Lost* or *The Rime of the Ancient Mariner*, or, to stick to Nussbaum's genre of the novel, *Pride and Prejudice*, inevitably produce better people? The oft-cited examples of S. S. guards delighting in Goethe and other monuments

---

[8] Jesse Prinz, *The Emotional Construction of Morals* (Oxford: Oxford University Press, 2007. And, more recently, "Is Empathy Necessary for Morality," in *Empathy: Philosophical and Psychological Perspectives*, ed. Amy Coplan and Peter Goldie (Oxford: Oxford University Press, 2011), pp. 211–29.
[9] See especially Antti Kauppinen, "Empathy, Emotion Regulation, and Moral Judgment," in *Empathy and Morality*, ed. Heidi L. Maibom (Oxford: Oxford University Press, 2014), pp. 97–121.

of German culture between murders gives immediate pause, but the confirmation of less egregious examples are certainly ready-to-hand. A quick and informal look at the lives of English profs might be enough to check our enthusiasm. Yet, Aristotle's virtue ethics makes plain that virtue must issue in appropriate behavior; were it merely a matter of passively building character, we might be virtuous while we were asleep, as he tartly observes. So, perhaps our question might be recast to ask whether literature can alter character, with character understood to be the stable agent of action patterns. The development of character construed in this way is a slow, arduous process of intellectual and emotional discrimination for which the growing child relies on parents, teachers, and, more broadly, cultural norms. Gradually one learns to detect the morally salient and what sort of response, both in kind and degree, is appropriate. The role of literature is to refresh and refine this set of responses. We do not look to literature for new first principles, nor – except in rare cases, perhaps certain instances of the Longinian sublime – is it transformative. We can be, and often are, deeply moved by literature in the sense of Emily Dickinson's metaphor of having the tops of our heads taken off by poetry, but this should be understood to be an intense and, in the case of poetry, often strikingly immediate, subtilization of responses already in our repertoire. Thus, to demand, or even look for, a *direct* correspondence between the reading experience and subsequent moral behavior is a misguided enterprise.[10] More properly, we should regard a good book in the hands of an attentive reader as a means to refine moral knowledge in ways that we are unlikely to get from even careful parents or other guiding sources. If literature can be said to change character it is only in this quietest of ways. It is unlikely to much change the patterns of our interactions, but it can potentially enlarge our understanding of why these interactions are the way they are, and, when we get them right, why this ought to have been so.

---

[10] One would like to concur with Nussbaum's optimistic opinion that reading the best novels will make us better participants in a democracy, insofar as we get involved sympathetically with a range of other lives, but I do not think this tight causal connection can hold. She singles out realist novels as the prime source of literary influence in this regard, but one could certainly read perhaps the greatest of realist novels, *War and Peace*, with its vast array of characters sympathetically rendered, and not emerge any the more democratic for the experience. See Nussbaum's *Poetic Justice: The Literary Imagination and Public Life* (Boston: Beacon Press, 1995) for a sustained defense of her position.

# *Index*

Abrams, M. H., 53
the Absolute, 53–54, 55–56
Adamowski, T. H., 104
Adorno, Theodor, 7
aesthetics
   Hume on, 47
   Kant on, 21–25
affect, 40–44, 131–32
*After Strange Gods* (Eliot), 76
*akrasia*, 27
alienation, 127
Althusser, Louis, 4–5
Altieri, Charles, 34, 37
   on affect, 40–44
   on authenticity, 41
   on Eliot, 53
   on Nussbaum, 40–41, 45, 49
   on *Othello*, 41–42
   on Proust, 43
*Anabase* (Perse), 72
*Anatomy of Criticism* (Frye), 148
Apollo, 143, 147
the Apollonian, 140, 161
appetitive desires, 15
Appiah, Anthony, 8
*Ariel Poems* (Eliot), 73
Aristotle
   on *akrasia*, 27
   on character, 150
   on comedy, 147
   on emotions, 26, 27–29, 62, 173–74
   on ethics, 12
   on fear, 29
   on history, 30–31, 176
   on *katharsis*, 27–29, 30
   Lawrence and, 107–9
   moral psychology of, 20, 25–27, 48
   on pity, 29
   on poetry, 30–31, 176
   on rhetoric, 32–33
   on tragedy, 27–29, 31, 173

   on virtue, 25–26, 29–30, 179, 180
   Woolf and, 111
Armenian Genocide, 123–24
Arnold, Matthew, 2, 69
art
   Kant on, 24–25
   Shaw on, 166–67
*As You Like It* (Shakespeare), 149, 164
Auerbach, Erich, 129
Austen, Jane, 31, 179
authenticity, 41

Babbitt, Irving, 51–52
*Back to Methuselah* (Shaw), 152, 165–67
Baier, Annette, 10
Banfield, Ann, 112
Barrès, Maurice, 7
Baumgarten, Alexander Gottlieb, 21–22
beauty, 24
Beerbohm, Max, 170
belief, 78
Bergson, Henri, 151
Berman, Jessica, 124
Berst, Charles, 163
Bible, 37
biography, 176–77
*The Birth of Tragedy* (Nietzsche), 161
Bloom, Harold, 43
Bradley, F. H., 12
   on the Absolute, 53–54, 55–56
   Eliot and, 52–54, 57
   on feelings, 55
   intersubjectivity and, 57–58
   on primitive feeling, 55–58
   on the self, 56–57
   solipsism and, 57–58
Brontë, Emily, 40
Brooks, Cleanth, 42
Buddhism, 75
Buell, Lawrence, 3
Bush, Ronald, 73

Butcher, S. H., 28, 147
Butler, Judith, 9
Butler, Samuel, 151–52

*Caesar and Cleopatra* (Shaw), 158, 165, 167, 171, 173
Calvinism, Lawrence and, 93
Campbell, Sue, 78
care, ethics of, 9–10
catharsis, 62. *See also katharsis*
Cézanne, Paul, 112, 115
character
  Aristotle on, 150
  comedy and, 149
  Lawrence on, 82–84, 96
  literature altering, 180
  Shaw and, 144, 150–51, 166, 170–71, 173–74
  Woolf and, 111, 113, 118, 125, 142
childhood, 97
Christianity. *See also* Protestantism
  Eliot and, 73, 76–78
  Shaw and, 170
  Woolf and, 121
chronology, Eliot and, 71–72
Coleridge, Samuel Taylor, 179
Collier, Mark, 45
comedy, 176
  Aristotle on, 147
  character and, 149
  Frye on, 148
  lightness or darkness of, 147–48
  Molière and, 147, 149
  Shakespeare and, 148, 149
  sympathy and, 148
common culture, 69–77, 79, 119–20
communication, Woolf and, 124–25
community. *See also* linguistic community
  Woolf and, 117, 119–20, 124
consciousness. *See also* mental consciousness; primal consciousness
  Freud on, 105
  in Woolf, 137–42
consensus, 80–81
constructivism, feminism and, 9–10
Cooper, John, 15
Corneille, Pierre, 28–29
cosmology, 84–85
cosmopolitanism, 8
Creative Evolution, 165–67
*Critique of Judgment* (Kant), 22–23
Crompton, Louis, 164

Dante Alighieri, 63, 148
  Eliot on, 63–64, 65–66, 77–78
  Maurras on, 63

Darwin, Charles, 105, 151
De Man, Paul, 1–2
*Decline of the West* (Spengler), 84
deconstruction, 1, 2–4, 6–7
Defoe, Daniel, 165
Demosthenes, 34, 37
Derrida, Jacques, 3–4, 175
Descartes, René, 140–41
*Dialectic of Enlightenment* (Horkheimer and Adorno), 7
"A Dialogue on Dramatic Poetry" (Eliot), 171
Dickens, Charles, 91, 149, 150
Dickinson, Emily, 180
the Dionysian
  Shaw and, 145, 146–47, 161
  Woolf and, 114–15
discourse. *See also* free indirect discourse
  Foucault on, 4–5
disinterested interest, 22–23
*Divine Comedy* (Dante), 63, 148
Doestoevky, Fyodor, 137
drama, Eliot and, 73–74
Dreyfus affair, 7

education, Lawrence and, 88
"Education of the People" (Lawrence), 84
Eliot, T. S., 12, 79–81, 176
  Altieri on, 53
  on Arnold, 69
  Bradley and, 52–54, 57
  Buddhism and, 75
  catharsis and, 62
  Christianity and, 73, 76–78
  chronology used by, 71–72
  common culture and, 69–77, 79
  on consensus, 80–81
  on Dante, 63–64, 65–66, 77–78
  drama and, 73–74
  emotions and, 52, 62, 63
  on ethics, 51–52
  on feelings, 59–60, 63
  Greek tragedy and, 74
  on habit, 77
  on interpretation, 64–65
  on intersubjectivity, 58–60
  on Jonson, 64
  on Joyce, 72
  Lawrence and, 105
  on linguistic community, 75–76
  on Marvell, 67
  on Massinger, 69
  on Middleton, 67–68
  Miller on, 53
  on Morris, 67
  on object, 60–61

on objective correlative, 60
on Perse, 72
on poetry, 50, 61–69, 77–78
Pound and, 67, 72
religion and, 73–75, 78–79
Romanticism and, 50–51
on Sappho, 35
on the self, 58–59
on Shakespeare, 64, 68, 77
on Shaw, 144, 171
on Swinburne, 66–67
on taste, 65–69
on Tennyson, 65–66
on Tourneur, 66
*Emma* (Austen), 31
emotions, 14. *See also* affect; feelings; primitive feeling
   Aristotle on, 26, 27–29, 62, 173–74
   basic, 177
   belief and, 78
   Eliot and, 50, 52, 61–69, 77–78
   ethics and, 13, 25–26
   Hegel on, 62
   Hume on, 44–45
   Kant on, 18–21
   Lawrence and, 102, 103–4, 106–9
   literature and, 10–13
   Nussbaum on, 11, 44, 48, 175
   Plato on, 14–18
   poetry and, 50, 61–69, 77–78
   Shaw and, 147, 159–61, 170, 173–74
   Woolf and, 120–21, 142
empathy, 177–79
   Hume and, 46
   morality and, 178–79
   sympathy and, 178
Enlightenment, 7
epistemology, 112–15
eroticism, Shaw and, 164–65
essentialists, feminism and, 9
ethics. *See also* specific topics
   Aristotle on, 12
   of care, 9–10
   De Man and, 1–2
   deconstruction and, 1, 2–4
   Derrida on, 3–4
   Eliot on, 51–52
   emotions and, 13, 25–26
   as Enlightenment ideology, 7
   feminism and, 8–10
   Foucault on, 4–5
   *katharsis* and, 30
   Lawrence and, 104–5, 108–10
   Lévinas on, 3–4
   literature and, 10–13, 25, 175

   love and, 40, 42
   lyric poetry and, 12
   Miller on, 2–3
   modernist literature and, 12–13
   morality and, 16
   poetry and, 175–76
   postcolonial studies and, 7–8
   religion and, 51–52
   Woolf and, 111–12, 123–24, 132, 142–43
*Ethics* (Aristotle), 20
*The Ethics of Reading* (Miller), 2–3
Euripides, 159–60
evil, Shaw and, 152–53, 162–63

*Fantasia of the Unconscious* (Lawrence), 84, 87, 88–89, 106
fear
   Aristotle on, 29
   Lawrence on, 107
   Woolf and, 127–28
feelings
   Bradley on, 55
   Eliot on, 59–60, 63
   Lawrence on, 82, 102–4
feminism, 8–10
Fichte, Johann Gottlieb, 136
Ford, John, 67–68
Foucault, Michel, 4–5, 175
*Foundation of the Metaphysics of Morals* (Kant), 3
*Four Quartets* (Eliot), 78–81
free indirect discourse, Woolf and, 135
French Revolution of 1789, 50–51
Freud, Sigmund
   on consciousness, 105
   Lawrence and, 87–88, 101, 105
   Nietzsche and, 87–88
   Shaw and, 146–47
*From Ritual to Romance* (Weston), 72
Fry, Roger, 112
Frye, Northrop, 148

genre, Woolf and, 134, 142–43
"Gerontion" (Eliot), 71–72
Gilligan, Carol, 9
Goldie, Peter, 57
Gordon, Lyndall, 53
Gottfried von Strassburg, 109
Graham, J. W., 136
Greek mythology, Shaw and, 158–60
Greek tragedy, Eliot and, 74
Greenblatt, Stephen, 5–6
Griffith, Garret, 152, 153, 154
Guiguet, Jean, 135
Guth, Deborah, 123

habit, Eliot and, 77
Hafley, James, 119, 129, 135
*Hamburg Dramaturgy* (Lessing), 28–29
*Hamlet* (Shakespeare), 64
happiness, Kant and, 20–21
*Hard Times* (Dickens), 91
*Heartbreak House* (Shaw), 155, 156–65, 167, 173
Hegel, Georg Wilhelm Friedrich, 62, 151–52
Heidegger, Martin, 3–4, 7, 141–42
Held, Virginia, 10
Henke, Suzette, 141–42
Herder, Johann Gottfried, 7
Hertz, Neil, 37
history
    Aristotle on, 30–31, 176
    Shaw and, 167–68, 173
Hite, Molly, 123
Homer, 16–18, 25, 35–36
Horkheimer, Max, 7
Hume, David, 10, 48
    on aesthetics, 47
    on emotions, 44–45
    empathy and, 46
    Hutcheson on, 48
    moral psychology of, 47–48
    on motivation, 21, 45
    on reason, 44–45, 48
    on the self, 47
    on sympathy, 45–46
Husserl, Edmund, 3, 141–42
Hutcheson, Francis, 19, 48

Ibsen, Henrik, 146
*The Idea of a Christian Society* (Eliot), 75, 76–77
identity, Woolf and, 139
ignorance, Shaw and, 169
*Iliad* (Homer), 35, 36
*The Importance of Being Earnest* (Wilde), 160
individuality
    Lawrence on, 85, 86
    primal consciousness and, 89–90
innate difference, Lawrence and, 99
intention, 19
interpretation, Eliot and, 64–65
intersubjectivity, 57
    Bradley and, 57–58
    Eliot on, 58–60
    narrator and, 118–19
    Woolf and, 114–33
*Ion* (Plato), 31–32
Iser, Wolfgang, 46–47, 65, 176
isolation, Woolf and, 126–27

James, Henry, 11
Jonson, Ben, 64, 147

"Journey of the Magi" (Eliot), 73
Joyce, James, 72, 123
*Julius Caesar* (Shakespeare), 167–68

*Kangaroo* (Lawrence), 84
Kant, Immanuel, 3
    on aesthetics, 21–25
    on art, 24–25
    on disinterested interest, 22–23
    on emotions, 18–21
    on happiness, 20–21
    on morality, 18–21
    on motivation, 21
    Newton and, 18
    on reason, 19
    on *sensus communis*, 23
*katharsis*, 27–29, 30
Keats, John, 39, 177–78
Kierkegaard, Søren, 168–69
*King Lear* (Shakespeare), 158, 161–63
Knafo, Ariel, 178
Kristjánsson, Kristján, 48, 177

Lacan, Jacques, 48–49
*Lady Chatterly's Lover* (Lawrence), 102, 144–45
language, morality and, 2
Lawrence, D. H., 12, 96–101, 102–4, 106–7, 163
    Aristotle and, 107–9
    Calvinism and, 93
    on character, 82–84, 96
    childhood and, 97
    cosmology of, 84–85
    on education, 88
    Eliot and, 105
    emotions and, 102, 103–4, 106–9
    ethics and, 104–5, 108–10
    on fear, 107
    on feelings, 82, 102–4
    Freud and, 87–88, 101, 105
    on individuality, 85, 86
    on innate difference, 99
    on love, 107
    on mental consciousness, 91–92
    on morality, 92
    on mothers, 92–93
    Nietzsche and, 87–88, 93–95, 99, 102, 103, 109
    on primal consciousness, 85, 86–91, 108
    on psychic health, 95–97, 99–101, 107
    on rationalism, 86
    on relativism, 85–86
    Rousseau and, 92, 93–95, 99
    the self and, 105, 106
    on sexual pathology, 101
    on Shaw, 144–45

on will, 92–95, 97–99
on World War I aftermath, 84
"Leda and the Swan" (Yeats), 35
Lessing, G. E., 28–30
Lévinas, Emmanuel, 3–4
Levinson, Michael, 53
Life Force
    Shaw and, 151–55
    World War I and, 156
linguistic community, Eliot and, 75–76
*Literary Theory and the Claims of History* (Mohanty), 7–8
literature. *See also* modern literature; modernist literature
    biography and, 176–77
    character altered by, 180
    emotions and, 10–13
    ethics and, 10–13, 25, 175
    moral imagination and, 46–47
    Nussbaum on, 11–12, 34, 48, 175–76
    virtue and, 48
Loftis, Sonya Freeman, 158
logocentrism, 2
Longinus, 32–34
    on Bible, 37
    on Demosthenes, 37
    on the sublime, 33–38, 39
love
    ethics and, 40, 42
    Lawrence on, 107
    primal consciousness and, 90
"The Love Song of J. Alfred Prufrock" (Eliot), 70–71
lyric poetry, 12

MacIntyre, Alasdair, 10
de Maistre, Joseph, 7, 50
*Major Barbara* (Shaw), 150, 155
*Man and Superman* (Shaw), 145, 151, 152, 153, 164, 166
Mann, Thomas, 170
"The Mark on the Wall" (Woolf), 113–15
Marvell, Andrew, 67
Marx, Karl, 151, 153–54
Massinger, Philip, 69
Maurras, Charles, 50, 63
*Measure for Measure* (Shakespeare), 148
memory, Woolf and, 129–31, 132–33
mental consciousness
    Lawrence on, 91–92
    primal consciousness and, 91–92, 108
Michael, Walter Benn, 53
Middleton, Thomas, 67–68
*Midsummer Night's Dream* (Shakespeare), 153
Mill, John Stuart, 58

Miller, J. Hillis, 2–3, 53
Milton, John, 28, 179
modern literature, 145, 155
modernist literature, 12–13
Mohanty, Satya, 7–8
Molière, 147, 149–50, 172–73
*Moll Flanders* (Defoe), 165
Moore, G. E., 111–12
moral imagination, 46–47
moral psychology
    of Aristotle, 20, 25–27, 48
    of Hume, 47–48
morality
    beauty and, 24
    empathy and, 178–79
    ethics and, 16
    intention and, 19
    Kant on, 18–21
    language and, 2
    Lawrence on, 92
    Shaw and, 166
    Williams on, 16
Morris, William, 67
mothers, Lawrence and, 92–93
motivation
    Hume on, 21, 45
    Kant on, 21
*Les Mots et Les Choses* (Foucault), 5
"Mr. Bennett and Mrs. Brown" (Woolf), 113, 142
*Mrs. Dalloway* (Woolf), 115–19, 120
*Mrs. Warren's Profession* (Shaw), 145, 163, 165, 173
*Much Ado About Nothing* (Shakespeare), 164

Nagel, Thomas, 109
narrative voice, Woolf and, 135–36, 137
narrator
    intersubjectivity and, 118–19
    in Woolf, 117–19, 133–34
New Criticism, 24, 42–43
New Historicism, 5–6
Newton, Isaac, 18
Nietzsche, Friedrich, 5
    De Man on, 2
    Freud and, 87–88
    Lawrence and, 87–88, 93–95, 99, 102, 103, 109
    Shaw and, 145, 151, 152, 153–54, 161
    on Socrates, 146
9/11, 4
Noddings, Nell, 9
*Notes Towards the Definition of Culture* (Eliot), 75, 76
novel
    Nussbaum on, 11, 175, 176, 180
    Woolf on, 142
"The Novel and the Feelings" (Lawrence), 102–3

Nussbaum, Martha, 8, 10–11
  Altieri on, 40–41, 45, 49
  on emotions, 11, 44, 48, 175
  on literature, 11–12, 34, 48, 175–76
  on novel, 11, 175, 176, 180
  on Proust, 43–44
  Shaw and, 172–74, 176
  the sublime and, 39–40
  on Woolf, 11–12
"The Nymph's Song to Hylas" (Morris), 67

object, Eliot and, 60–61
objective correlative, 60, 71, 72, 79, 81, 176
*Odyssey* (Homer), 35–36
"On Taste" (Hume), 47
*On the Sublime* (Longinus), 32–34
ontology, Woolf and, 137–38
Orwell, George, 149
Oser, Lee, 115
*Othello* (Shakespeare), 41–42, 44, 179

*Paradise Lost* (Milton), 179
Pater, Walter, 41
*Peloponnesian War* (Thucydides), 17
perception, Woolf and, 111–14, 125–26, 140–41
Perse, St. John, 72
Pettet, Edwin, 154
*Phaedrus* (Plato), 14
*The Phantom Table* (Banfield), 112
*phronesis*, 39–40
*Pickwick Papers* (Dickens), 150
pity, Aristotle and, 29
Plato, 166
  on appetitive desires, 15
  on emotions, 14–18
  on Homer, 17–18, 25
  on poetry, 16–18, 31–32
  on reason, 15, 18
  on rhetoric, 33
  Taylor on, 18
  on *thumos*, 15
*Plays for Puritans* (Shaw), 165
*Poetics* (Aristotle), 27–29, 30–31, 147
poetry. *See also* lyric poetry
  Aristotle on, 30–31, 176
  Eliot on, 50, 61–69, 77–78
  emotions and, 50, 61–69, 77–78
  ethics and, 175–76
  Plato on, 16–18, 31–32
  Romantic theory of, 61
  *technê* and, 31–32
*Politics* (Aristotle), 30
"Portrait of a Lady" (Eliot), 71

postcolonial studies, 6–8
Post-Impressionism, 112
Pound, Ezra, 67, 72, 144
*The Prelude* (Wordsworth), 38–39
"Preludes" (Eliot), 69–70, 71
*Pride and Prejudice* (Austen), 179
primal consciousness
  basic schema of, 89–90
  individuality and, 89–90
  Lawrence on, 85, 86–91, 108
  love and, 90
  mental consciousness and, 91–92, 108
  psyche and, 90–91
primitive feeling, 55–58
*Principia Ethica* (Moore), 111–12
Prinz, Jesse, 178–79
Protestantism, Shaw and, 167
Proust, Marcel, 43–44
psyche
  health of
    impact of era on, 99–100
    Lawrence on, 95–97, 99–101, 107
    sexual pathology and, 101
    therapy and, 101
  primal consciousness and, 90–91
*Psychoanalysis and the Unconscious* (Lawrence), 84, 87

*qualia*, 40–41

*The Rainbow* (Lawrence), 97
rationalism, Lawrence and, 86
reason
  Hume on, 44–45, 48
  Kant on, 19
  Plato on, 15, 18
*The Red and the Black* (Stendhal), 109
relativism, Lawrence and, 85–86
religion, 51–52, 73–75, 78–79. *See also* Christianity
*Republic* (Plato), 15, 16, 166
"The Resistance to Theory" (De Man), 1
revelation, Shaw and, 168–69
*The Revenger's Tragedy* (Tourneur), 66
"Rhapsody" (Eliot), 71
rhetoric
  Aristotle on, 32–33
  Plato on, 33
*Rhetoric* (Aristotle), 26, 32–33
*The Rime of the Ancient Mariner* (Coleridge), 179
Romanticism
  Eliot and, 50–51
  French Revolution of 1789 and, 50–51
  on poetry, 61
  Rousseau and, 50–51
*A Room of One's Own* (Woolf), 111

Rousseau, Jean-Jacques, 19
    Lawrence and, 92, 93–95, 99
    Romanticism and, 50–51

sacrifice, Shaw and, 155–56
Said, Edward, 4
*Samson Agonistes* (Milton), 28
Sappho, 34–35, 44
Sartre, Jean-Paul, 106
Schneewind, J. B., 21
Schopenhauer, Arthur, 151, 152
the self
    Bradley on, 56–57
    Eliot on, 58–59
    Hume on, 47
    Lawrence and, 105, 106
    primitive feeling and, 56
    Shaw and, 157
    Woolf and, 112, 134, 140–41
*The Self and Its Emotions* (Kristjánsson), 177
*sensus communis*, 23
sexual pathology, Lawrence and, 101
sexuality, Shaw and, 164–65
Shakespeare, William, 25, 41–42, 44, 153, 179
    comedy and, 148, 149
    Eliot on, 64, 68, 77
    Shaw and, 156, 158, 161–63, 164–65, 167–68, 172–73
"Shakespeare and the Stoicism of Seneca" (Eliot), 68, 77
Shaw, George Bernard, 12, 152, 156–72
    Apollo and, 147
    the Apollonian and, 161
    on art, 166–67
    character and, 144, 150–51, 166, 170–71, 173–74
    Christianity and, 170
    Creative Evolution and, 165–67
    Defoe and, 165
    on Dickens, 150
    the Dionysian and, 145, 146–47, 161
    Eliot on, 144, 171
    emotions and, 147, 159–61, 170, 173–74
    eroticism and, 164–65
    evil and, 152–53, 162–63
    Freud and, 146–47
    Greek mythology and, 158–60
    Hegel and, 151–52
    history and, 167–68, 173
    on Ibsen, 146
    ignorance and, 169
    Lawrence on, 144–45
    Life Force and, 151–55
    Molière and, 149–50, 172–73
    morality and, 166

Nietzsche and, 145, 151, 152, 153–54, 161
Nussbaum and, 172–74, 176
Pound on, 144
Protestantism and, 167
revelation and, 168–69
sacrifice and, 155–56
the self and, 157
sexuality and, 164–65
Shakespeare and, 156, 158, 161–63, 164–65, 167–68, 172–73
socialism and, 154
Socrates and, 146
tragedy and, 145, 156, 168, 172–73
unconscious and, 153
virtue and, 146
will and, 151
Woolf on, 144
World War I and, 155, 156–57
Yeats on, 145
socialism, Shaw and, 154
Socrates, 92, 146. *See also* Plato
solipsism, Bradley and, 57–58
*Sons and Lovers* (Lawrence), 93
Spengler, Oswald, 84
Spitzer, Jennifer, 83–84
Spivak, Gayatri, 6–7
*St. Joan* (Shaw), 155, 156, 167–72, 173
St. Thomas, 74
Stendhal, 109
Stern-Gillet, Suzanne, 32
sublime, 33–38, 39–40
suicide, Woolf and, 121–23
Swinburne, Algernon Charles, 66–67
sympathy
    comedy and, 148
    empathy and, 178
    Hume on, 45–46
*Symposium* (Xenophon), 17

Tague, Gregory, 104–5
*Tartuffe* (Molière), 149–50
taste, Eliot and, 65–69
Taylor, Charles, 18
*technê*, 31–32
Tennyson, Alfred, 65–66
tense, Woolf and, 136
therapy, 101
Thucydides, 17
*thumos*, 15
time, Woolf and, 127–28, 134
"To His Coy Mistress" (Marvell), 67
*To the Lighthouse* (Woolf), 111, 124–33
Tolstoy, Leo, 180
Tourneur, Cyril, 66
Townsend, Dabney, 47

tragedy, 176. *See also* Greek tragedy
  Aristotle on, 27–29, 31, 173
  Frye on, 148
  Shaw and, 145, 156, 168, 172–73
Trilling, Lionel, 145, 155
*Tristan* (Gottfried), 109
*The Trojan Women* (Euripides), 159–60
Tronto, Joan, 10

"Über Wahrheit und Lüge im Außermoralischen Sinn" (Nietzsche), 2
*Ulysses* (Joyce), 72
unconscious. *See also* primal consciousness
  Shaw and, 153

virtue
  Aristotle on, 25–26, 29–30, 179, 180
  literature and, 48
  Shaw and, 146
*A Vision* (Yeats), 84–85

*War and Peace* (Tolstoy), 180
*The Waste Land* (Eliot), 72, 156
*The Waves* (Woolf), 133–43
Weintraub, Stanley, 158–59, 172
Weston, Jessie, 72
"What is an author?" (Foucault), 5
Wilde, Oscar, 160
will
  disruption of, 92–95
  Lawrence on, 92–95, 97–99
  mental, 98–99
  Shaw and, 151
Williams, Bernard, 16
Wilson, Edmund, 168
"The Window: Knowledge of Other Minds in Virginia Woolf's *To the Lighthouse*" (Nussbaum), 11–12
Wollheim, Richard, 53
*Women in Love* (Lawrence), 84, 93–94, 95–101, 102–4, 105, 106–7
Woodbridge, Homer, 171
Woolf, Virginia, 115–16, 120, 133–43

affect and, 131–32
alienation and, 127
Apollo and, 143
the Apollonian and, 140
Aristotle and, 111
Armenian Genocide and, 123–24
character and, 111, 113, 118, 125, 142
Christianity and, 121
common culture and, 119–20
communication and, 124–25
community and, 117, 119–20, 124
consciousness in, 137–42
the Dionysian and, 114–15
emotions and, 120–21, 142
epistemology and, 112–15
ethics and, 111–12, 123–24, 132, 142–43
fear and, 127–28
free indirect discourse and, 135
genre and, 134, 142–43
Heidegger and, 141–42
Husserl and, 141–42
identity in, 139
intersubjectivity and, 114–33
isolation and, 126–27
memory and, 129–31, 132–33
narrative voice in, 135–36, 137
narrator role in, 117–19, 133–34
on novel, 142
Nussbaum on, 11–12
ontology in, 137–38
perception and, 111–14, 125–26, 140–41
the self and, 112, 134, 140–41
on Shaw, 144
suicide and, 121–23
tense in, 136
time and, 127–28, 134
Wordsworth, William, 38–39, 50
World War I, 84, 155, 156–57
*Wuthering Heights* (Brontë), 40

Xenophon, 17

Yeats, William Butler, 35, 84–85, 145